# LEARN TO DRIVE

# LEARN
## TO
# DRIVE

## in 10 Easy Stages!

### 6TH EDITION

**JOHN WELLS**
**MARGARET STACEY**

KoganPage

LONDON  PHILADELPHIA  NEW DELHI

**Publisher's note**

Every possible effort has been made to ensure that the information contained in this book is accurate at the time of going to press, and the publisher and authors cannot accept responsibility for any errors or omissions, however caused. No responsibility for loss or damage occasioned to any person acting, or refraining from action, as a result of the material in this publication can be accepted by the editor, the publisher or either of the authors.

First published in Great Britain in 1987
Revised edition 1990
Second edition published in 1993
Revised edition 1998
Third edition published in 1999
Fourth edition 2009
Fifth edition 2013
Sixth edition 2016

Kogan Page Limited
2nd Floor, 45 Gee Street
London EC1V 3RS
United Kingdom
www.koganpage.com

**British Library Cataloguing in Publication Data**

A CIP record for this book is available from the British Library.

ISBN      978 0 7494 7478 2
E-ISBN   978 0 7494 7479 9

Typeset by Graphicraft Limited, Hong Kong
Printed and bound in India by Replika Press Pvt Ltd

# Contents

## PART 3  Appendices  319

# About the authors

**Dr John Wells** is well known in the driver training profession as a specialist author of training materials for driving instructors. Used nationwide by independent instructors and training establishments, John's materials are recommended by the leading trade body in the industry, the Driving Instructors Association (DIA). John has also provided a consultancy service, advising on training and quality for those wishing to register with ORDIT (The Official Register of Driving Instructor Trainers whose members provide training and professional development courses for other driving instructors). He is a member of the DIA Education Committee and adviser to BUSK, the school transport safety consultancy.

**Margaret Stacey** was the co-author of *The Driving Instructor's Handbook* and *Practical Teaching Skills for Driving Instructors*, both of which are published by Kogan Page. These books are recommended by the Driving Standards Agency to those preparing for the Approved Driving Instructors' exam and also to experienced instructors. Margaret also supplied establishments throughout the UK with other training materials including *The Advanced Driver's Handbook* and the *Autodriva Instructor Home Study Programme*. Margaret represented the Approved Driving Instructors' National Joint Council on various national committees and served on the management committees of ADITE, ORDIT and the NVQ Steering Group.

# Acknowledgements

The authors thank all those who gave feedback on previous editions of this book, Jared Fortin for assistance with the diagrams, and Theory First Publishing for permission to include diagrams from the *Colourfile* range of products.

# Introduction

This book has been written by leaders in the driver training profession. It is a comprehensive course designed to help provisional licence holders prepare for both the theory and the practical parts of the driving test and is linked to the Driver and Vehicle Standards Agency (DVSA) recommended syllabus for learner drivers.

This book has been written to:

- help with your studies for the theory and hazard perception test;
- supplement your practical driving lessons;
- provide guidance for you and your supervisor when you are practising.

It shows you:

- what to expect on your lessons;
- how to develop driving as a life skill;
- what you need to know to pass the theory and practical driving tests.

## Your provisional licence

Before you can start driving for the first time you need to have received your provisional driving licence. The minimum age for driving a car is normally 17. However, you can drive a car at 16 if you get, or have applied for, the enhanced rate of the  mobility component of Personal Independence Payment (PIP). A provisional licence allows you to drive only whilst supervised by a suitably qualified driver or professional driving instructor.

The Driver and Vehicle Licensing Agency (DVLA), or Driver and Vehicle Agency in Northern Ireland, issues driving licences. You can get an application form (D1) from any post office. All new licences issued are of the photocard type shown here. You will need to include a passport-style photo with your application. When you receive the licence, check that the details are correct. If not, you will need to contact the issuing agency.

## Your eyesight

**HK55 WES**

**W123 ABC**

You must be able to read a number plate at the prescribed distance with glasses if worn

When you apply for your provisional driving licence, you sign to the effect that you can read (with glasses or contact lenses, if necessary) a car number plate in the format XX50 XXX from 20 metres (66 feet). Make sure that you can. In today's busy conditions you need to be looking well ahead. If you need glasses or contact lenses to read the number plate, you must also wear them for driving. If you are in doubt, get your eyes tested professionally. Your driving instructor should also check your eyesight on your first lesson!

## Essential reading

The best way of preparing for both parts of your driving test and to become a safe and competent driver is to combine theory with practice. To help you prepare for both the theory and the practical tests you need to study the following books:

- *The Highway Code* – rules of the road for all. You can read the complete *Highway Code* rules at www.gov.uk/highway-code
- *The Official DVSA Guide to Learning to Drive* – tells you how to apply for your provisional licence, details the key skills required and explains what a driving examiner is looking for.
- *The Official DVSA Guide to Driving: The essential skills* – advice for all drivers, skilled or novice, on how to make driving 'safe for life'.

These books will help you to understand the rules so that you can apply them during your practical lessons. If your driving instructor doesn't keep a stock you should be able to buy them at any good bookshop or online. The books are a worthwhile investment. The more you can read and understand, the less time your instructor needs to spend explaining, and the more time you have for practice! There are also a number of interactive DVDs covering some of the material you need to learn. Ask your instructor to recommend the products that best suit your learning needs.

## Reducing the risk of accidents

A high percentage of newly qualified drivers are involved in accidents. Under the New Driver Act, if you accumulate more than six penalty points within two years of passing your test you will have to:

- go back to using a provisional licence;
- display L plates; and
- take another driving test.

This book explains how to develop your control skills so that you will be able to handle your car safely and efficiently. This will make learning to drive an enjoyable experience.

Your instructor will explain how to apply the rules you are learning and teach you to plan ahead and anticipate what could happen. This will help you to learn how to avoid problems of conflict with other road users, which in turn will help you keep your full licence and enjoy 'safe driving for life'.

# How to use this programme

## Organizing your course of training

This training programme has now been in use for many years. By following this programme, and combining learning the theory with your practical lessons, you will soon learn how to apply the rules to different road situations more easily. This book includes common-sense advice, starting with how to choose your instructor and progressing to the driving test itself and further training. The task of learning to drive is broken down into easy stages that will enable you to plan and pace yourself according to your own natural aptitude and driving ability.

## Charting your progress

The systematic step-by-step programme of learning in this book is designed to take the panic and confusion out of your practice and therefore make more effective use of your time. You can map your progress through the course by completing the assessment sections and entering your scores at the end of each stage of learning.

## Key points

Each stage identifies key learning points. Before your lessons, study these points carefully along with any relevant Highway Code rules. If your next session is private practice get your supervisor to study the key points and the rules as well. Read the introduction to each stage and follow the instructions carefully.

## The DVSA syllabus for learners

The book *The Official DVSA Guide to Learning to Drive* has been compiled by the Driver and Vehicle Standards Agency. Their motto is 'Safe Driving for Life'. This book is essentially the syllabus for learner drivers. Read the pages listed at the beginning of each stage of *Learn to Drive* and make sure you get lots of practice at all of the skills involved.

## Completing the checkpoint

At the end of each stage there are some multiple-choice and multiple-response questions similar to those you will take in your theory test. The questions are designed to help you judge how well you have learned from this book, your lessons and the rules of driving from *The Highway Code*. Choose the most appropriate answers and check with the answer list in Appendix 2 (page 331). Record your scores and try again if you need to.

## Using illustrations to help you understand

Most of the key learning points are illustrated with diagrams. This will help you to:

- understand more easily;
- recognize risks earlier;
- predict danger; and
- avoid conflict with other road users.

Many of the illustrations in this book are adapted from the *Colourfile* series of driver training aids by John Wells, which is approved by the lead body in the driver training profession, the Driving Instructors Association (DIA). These tried-and-tested diagrams are clear, easily understood and used by thousands of professional instructors.

## Learning in stages

Try to follow the sequence of the stages, making sure you have learned and practised all of the points before going on to the next. Sometimes the area you live in may mean that some topics will need to be covered in a different order. For example, if you live near roundabouts and dual carriageways you will have to be taught how to drive on them fairly early on in your course of lessons. The manoeuvre exercises can be introduced at any point. However, it is advisable that your clutch control skills are fairly well developed before you start learning how to reverse, as you will be more confident and achieve success more easily.

## Using this guide as your personal logbook

When learning, your instructor/supervisor should help you to take responsibility for new driving tasks. He or she should encourage you to think things through for yourself by asking questions to find out how much you know already and what additional explanation is needed. At first you might benefit from 'talk-through' practice, then as your skills improve, you should progress and carry out the various tasks with less assistance. Finally, you should be able to complete the exercises without any help at all.

Use this book to chart your progress when you have studied and then practised each exercise. You can get your instructor/supervisor to help by adding their constructive comments as well. Keep practising each skill until you and your instructor are happy with your progress in each topic. You should be ready for a practical test when you are confident that you can complete all the exercises in this book without any help from your instructor.

Notes:
I've studied it

Notes:
I can do it with help from my instructor

Notes:
I can do it without help

**Use this book as your personal progress logbook**

## In-car lessons and practice

You must feel confident in yourself. Be prepared to take your instructor's advice and have enough lessons and practice on all of the subjects covered.

If you are unsure of a topic or don't understand the reasons for it, agree with your instructor to go over it again. Remember, you must feel confident that you can carry out driving tasks safely and efficiently to become a responsible driver.

## Concentration

It is important that you maintain your concentration all of the time. When learning a new skill, don't try to practise for too long. Take short breaks to discuss your performance and then practise again. Following this system will help you to keep your concentration and therefore make your learning more effective.

## Recapping at the start of each lesson

At the beginning of each lesson or practice session, your instructor or supervisor should spend a few minutes going over what you learned previously. This will help you and your instructor agree on what you should achieve in the current lesson.

## Keeping a check on appointments and progress

Your instructor will probably use a record system to keep a note of your lesson appointments and progress, but you can keep your own record by filling in the 'Can do' statements in Appendix 2 (page 327).

# The driving test

There are two parts to the driving test: the theory and hazard perception test and the practical test.

## The theory and hazard perception test

You can apply for the theory and hazard perception test as soon as you have received your provisional driving licence. However, the test requires more than just theoretical knowledge of the rules of driving. You will also need some driving experience. Your instructor will help you understand how to apply the rules so that you develop 'defensive' driving techniques. Take advice from your instructor on when you will be ready to take your test.

The theory and hazard perception test is computer-based, and you have to pass each element in one sitting. All of the subjects tested are dealt with in this book. The theory test comprises 50 multiple-choice questions that are displayed on-screen one at a time. You touch the screen to select your choice, and some of the questions have more than one correct answer. At the time of writing, to pass this element, you must score at least 43 correct answers within 57 minutes. As a learning resource we have provided sample theory tests for you in Part 2. The checkpoint questions at the end of each stage are also in the same style as the theory test, so by studying *Learn to Drive* you will have had plenty of practice by the time you take your theory test for real.

When you have completed the theory section of the test, there will be a short break before you move on to the hazard perception test. Fourteen 'film clips' will be shown featuring various types of hazard as seen from the driver's seat of a moving car. These are very lifelike computer-generated scenes. Each clip lasts for about a minute, and you will need to 'click' when you see a potential hazard *developing* into a moving hazard, ie a situation which you would have to change speed or course to deal with. At the time of writing, up to five marks can be scored for each hazard, and the more quickly you respond to the developing hazard the more you will score. However, you must be careful not to go 'click-crazy', because the programme is designed to disqualify your score if you do so. To pass this part of the test, you must score 44 out of the possible 75 marks. Your instructor will advise you of any changes in the criteria for passing this part of the test.

A theory test pass certificate is valid for two years. You must pass the practical driving test within the two-year period; otherwise you will have to take the theory part again.

## *The practical test*

When you have passed the theory test, only apply for the practical test when you and your instructor agree that you will be ready.

Be prepared to have enough professional driving tuition. It is far better to be properly prepared and pass first time than be disappointed! Remember, a failed practical test means extra cost in terms of:

- another test fee;
- more driving lessons;
- time – there may be a long waiting list for a test at your local centre.

At the start of the test your examiner will check your eyesight by asking you to read a number plate. Once at your vehicle, you will be asked to explain or demonstrate how you would carry out certain safety checks. Referred to as 'show me, tell me', this part of the test will ensure that you are familiar with the vehicle you are driving and are aware of safety checks you must be able to make. Whilst dependent on the car you take for your driving test, most of the information you need to answer these questions is contained in this book, and you will learn it as you proceed with your course of tuition.

The practical part of the test lasts about 40 minutes, and the route will cover as many road and traffic conditions as possible. You will have to perform some 'set manoeuvres' to show that you can control the vehicle correctly and safely. You will also need to demonstrate that you can drive 'independently' without directions from the examiner for part of your practical test. The examiner will try to put you at ease and give you directions and instructions clearly and in good time. More detailed information on the practical part of the test is given in Stage 10. By following the structured approach to learning in this book and applying for your test only when you are thoroughly prepared, you should have no difficulty in passing first time!

Take advice from your instructor on when and how to apply for your theory and practical tests.

## Changes to the driving test

From time to time, and in line with government consultation, the Driver and Vehicle Standards Agency may introduce changes to the content of the theory and practical parts of the driving test. Your instructor should be able to give you up-to-date information but you can also check online by searching for 'DVSA'.

# PART ONE
# DRIVING SKILLS

# Stage 1
# Before you drive

*W*hat do I need before I can start learning? How do I choose a good driving instructor? How can I practise what I'm learning? What do I need to study? How much is it all going to cost? These are some of the questions that you will have asked yourself when you decided to learn to drive. So, before you drive, read through Stage 1 and start preparing yourself for a lifetime of safe driving!

Before driving you should read:

- *The Official DVSA Guide to Driving: The essential skills*, Section 1 – The driver, and Section 2 – The driver and the law.
- *The Official DVSA Guide to Learning to Drive*, Section 1 and Section 2, Legal responsibilities.

These emphasize the importance of a structured approach to learning and outline the qualities of the 'good driver'.

Remember that you must be in possession of your provisional driving licence before you can begin driving!

## The Highway Code

Learning the rules by heart will not necessarily make you a good driver! Your instructor should teach you how the rules apply in different situations, so that you can put them into practice safely.

Make sure that you have an up-to-date edition of *The Highway Code* book (or online access) and read up on the rules in the following sections:

- Rules about animals:
  - animals in your vehicle.
- Rules for drivers and motorcyclists:
  - vehicle condition;
  - fitness to drive;

- – alcohol and drugs;
- – seat belts and child restraints;
- – children in cars.
- General rules:
  - – lighting requirements.
- Annex 3:
  - – documents;
  - – learner drivers.
- Annex 5:
  - – penalties.

When you have studied the rules in *The Highway Code*, work through this chapter and complete the checkpoint at the end of it. Your instructor should be able to help if you have any problems or don't understand some of the rules.

# Who should I get to teach me?

The best way to learn to drive safely and with confidence is to combine professional tuition with private practice. In law, the only people who can accept payment in money or money's worth for giving driving instruction are those on the DVSA register of approved instructors. They have the qualification 'Driver and Vehicle Standards Agency Approved Driving Instructor (car)' and are usually known as 'ADIs'. It is unlikely that anyone

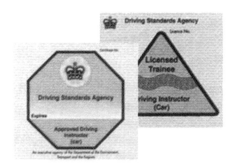

**If you are paying for driving instruction make sure that the person teaching you is on the DVSA register of driving instructors. Note that badges may bear the newer title 'Driver and Vehicle Standards Agency'.**

other than an ADI would have the skills, knowledge and experience to help you reach the standard required for the driving test.

ADIs must pass challenging theory and practical tests to join the DVSA register. They must maintain a satisfactory standard to remain on the ADI register. Their tuition is regularly checked by a DVSA examiner. Your instructor should display his or her green ADI certificate in the left-hand side of the windscreen. It shows:

- the instructor's photograph;
- his or her ADI number;
- the date of issue and date of expiry.

Your instructor may display a red triangular certificate. This means that the instructor is a 'licensed trainee driving instructor', who is part-qualified. He or she can use the trainee badge to gain teaching experience before taking the final part of the register qualifying examinations.

Ask around for recommendations and go to a school with a good reputation and a high pass rate. It is a good idea to speak with the instructor who will be teaching you before committing yourself to paying for a course of lessons. You need to be sure that you will feel comfortable with your instructor and be able to communicate easily.

Driving schools and instructors vary in the way they give tuition and the order in which subjects are taught, but all should cover the syllabus outlined in *The Official DVSA Guide to Learning to Drive*.

# Safe driving for life

Gaining a full driving licence can seem expensive. Passing the 'L' test means you have reached a basic minimum standard to be able drive by yourself. Remember that inexperienced drivers are at the highest risk of accident involving serious or fatal injury. It is worth investing in quality tuition that will keep you safe on the road for the rest of your life. You should avoid falling into the trap of wanting to have as few lessons as possible and at the cheapest possible price!

Older drivers are often aghast at the number of lessons it could take to pass the modern-day driving test, particularly if they are parents or guardians paying the bill! DVSA research has shown that on average a newly qualified driver will have had about 70 hours of driving experience, including some 45 hours' professional tuition. Driving is a skill that improves with practice and experience, but not everyone will master these skills at the same rate. Providing that you are getting good instruction, you should not be worried if you take longer to learn than others. Younger learners often feel under pressure from their friends or relatives to get through the test as quickly as possible. You shouldn't feel pressurized into applying for a test before you are ready. You will be wasting your time and money!

# Pass Plus

After passing your test your instructor may offer you extra training under the Pass Plus scheme. Designed by the DSA with the help of the motor insurance industry and driver training profession, the course comprises a minimum six hours' additional tuition. You will be able to gain experience in a wider variety of situations, for example driving on more rural roads and on motorways. Your instructor will assess your progress and issue a certificate on satisfactory completion. Participating insurance companies can offer a reduction in your insurance premium if you have completed the Pass Plus course.

# How often should I have driving lessons?

This will depend largely on your budget and time commitments and the availability of your instructor. However, one of the most effective ways of learning is to have two or three lessons each week, with practice in between. As you have to pass the theory test before you can apply for the practical driving test, combining your lessons with your studies helps you prepare for both elements at the same time. Some people do need to learn more quickly, for example if a job depends on having a driving licence. In these cases an intensive course leading up to a pre-booked practical test can seem an attractive option. Before committing yourself, however, it would be sensible to arrange for an assessment so that your instructor can establish whether or not you are likely to be up to the required standard in time. Even then, you need to bear in mind that learning to drive over a relatively short period can be stressful and tiring. Remember that you will still have to pass the theory test first!

# How much will it cost?

Whilst the cost will vary with where you live, a quick scan of your local newspaper will show you that driving lessons can be had at remarkably low prices. Driving schools can sometimes seem desperate to get your business, with offers of cheap tuition and 'free lesson' deals. Whilst some offers will be genuine promotions from successful ADIs (their students have passed!), consistently low prices may just reflect the quality of the tuition you will get.

Think about how much it costs to run a driving school – typically between £9 and £10 per lesson to cover fuel, insurance, servicing and depreciation. That's just for the vehicle. If you are booking lessons at, say, 10 for £120, how motivated is your instructor going to be earning less than £30 for 10 hours' work? That's less than the legal minimum wage!

The lead body in the profession, the Driving Instructors Association, suggests that, to earn an average wage, an instructor should be charging around £33 per hour. The reality is that you will pay less than this. Budget for between £20 and £28 per hour according to region.

Choosing the wrong school, because lessons are cheap, may cost you more in the long run. So if you must ring round to compare schools, don't just ask 'How much are your lessons?' Ask how long the lessons are, what vehicle is used and what the instructor's pass rate is. Does the instructor have qualifications over and above the ADI certificate?

Go for quality, not quantity.

## Are you learning already?

If you are already learning to drive but are not quite sure about the quality of training you are getting, ask yourself whether your instructor:

- gives an outline of the course;
- arrives on time for your lessons;
- behaves professionally;
- helps you with your studies for the theory test;
- recaps on your previous lesson;
- agrees with you what you will be learning at the start of lessons;
- encourages you to take responsibility;
- explains things in simple and understandable terms;
- demonstrates when you don't understand;
- assesses your progress and gives you feedback;
- praises you when you get things right;
- helps you to understand when you get things wrong;
- encourages you to reflect on your own performance;

- helps you record your progress for each lesson;
- allows you to ask questions without feeling awkward;
- guides you in what to study before the next lesson;
- shows a real interest in your progress.

If you have a good instructor, you should have been able to answer yes to most of these questions. If you can't, then you should try to discuss the problems. If you are offered no remedy, you should perhaps consider looking for another driving instructor. Remember – it's your money and your choice.

If you feel you have a justifiable complaint, contact:

DVSA, PO Box 280, Newcastle-Upon-Tyne, NE99 1FP

E-mail: adireg@dsa.gsi.gov.uk.

Sometimes it happens that you just can't get on well with an instructor. You can always change to another school or an instructor who suits your learning style.

# Ready for your lesson?

Learning to drive takes a great deal of concentration, especially in the early stages. To maintain your concentration you must be comfortable when driving. Visit the toilet before your lessons. Get ready in plenty of time so that you can spend a few minutes relaxing. This will help you collect your thoughts and prepare yourself mentally for driving.

Being worried or stressed will not help your concentration. Try to avoid any arguments before going out – they will put you in the wrong mood for learning. Even just feeling 'under the weather' will affect your mood and ability to concentrate. If you are ill it probably isn't worth having a lesson – but do try to give your instructor adequate notice if you need to cancel.

You must concentrate all the time. You should not drive if you're not feeling well. You'd be surprised how even a common cold can affect your concentration.

Modern cars have very effective heating and ventilation systems that allow you to keep a comfortable temperature in the car whatever the weather, so there's no need to wear heavy coats or sweaters. Wear light, comfortable clothes. Avoid anything that is heavy or tight-fitting when driving, as this could either distract you or restrict your body movements. You might find yourself getting 'hot and bothered' in the early stages no matter what you've chosen to wear. If this happens, open a window to get some fresh air and keep you alert.

Flat shoes are normally the best for driving. Heavy boots or fashion shoes may make controlling the pedals difficult. The ridged soles of some trainers can catch on the pedals and make driving difficult.

## Are you fit to drive?

**Drinking and driving don't mix!**

Driving whilst impaired through alcohol or drugs is against the law. Apart from the dangers you could cause on the road, the penalties are heavy and can cost you your licence. Alcohol is a drug. It can make you feel overconfident and less aware of danger. It makes people think they can achieve the impossible and adversely affects judgement of speed and distance. Even small amounts of alcohol will slow down your reactions. If you drink the night before a lesson, the amount of alcohol in your body may still exceed the legal limit in the morning!

If you are taking medicines or drugs (whether prescribed or not!), ask your doctor if they are likely to affect your driving. Just because a drug can be legally taken doesn't mean it will be safe to drive afterwards. Regular medicines like common cough and cold remedies can cause drowsiness – read the directions carefully. If unsure, ask the pharmacist for advice. Even if a medicine is not supposed to affect your ability to drive, remember that some people respond differently. If in doubt, don't drive!

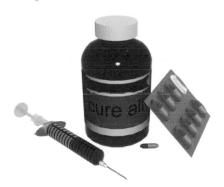

**Even over-the-counter medicines can affect your ability to drive!**

## Practising with friends and relatives

The DVSA recommends that you get plenty of practice to supplement your lessons. However, you should take advice from your instructor on when you are safe and confident enough to practise in another car. Starting private practice too soon could ruin your confidence or result in a serious loss of control.

**Full photocard licence**

In law, anyone supervising a learner driver must be over 21 and have held a full EC/EEA driving licence (European standard licence) for at least three years for the group of vehicle you will be driving.

Recommended driving techniques have changed over the years and it can be that there is conflict between what you have learned with your driving instructor and what the person supervising your private practice tells you. Furthermore, your supervisor may well have developed some bad habits that could be passed on to you. To avoid these conflicts, both you and your supervisor should follow the guidance in this book. You will both then be using up-to-date methods and following the latest rules.

Involve your driving instructor: he or she should have no objection to allowing your friend or relative to sit in on a driving lesson to find out what to expect. Ask your instructor to help you plan and advise what skills you are ready to practise.

Very often, close relatives and friends are too personally involved and may find it unnerving and frustrating to accompany you in private practice. Try to avoid conflict by staying calm. Friction between learner and supervisor will only lead to loss of concentration that will impede your progress.

The vehicle you use for private practice may be different from the car you are taking professional lessons in. This shouldn't present a problem providing you've mastered the basic control skills. However, do take the time to familiarize yourself with the practice vehicle and make sure you know where all the controls are and how they operate. Remember:

- The practice vehicle must display L plates (or D plates in Wales) clearly visible at the front and rear of the vehicle. Do not attach them to the car windows, as they will obscure your view. L plates must be removed or covered up when a learner is not driving the car.

- Your accompanying driver will need an additional rear-view mirror to keep track of what's happening behind. These are available from car accessory shops.

- It is illegal to give payment of any kind, either in money or in goods, to anyone supervising your driving unless they are on the Register of Approved Driving Instructors.

## Documents

Make sure that the vehicle can be legally driven by you before commencing practice. Check the insurance certificate. If it is not clear whether you are covered, the policyholder needs to check with the insurance company.

**Is your vehicle taxed?**

If the vehicle is more than three years old, make sure it has a current MOT certificate. If it does not, your insurance could be invalid! You also need to make sure the vehicle you are driving is taxed. You can check both online at https://www.vehicleenquiry.service.gov.uk/

## Is your vehicle roadworthy?

It is your responsibility as the driver to make sure your vehicle is in a road-worthy condition before driving. Get into the habit of making regular checks for obvious faults:

- Tyres (including spare). It is a good idea to walk round the car and check that the tyres appear to be properly inflated and undamaged and that there is nothing wedged in the tyre treads. You should also check that the tread depth is legal and that tyre pressures are correct at least once a week.

- Windscreen, windows and mirrors should be clean and free from defects. Scratched or dirty windows are a hazard, adding to glare in bright sunlight and dazzle from the headlights of other vehicles at night. Condensation can restrict your vision, particularly in damp or cold weather. Do not drive away if any of the windows are steamed up. Clear the windows before driving with a cloth or with the demister and rear screen heater. A slightly open window can help prevent condensation from reforming once you are on the move.

- Check windscreen wiper blades and that the wipers operate correctly. The wash bottle should also be topped up.

- Lights (including indicators). Check that the lenses are clean and free from defects and that the bulbs are working. Get someone to help you if necessary. Replace any dead bulbs immediately. It is a good idea to carry spares in the car.

- Check that the horn is working.

- Brakes. Check that the brakes are working at the first safe opportunity. Stop driving if you think the brakes may be faulty.

## Practising safely

Your instructor should advise you on the parts of this book to study with your supervisor before going out to practise. Remember that the car in which you practise is unlikely to have dual controls – don't be tempted to try too much too soon.

To help you during the early stages of learning, you and your supervisor need to give some thought to the time and the place for practice. Choose a level road in a quiet area where there won't be too much traffic and where you won't irritate other road users or local residents. Although your practice sessions may have to suit your supervisor's availability, try to avoid peak traffic times – rush hour and the school run! Be aware of any traffic problems that might be caused by road works or local events and plan accordingly. When you first start practising, it's best to avoid driving in bad weather conditions.

Avoid problems by asking your supervisor to select routes that you will be able to cope with. Your supervisor should also help by planning well ahead and giving you instructions and directions in plenty of time. If things get too complicated your supervisor should be prepared to compensate, for example with steering corrections.

Being a learner is no excuse for breaking the law – careless driving could result in disqualification for you and your supervisor. Make sure that you are able to stop under control before you drive in traffic. If you feel you can't cope ask your supervisor to take over. If you find something is too difficult, ask for a further explanation or a demonstration. If you still have difficulty in understanding or carrying out a routine, ask your instructor to work on it with you on your next lesson.

As your driving skills improve, your supervisor should be able to widen the range of road and traffic conditions you experience. Providing you have mastered control of the vehicle and weather conditions aren't dangerous, there is nothing to stop you gaining experience in heavier traffic, on faster roads and in windy or wet conditions.

## Don't get distracted

De-clutter your vehicle. You don't want any unnecessary window stickers, dangling mascots or other loose articles in the car. Loose articles may move about whilst you are driving, causing you distraction. Make sure there is nothing on the floor likely to roll around, such as a child's toy or an aerosol can. Apart from being a distraction, it could roll under the pedals and prevent you from applying the brakes properly.

It is not normally a good idea to carry extra passengers during the early stages of learning. It could affect your concentration. If this is unavoidable, make sure they get in safely and sit where they will not restrict your view in the mirrors. Children can get bored travelling in cars. This will make it difficult for you to concentrate on your driving. If they must go with you, make sure they are properly restrained and kept under control. This also applies if you take your pets in the car.

# Checkpoint 1

Before going out to practise, answer the following questions. Just as with the theory test, some of them will have more than one correct answer. If you can't answer a question, or you don't understand what it means, refer back to the books or *Highway Code* rules listed at the beginning of this stage. If you still don't understand, ask your instructor for help.

1   You want to pay someone to give you driving tuition.
    You must be certain that the person:
    *Choose one answer*
    a.   is old enough and has the correct driving licence
    b.   is an approved driving instructor (ADI) or holds a trainee
         licence
    c.   has dual controls in his or her car
    d.   has held a driving licence for at least two years

**2**   Anyone supervising a learner driver must be:
*Choose one answer*

a.   18 and have passed the L test
b.   18 and have held a full licence for six months
c.   21 and have held a full licence for two years
d.   21 and have held a full licence for three years

**3**   Before applying for your theory test you must:
*Choose one answer*

a.   apply for your driving licence
b.   apply for your practical driving test
c.   have had at least 10 driving lessons
d.   have received your provisional licence

**4**   A relative offers the use of his or her car for private practice. Before driving it you must make sure that:
*Choose one answer*

a.   the vehicle has insurance cover
b.   your use of the car is insured
c.   your relative has third-party insurance
d.   you have the insurance documents for the car

**5**   Before driving a car for the first time you must: *Choose two answers*

a.   have applied for your photocard licence
b.   make sure your eyesight is up to the required standard
c.   have received your provisional licence
d.   pass the theory test

**6**   To meet the legal eyesight requirements, you should be able to read a car number plate in this format from:

**HK55 WES**

*Choose one answer*

a.   10 metres
b.   15 metres
c.   18 metres
d.   20 metres

**7** If you need to wear glasses or contact lenses to read a car number plate at the distance required for driving, you:
*Choose one answer*

  a.  must keep them in the car
  b.  needn't wear them when driving
  c.  might need to use them in poor weather or when driving at night
  d.  must wear them at all times when driving

**8** Cars used for driving lessons must be:
*Choose one answer*

  a.  fitted with dual controls
  b.  roadworthy
  c.  less than three years old
  d.  saloon models

**9** You are using your own car for private practice. The L plates displayed on the car:
*Choose two answers*

  a.  can be made up to a size of your choice
  b.  must be clearly visible to the front and from behind
  c.  are best placed in the front and rear windows
  d.  must conform to legal specifications

**10** Cars being driven on the road must:
*Choose one answer*

  a.  be taxed
  b.  not require a current MOT certificate
  c.  be capable of carrying at least three passengers
  d.  display an insurance certificate on the windscreen

**11** You have been to a party the night before a driving lesson and had a few alcoholic drinks. In the morning you:
*Choose one answer*

  a.  should be all right to drive
  b.  could still be over the legal limit
  c.  should have more confidence
  d.  should ask your ADI to test your breath

**12** You should apply for your practical test:
*Choose two answers*

    a.   when your instructor says you are ready

    b.   when you've had a minimum of 10 lessons

    c.   after you've passed the theory and hazard perception tests

    d.   as soon as you've read *The Highway Code*

**13** The driver is legally responsible for the wearing of seat belts by:
*Choose one answer*

    a.   all passengers, regardless of age

    b.   children over 14 but under 16

    c.   all children under 14

    d.   any adult with a disability

**14** The most effective ways to counter sleepiness when driving are to:
*Choose three answers*

    a.   avoid driving at night

    b.   avoid driving for too long without a break

    c.   keep fresh air circulating in the car

    d.   take regular breaks

    e.   play loud music on the car audio system

**15** Driving after drinking alcohol will:
*Choose three answers*

    a.   reduce your sense of confidence

    b.   speed up your reaction time

    c.   make you more likely to take risks

    d.   slow down your reactions

    e.   affect your judgements

**16** If carrying children in a vehicle the driver should ensure that they:
*Choose two answers*

    a.   enter by the door nearest their seat

    b.   enter by the door nearest the kerb

    c.   all wear an adult seat belt

    d.   use a child restraint appropriate for their height and weight

**17** Which of these statements apply when deciding whether you can legally drive a car? *Choose three answers*

   a.  You must have fully comprehensive insurance

   b.  You must have a valid driving licence

   c.  You must be in possession of the car registration certificate (logbook)

   d.  The vehicle must have a current MOT certificate if over three years old

   e.  The vehicle must be taxed

**18** Who has responsibility for seeing that a vehicle isn't overloaded? *Choose one answer*

   a.  the owner of the vehicle

   b.  the driver of the vehicle

   c.  the person who loaded the vehicle

   d.  the registered keeper of the vehicle

**19** You have arranged a practice session with your supervisor but find yourself very tired after a hard day at work. You should: *Choose one answer*

   a.  take some 'pep pills' to stay awake

   b.  not drive

   c.  drive faster to lessen the danger of falling asleep at the wheel

   d.  take a flask of hot coffee with you

**20** A full driving licence is valid until your: *Choose one answer*

   a.  60th birthday

   b.  65th birthday

   c.  70th birthday

   d.  retirement

You will find the answers on page 327.

Scores:     First try         Second try       Third try

Record your scores in Appendix 2 (page 330).

# Stage 2
# Get to know your car

In this stage you will learn about the 'cockpit drill' – the routine to go through each time you get into the driving seat. You will find out what the main car controls do and how they operate. You will also learn about the driving mirrors and other driving aids. Your instructor will refer to this stage as the 'controls lesson', and although you'll be anxious actually to get moving it is essential for safe driving that you understand the function and use of the main car controls before moving off for the first time.

To help you prepare for this stage, you can also read:

- *The Official DVSA Guide to Driving: The essential skills*, Section 3 – The controls, and Section 4 – Mirrors.
- *The Official DVSA Guide to Learning to Drive*, Section 2 – Cockpit checks, and Section 2 – Controls and instruments.

## The cockpit drill

Before you drive any vehicle you need to carry out the cockpit drill. This is a simple routine to ensure the safety of yourself, your passengers and other road users and is easily remembered as **DSMS**, which stands for Doors, Seat, Mirrors and Seat belt. Your instructor might teach you a variation of this routine.

**Take care getting into the driving seat!**

### Doors

The first thing to do is get in the driver's seat! Your instructor will probably have parked facing the traffic flow and put the seat back to make it easy for you to get in promptly. Open the driver's door from behind so you don't have to walk round it to get in. Beware of other traffic – you don't want to cause another road user to swerve when you open the door!

You should close the door as soon as you are seated and then check that the parking brake is applied – your instructor will show you how to do this.

**Make sure all the doors are closed**

Pull the door to make sure there's no movement. Check in the outside mirrors that the doors are flush with the bodyline of the car. Listen to make sure that passengers (including your instructor!) have closed their doors properly. Remember – you are responsible for the safety of your passengers. A door not closed properly will rattle. It could fly open as you drive along or go around a bend.

## *Seat*

The next thing to do is adjust the driving seat so that you can see all round and reach the hand and foot controls comfortably and easily. To do so, hold the steering wheel with one hand and pull the lever at the side/beneath the seat with your other hand so that you can move the seat to the correct position. You need to be able to push the left foot pedal down fully with your left foot without stretching.

Release the lever when you are happy with the seat position and push yourself back in the seat to make sure it is locked in place. You can then adjust the angle of the back of the seat by the lever/knob on the side of the seat so that you are comfortable, can see clearly over the steering wheel and can move your arms freely.

*Can you reach all around the steering wheel?* If not, you may need to adjust the back of the seat or move the steering wheel if the car you are in has that option. Your instructor will guide you.

The next thing to do is adjust the head restraint so that it will protect your head and neck. Reach behind you and raise or lower the restraint so that the

**Make sure you can reach and use all the controls comfortably and easily**

rigid part is at least as high as the top of your ears and as close as is comfortable to the back of your head (note that in some vehicles the position of the head restraint is fixed).

## Mirrors

The mirrors are your most important visual driving aid, which must be checked at regular intervals as you drive along. It's as important to know what's happening behind as it is to see what's happening ahead. There will be more about using the mirrors later. For now you need to know how to adjust them.

**Adjust the interior mirror to give the best possible rear view**

Only adjust the mirrors when the car is stationary and you are seated in your normal driving position. Start with the interior mirror. Hold the mirror by the edges to avoid finger marks. Adjust the mirror so that you get the best possible view through the back window without having to move your head. You should be able to frame the whole of the rear window in the interior mirror, but, if you can't, make sure you can see the top and right-hand side of the rear window.

Adjust the exterior mirrors so that you can get the best rear view with minimal head movements. You should be able to see a small strip of the

side of the car, and the horizon should appear about in the middle of the mirror.

## Anti-dazzle

Most interior mirrors have an anti-dazzle lever. This is for use at night so that you are not blinded by the glare of headlights from vehicles behind.

## Seat belt

Having adjusted the mirrors, you should now put on the seat belt. You must use the seat belt whenever you drive, no matter how short your journey. Use your left hand to reach for the buckle and stretch it across. Ensure that the belt is not twisted and that it lies flat across your chest and stomach. Secure the belt in the buckle at the side

of your seat. To remove it again you need simply press the button on top/at the side of the buckle. When putting the belt on and taking it off, hold the buckle so that it doesn't fly up and hit you in the face or bang into the window. Your instructor will demonstrate how to do this if needed.

Seat belts save lives and reduce the risk of serious injury. The law requires that all drivers and passengers (unless they have an exemption certificate) must wear a seat belt. As the driver, you should encourage all of your passengers to wear their seat belts. If you are carrying passengers under 14 years of age, it is your responsibility to make sure they wear seat belts.

## Fuel

On your first lesson your instructor will have made sure that there is enough fuel in the car, but you should get into the habit of checking the fuel gauge before setting off.

## Parking brake and neutral

After you have completed the DSMS routine, it is good practice to check once more that the parking brake (sometimes referred to as the handbrake) is applied and that the gear lever is in the neutral position. You'll learn how to do this a little later in this stage as you go through the main controls.

It is very important that you complete the cockpit drill *before* starting the engine and moving off. It would be very dangerous to adjust the seat, steering column or mirrors whilst the vehicle was moving.

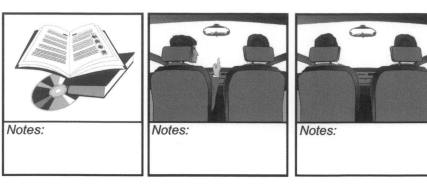

**Assessment – the cockpit drill**

# The main controls

Now that you're seated correctly and the vehicle is secure, it's time to learn about the main controls and driving aids.

## *Foot controls*

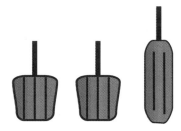

Cars with manual transmission have three foot pedals. From right to left these are the accelerator, the footbrake and the clutch pedal.

The pedal on the right is the accelerator or 'gas' pedal and controls the rate at which fuel and air are supplied to the engine. The accelerator should only be used with the right foot.

The harder the pedal is pressed, the faster the engine will run and the more power is generated. You should press the pedal lightly, using gentle changes of pressure in normal driving. It takes practice and experience to know how much to press the pedal to make the car speed up. Easing the pressure on the pedal will make the car slow down.

Accelerator or 'gas' pedal

The footbrake

The middle pedal is the footbrake and is used to slow down and stop the car by applying pressure to the front and rear brakes. The footbrake should normally only be used with the right foot, as you would not have to use both the accelerator and brake at the same time.

## Using the accelerator and footbrake

Position your right foot so that it will pivot comfortably between the accelerator and brake pedals. To do this, cover the brake pedal with your right foot. Without looking down or moving your heel, practise pivoting between these pedals. When you have found a comfortable position for your foot, get a feel for the brake pedal by pressing it lightly.

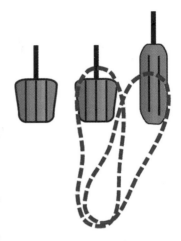

You should be able to pivot your foot between the accelerator and footbrake

The first pressure puts the brake lights on at the back of the car. When driving along, this will let anyone behind know you are slowing down. The harder you press the pedal, the more the car will slow down. You should brake progressively, using the ball of your foot to press the pedal lightly, increasing pressure gradually as the car slows, and easing the pressure just before stopping so that the vehicle halts smoothly.

Brake light signals come on when you press the footbrake

The left foot pedal operates the clutch. The main purpose of the clutch is to connect and disconnect the power from the engine to the road wheels. It is needed so that changes can be made smoothly from one gear into another. The clutch pedal should only be pressed with the left foot.

## How the clutch works

In its simplest form, the clutch is made up of two circular friction plates, held firmly together by spring pressure. One of these plates is attached to the engine and rotates all the time that the engine is running. The other plate is attached, through the gearbox, to the drive wheels. Pressing the clutch pedal down forces the plates apart, breaking the link between the engine and the wheels. Controlling the clutch pedal correctly is a vital part of safe and skilled driving and takes practice and experience.

The Clutch Pedal

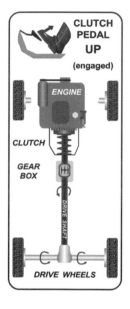

CLUTCH PEDAL **UP** (engaged)

CLUTCH

GEAR BOX

DRIVE SHAFT

DRIVE WHEELS

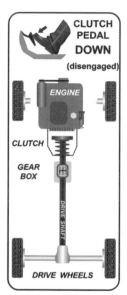

CLUTCH PEDAL **DOWN** (disengaged)

CLUTCH

GEAR BOX

DRIVE SHAFT

DRIVE WHEELS

**Controlling the clutch is an important driving skill that takes practice to learn**

## Using the clutch

To move off, change gear and stop, you should be able to use the clutch smoothly and without looking at your feet. To begin with, cover the clutch with your left foot and then press it down. This will disconnect the engine from the gearbox. You will have to do this when changing gear and just before stopping. Next let the pedal up smoothly. You will feel a powerful spring pushing your foot up.

Only a small part of the total pedal travel, known as the biting range, has any noticeable effect on the car. To move off and control very low speeds, you must be able to find the **biting point** (sometimes called the holding point) at the bottom of this range. The biting point is where the two clutch plates are just in contact so that they slip against one another. Lifting the clutch pedal up beyond this point brings the plates into full contact, causing the engine to drive the road wheels.

# Hand controls

## Parking brake

The parking brake is used to secure the car when you park it or are stationary for more than a few moments. The parking brake is usually operated by a lever positioned beside the driver's seat usually operates the parking brake. You must make sure the car has stopped before applying the parking brake, and you must be able to apply and release it promptly, without looking down.

**Only use the parking brake when the vehicle is stationary**

To practise, first press the footbrake with your left foot and keep it pressed down so that the car won't move. To release the parking brake, put your hand on to it with your thumb on the button. Pull the lever up slightly and press the button in. Keep the button pressed in whilst you lower the lever.

To apply the parking brake, press in the button, pull the lever firmly upwards and release the button. The button will lock against a ratchet. You should try not to forget to push in the button, as this would cause unnecessary wear.

In some vehicles the lever operating the parking brake can be an additional foot pedal or even electrically operated. Your instructor will show you how these work if fitted in your tuition vehicle.

## Gear lever

The purpose of the gears is to allow the car to be driven with minimum strain on the engine, just the same as the gears on a pushbike! The gear lever enables you to change from one gear to another.

Modern cars usually have five or six forward and one reverse gear. Older cars may only have four forward gears.

The speed ranges overlap, so there is no fixed speed at which to change gear. With experience you will know from the sound of the engine when a gear change is needed. First gear is the lowest and most powerful gear, which is used to move the car from rest. The highest gear is the least powerful and is used for cruising at higher speeds. Low gears

**The gear lever is usually marked with the gear positions**

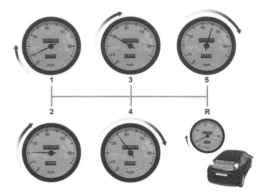

**The speed ranges for the gears overlap**

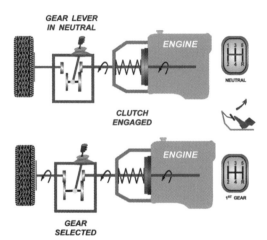

**In 'neutral' the link between engine and road wheels is broken in the gearbox**

are used at low speeds and when the engine has extra work to do, for example climbing a steep hill. Higher gears are selected at higher speeds when the engine has less work to do. Reverse gear is only used as low speeds. Selecting reverse gear causes the reversing lights to come on at the rear of the car.

The gear lever also has a **neutral** position where no gear is selected. In the neutral position the link between the engine and the driven wheels is broken in the gearbox. This allows the engine to run without turning the road wheels even if the clutch pedal is up. To check that the gear lever is in the neutral position, move it from side to side.

## How to select a gear

You need to be able to select each gear without looking down at the lever.

The gear lever in most modern cars is 'spring-loaded' and, when in neutral, rests between third and fourth gears. To select a gear, use the palm

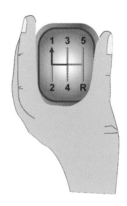

of your hand on the lever. This will allow you to push the lever forwards, backwards and sideways as needed. Your instructor will demonstrate the gear positions for your car and let you practise with the car stationary and the parking brake applied.

To find first gear, push the lever across and forwards. From first gear push the lever straight back to second gear. To find third gear, palm the lever out of second and forward into the correct position, and so on for each gear. It will take practice to make smooth and unhurried gear changes. You usually change through the gears in order as you increase in speed. When you slow down, however, you usually select the appropriate gear for the new speed, and it is safe to miss one or more gears in between.

Practise changing up and down the gears until you are confident you can do so without looking at the lever. You will need to coordinate this skill with foot pedal movements when you start to drive.

## Steering wheel

The steering wheel is used to control the direction of the car by turning the front wheels. Imagine the wheel as a clock face. You should hold the steering wheel lightly but firmly with your hands in the 'ten-to-two' or 'quarter-to-three' position. You should keep both hands on the wheel all the time the car is moving unless operating another hand control or giving a signal. You should never take both hands from the wheel whilst the vehicle is moving.

**Hold the steering wheel at the 'ten-to-two' or 'quarter-to-three' position as you drive ahead**

To steer a straight course, look well ahead – you will always tend to 'go where you are looking'! You must be able to operate the main controls without looking at them. Looking down will result in your car wandering from side to side.

To turn the car you should use the 'pull–push' technique. This means feeding the rim of the steering wheel through your hands so that one hand is always gripping the wheel. For example, to turn right, move your right hand to the top of the wheel but not beyond the 12 o'clock position. Pull the wheel downwards with your right hand and at the same time slide your left hand down the rim so that both hands end up at the same height on the wheel. Then change the grip to your left hand

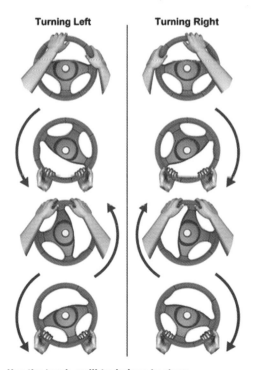

Turning Left    Turning Right

**Use the 'push–pull' technique to steer**

and push the wheel further round, at the same time allowing your right hand to slide up the rim of the wheel. You may need to repeat these steps according to the angle through which the front wheels need to turn. You can vary your hand movements according to the amount you need to turn.

To turn the wheel back again, or to turn left, use the same procedure, but the left hand goes to the top of the wheel first. You should not let the wheel slip back through your hands after a turn, as this lessens your control of the car.

Try not to cross your hands on the wheel, as this lessens control. You should also avoid steering when the car is stationary, as this can damage your tyres.

## Operating switches

The most frequently used switches, such as the direction indicators, lights and windscreen wipers, are usually on the column just behind the steering wheel. Other important switches include the horn, windscreen washer and demisters. Your instructor will show you how the switches operate. Practise using these and other ancillary controls when safe. It is important that you are familiar with their position and method of use. You will learn when to use each of the controls as your driving experience increases.

# The importance of mirrors

The driving mirrors are extremely important aids, and their use is vital for safe driving.

The purpose of the driving mirrors is to let you know what is happening behind. It is just as important to know what is behind you as what is in front of you. You must use the mirrors frequently when driving and act safely and sensibly on what you see.

**Compare the view in the interior and exterior mirrors**

The interior mirror is made of flat glass and gives a true picture of the following traffic. Most exterior mirrors are made with convex (curved) glass and make following traffic appear smaller and further away than it really is. You can see this effect from the driving seat when parked at the roadside. Choose an object or parked car behind you that you can see in the interior mirror. Compare this view with the view in the exterior mirrors. In practice this means that it can be difficult at first to judge the speed and position of vehicles behind.

Always remember that in a convex mirror the vehicle behind appears to be smaller and therefore will be closer than you think. With practice you will overcome this difficulty, particularly if you get into the habit of using the interior and exterior mirrors together.

You should always use the mirrors *well before* any manoeuvre, that is a change of speed or direction. This leads on to the golden rule of **mirrors–signal–manoeuvre**, referred to as **MSM**.

MSM means checking your mirrors well before signalling and doing both in good time before making your move. You need to check mirrors before:

- signalling;
- moving off;
- changing direction to overtake, turn left or right or change lane;
- slowing down or stopping;
- opening your car door.

It isn't possible to get a complete rear view with the driving mirrors. There are always areas that the mirrors don't cover. These areas are known as blind spots and can be caused by the body of the car, door pillars, etc. Here you can see that an overtaking motorcycle will momentarily disappear in your blind spot until you catch sight as it draws level with your seat. It is for this reason that you sometimes need to look round. This is especially important before moving off.

**Be aware of blind spots not covered by your mirrors**

As today's roads are getting busier and busier, looking round to check blind spots on the move can be dangerous, especially at speed. Every time you look behind, you are averting your eyes from what is happening in front of you. A quick sideways glance is necessary in certain circumstances. However, looking round on the move should be the exception rather than the rule.

You should normally check your interior mirror first and then, if changing direction, the exterior mirror on the side to which you will be moving or turning.

When you have looked in your mirrors you should assess the situation and decide whether it is safe to make your intended move. This means either making your move or waiting for a safe opportunity to do so. It is essential that you should never signal without first checking your mirrors and that you should never take it for granted that you can carry out these manoeuvres safely just because you've signalled.

When using your mirrors you should be asking yourself what's behind you, how near they are to you, what speed they are travelling at and what their intentions are. You must have enough time to decide, which makes early use of the mirrors essential.

Notes:     Notes:     Notes:

**Assessment – the main controls and driving aids**

# Driving an 'automatic'

Vehicles fitted with automatic transmission do not have a clutch pedal. This makes the physical task of driving easier, especially in heavy traffic. Automatic vehicles are increasing in popularity and are also particularly suitable for those with physical disabilities. Learning to start, steer and stop is much easier in a car with automatic transmission because the driver can concentrate more on planning ahead and steering.

Instead of a gear lever there is a **selector lever** that allows the driver to choose between Drive, Reverse and Neutral. In most automatic cars, the driver may engage a fixed low gear for carrying out low-speed manoeuvres and for better control on hills and in slow traffic. In an automatic you will normally only use your right foot to control the accelerator and footbrake. Gear changes are carried out automatically. They are regulated by the car's speed, the load on the engine and the pressure applied on the accelerator by the driver.

When driving an automatic car, the parking brake has to be used more often because the vehicle will have a tendency to creep forwards. If you are learning in an automatic, your instructor should explain about the extra use of the parking brake and the different techniques used to control the car at low speeds.

If you pass your test in an automatic car, you will only be entitled to drive this type of vehicle.

# Checkpoint 2

**1** Head restraints provide protection against:
*Choose two answers*

   a.  neck and spinal injuries
   b.  the effects of whiplash
   c.  severe headaches
   d.  fatigue on long journeys

**2** You should check your seat position:
*Choose two answers*

   a.  as soon as you drive away
   b.  if someone else has been driving
   c.  before you switch on the engine
   d.  when you have been driving for about five minutes

**3** When driving, you should:
*Choose two answers*

   a.  never take a hand off the wheel
   b.  never take both hands off the wheel if the car is moving
   c.  look where you want the car to go
   d.  let the wheel spin back after turning

**4** You should avoid:
*Choose two answers*

    a. applying the parking brake before the car has stopped
    b. applying the parking brake after the car has stopped
    c. releasing the parking brake until the car is moving
    d. releasing the parking brake until sure it is safe to move

**5** In an automatic vehicle, you:
*Choose one answer*

    a. only need to use the parking brake when parking
    b. will not need to apply the footbrake to stop
    c. will need to use the parking brake more frequently
    d. need to use the parking brake less frequently

**6** You can check that the seat is correctly positioned by:
*Choose one answer*

    a. driving a little way to ensure you have full control
    b. reaching all round the steering wheel
    c. asking your instructor
    d. asking a passenger

**7** You should understand the function of those controls that have a bearing on road safety. These include the:
*Choose three answers*

    a. indicators
    b. mobile phone
    c. radio
    d. lights
    e. demisters

**8** Most interior mirrors are made of flat glass. This:
*Choose two answers*

    a. gives a distorted picture
    b. gives a true picture
    c. makes it easier to judge the speed and distance of following traffic
    d. makes it difficult to judge the speed and distance of following traffic

**9** Most exterior mirrors have convex glass. This:
*Choose three answers*

a. gives a wider field of vision
b. makes things behind seem larger
c. makes things behind seem smaller
d. makes things behind seem to be nearer
e. makes things behind seem to be further away

**10** Blind spots:
*Choose three answers*

a. are caused by convex mirrors
b. can be fully overcome by mirrors
c. may be partially overcome by mirrors
d. may be caused by door pillars
e. are areas ahead, behind and to the side of the car that you can't see from your normal driving position

**11** The first thing to do when you've got into the driver's seat is:
*Choose one answer*

a. adjust the seat
b. apply the parking brake
c. switch on the ignition
d. close the door

**12** When the gear lever is in neutral, the engine:

*Choose one answer*

a. is disconnected from the road wheels
b. is connected to the road wheels
c. is disconnected from the gearbox
d. will slow the car down

**13** To adjust the interior mirror correctly you should:
*Choose three answers*

    a.  first make sure your seat is properly adjusted
    b.  operate the anti-dazzle device
    c.  hold the mirror by its edges
    d.  get the best possible rear view
    e.  lean forward slightly in your seat

**14** In a manual car, the left foot manually operates the:
*Choose one answer*

    a.  brake and clutch pedals
    b.  brake pedal only
    c.  clutch pedal only
    d.  accelerator pedal only

**15** In a manual car, the right foot operates the:
*Choose one answer*

    a.  clutch and brake pedals
    b.  accelerator pedal only
    c.  accelerator and brake pedals
    d.  brake pedal only

**16** To operate the parking brake lever you should:
*Choose one answer*

    a.  always listen for the ratchet
    b.  avoid wearing the ratchet
    c.  always press the footbrake
    d.  always press the clutch pedal down fully

**17** The best way to hold the steering wheel for driving along is: *Choose two answers*

    a.  at a 'ten to two' or 'quarter to three' position
    b.  at a 'twenty past eight' position
    c.  with your right arm resting on the door
    d.  firmly, but not too tightly

**18** Looking down at the gear lever or foot pedals when driving will:
*Choose two answers*

    a.  cause you to wander off course
    b.  distract you from the traffic situation ahead
    c.  help you avoid selecting the wrong gear
    d.  help you select the correct gear

**19** The main purpose of the clutch is to:
*Choose one answer*

    a.  judge where your seat should be positioned
    b.  disconnect power from the engine to the road wheels
    c.  control the speed of the engine
    d.  slow the car down

**20** First gear is the:
*Choose one answer*

    a.  least powerful gear
    b.  most powerful gear
    c.  most economical gear
    d.  best for driving at high speeds

You will find the answers on page 327.

| Scores: | First try | Second try | Third try |
| --- | --- | --- | --- |
| | | | |

Record your scores in Appendix 2 (page 330).

# Stage 3
# Starting to drive

During this stage you will be learning how to start the engine, move off, change gear, and stop the car. You will also get the feel of the steering and learn to use some of the ancillary controls. Make sure that you can carry out all of these skills reasonably well before going out to practise. Your instructor will advise you when you are ready to go out with someone else.

It is important that you learn the basic procedures in very quiet areas. Housing estates with lots of parked vehicles and other hazards are not really suitable. Your instructor will talk you through each exercise until you can manage on your own. Your instructor or supervisor should give you directions in plenty of time to allow you to carry out all of the individual skills without rushing. However, you may find that someone who isn't an ADI does not give you enough time, because of lack of experience with learners. If you find yourself becoming confused and rushed, ask your supervisor to give instructions much earlier.

Avoid talking whilst you are practising – this will only distract you. Concentrate, keep your eyes on the road and listen carefully to directions. The following are useful instructions:

- 'I would like you to take the next road on the right.'
- 'Take the second road on the right; this is the first one.'
- 'At the end of the road, turn left, please.'

To help you prepare for this stage, you can also read:

- *The Official DVSA Guide to Driving: The essential skills*, Section 5 – Starting to drive.
- *The Official DVSA Guide to Learning to Drive*, Section 2 – Moving away and stopping, Section 2 – Safe positioning, Section 2 – Mirrors – vision and use, Section 2 – Signals.

Look up and learn *Highway Code* rules about:

- Moving off, normal driving position and use of mirrors.
- Parking.

# Starting the engine and preparing to move off

Go through the cockpit drill that you learned in Stage 2. Once you are correctly seated you can learn how to start the engine and get the feel of the clutch and accelerator pedals by practising finding the biting point.

## *Starting the engine*

Before turning the ignition key it is important to make the safety checks of 'parking brake and neutral'. You must make sure the car is secure and that it won't move when you switch on the engine. If your car is in gear or if the handbrake is not properly set, when you switch on the engine you could move unexpectedly. Check that the parking brake is on firmly. Now check that the gear lever is in the neutral position. When you move the gear lever from side to side, it should feel quite free. If you are driving an automatic, check that the selector lever is in the P (park) or N (neutral) position.

The starter or ignition switch is normally on or near the steering column and usually combines an anti-theft steering lock. Most cars have an ignition switch with three positions. The first releases the anti-theft lock, the second position switches electrical power to the car's instruments and controls, and the third position operates  the starter. Place the ignition key in the switch and turn it to release the anti-theft steering lock. You may need to turn the steering wheel slightly whilst you do this.

Turn the key until you see some red warning lights appear on the instrument panel. The battery symbol is the ignition warning light. It only illuminates when the battery is not being charged by power from the engine. This light should go out soon after you start the car. The oil can symbol is the oil pressure warning light. It should also go out soon after you start the engine.   If the red lights do not go out you should switch off and investigate. Driving with any red light displayed on the dashboard usually indicates a mechanical fault that could damage the engine or compromise your safety.

If your car runs on diesel, you may have to wait until the pre-heater warning light goes out before you can switch on the engine.

Turn the key gently to operate the starter. When the engine starts release the key. If the engine does not start you might need to gently squeeze the accelerator pedal and try again. Do not pump the pedal, as this can flood the engine and make starting even more difficult.

Most modern cars have an automatic choke. This allows more fuel to flow into the engine in cold weather to help it start. If you're in an older car, you may need to pull the choke out manually, but remember to push this in once the engine is warm.

Once started, the engine should run smoothly without you having to press the accelerator pedal. The engine is said to be running at **tick-over** speed.

To stop the engine, simply turn the key anticlockwise. If you were leaving your car you would then remove the key and set the anti-theft lock by turning the steering wheel slightly until the lock engaged.

Some modern vehicles may have a keyless ignition system which will detect the presence of an electronic chip in your keyfob. This will permit you to start and stop the engine with a push button on the dashboard.

## *How to find the biting point*

**Finding the biting point**

With the engine running, press the clutch pedal fully down with your left foot and keep it pressed down. With the palm of your hand, select first gear. Then you need to **set the gas**. This means pressing the accelerator pedal lightly with your right foot until you get an even hum from the engine. You should only need to press the pedal down about the thickness of a £1 coin. Then hold your right foot steady. The engine speed should only be about half as fast again as the tick-over speed.

Raise the clutch pedal slowly by bending your ankle. Keeping your heel down will give you more support and positive clutch control. It may feel a little awkward at first, particularly if you have small feet or are in a car with high pedals. As you raise the clutch, listen for a slight drop in the engine speed. When you hear or feel this, you have found the holding point and should keep the pedal still. If you come off the clutch pedal a little further, you may see the bonnet begin to rise. When you try this exercise with the parking brake released you will find the car begins to creep forward as you lift the clutch pedal just beyond the biting point.

Push the clutch pedal down again and release the accelerator. Put the gear lever into neutral and relax your feet.

Setting the gas and holding the clutch at biting point for too long is a fault, which will waste fuel and wear the clutch unnecessarily. For this reason, as you get more experienced, you will learn to check all round before preparing the car to see that there will be a safe opportunity to move away reasonably soon.

Practise this exercise until you are confident you can find the biting point. If you let the clutch pedal up too far or too quickly the engine may stall. If this happens, go through your safety checks again (parking brake and neutral) before restarting the engine.

**Assessment – starting the engine and finding the biting point**

# Moving off and stopping

Now you know how to prepare the car for moving off. The next step is to learn the routine for moving away safely and how to stop in a safe place without causing danger or inconvenience to others. Initially, your instructor will get you to move off in first gear, drive a little way down the road and then stop again at the kerb.

## Using the clutch to manoeuvre at slow speed

Before practising moving off it is worth learning how to make the car creep forward slowly and stop it again using the clutch pedal. Choose a level road and prepare the car to move off by selecting first gear, setting the gas and finding the biting point. Keep your feet still and, when safe, release the parking brake. If you have correctly found the biting point, the car shouldn't move. If it starts to creep forward, you need to push the clutch pedal down very slightly to stop it again. Practise using the clutch pedal to move the car forward a couple of metres by raising the clutch pedal slightly and then stopping it again by dipping the clutch pedal back to the biting point. This procedure is known as clutch control and will help you to move off smoothly.

## Moving off

**Check in your mirrors and all round before moving away**

Take an initial look to the front and in the mirrors for traffic and pedestrians and then get ready to move. Remember to look ahead and to the sides of the car. As well as other vehicles, look out for pedestrians and cyclists who are in or approaching your blind spots. What are they going to do? Might someone be about to cross the road ahead of your car?

You normally move off in first gear, so you can prepare the car by selecting the gear, setting the gas and finding the biting point as above. Hold the clutch pedal still whilst you make your safety checks.

Make sure it's safe to move off. This means applying the mirrors–signal–manoeuvre routine. Check your mirrors and look all round to make sure there is no other road user in your blind spots.

You must then decide if a signal is necessary. You will need to give a signal when moving away if it will help, warn or inform another road user of what you intend to do. Timing the signal is important. You should not signal too early, too late or for too long. There is more about signalling later in this chapter.

Give a signal if needed; then be ready to release the parking brake.

It is very important to make a final safety check over your right shoulder to make sure there is no other road user in your blind area. If safe, release the parking brake and squeeze the gas pedal a little more. The car should start to move forwards. Smoothly raise your left foot fully from the clutch pedal as you build up speed.

**It is very important to make a final safety check over your right shoulder before moving off**

You will need to steer to your normal driving position – about a metre from the kerb. Turn the wheel slightly right as you move off. When you reach the correct road position, turn the wheel slightly left so that you end up steering a straight course.

It can be difficult to judge road position at first. Don't look at the kerb or the road just in front of the bonnet. Avoid staring at nearby objects; it will only make you steer towards them. Look well ahead to where you want the car to go. Plan your course well ahead by memorizing the position of any obstructions. Rely on your side vision to sense your position in the road and to judge the clearance you are leaving between your car and parked vehicles. Look ahead at the space at the side and in front of any obstruction – this will help you give enough clearance.

## *Stopping on the left*

**Except in an emergency the procedure for stopping is always the same**

Except in an emergency, the routine for stopping is always the same. Select a safe place to stop and use the MSM routine.

Check your mirrors and give a left indicator signal if necessary. Steer gently towards the kerb, remembering to correct the steering as you approach so you don't bump it.

Pivot your right foot from the accelerator pedal to the footbrake. Follow the rule of progressive braking: apply light pressure at first, gradually increasing pressure as the car slows.

Just before the car stops, you will need to push the clutch pedal down fully with your left foot so that the engine doesn't stall. For a smooth stop you should be easing the pressure on the footbrake as the car comes to rest. With practice you should be able to stop parallel to the kerb with the steering set straight.

Cancel the indicator signal if you've given one; then apply the parking brake and select neutral before taking your feet from the pedals.

# Changing gear

First gear provided the power you needed for pulling the weight of the car away. As you build up speed you don't need so much power, so you can change up through the higher gears. To gain confidence, practise gear changes on fairly quiet, level roads.

## *Changing up*

**First to second**

**Second to third**

The procedure for changing up from a low to a higher gear is always the same.

To change from first to second, grip the wheel a little more firmly with your right hand and, keeping your eyes on the road, cup your left hand over the gear lever ready. Push the clutch down quickly and at the same time take your foot off the gas pedal. Using gentle pressure, move the gear lever from first into second.

Raise the clutch smoothly to the top and then press the accelerator gently to increase the engine speed. Put your left hand back on to the wheel.

Second gear will allow you to accelerate a little more until you are ready to move to third and so on. Remember to use the palm of your hand to move the gear lever.

## *Changing down*

The procedure for changing down from a high to a lower gear will depend on whether or not the car has been slowed by braking. As a general rule, you should use the footbrake to reduce speed before changing down to the appropriate gear. However, braking need not always precede a downward gear change. You may slow down simply by easing off the gas as you approach a hazard.

To practise changing down the gears you will need to move off and build your speed up until you are driving at about 30 mph in fourth gear. Your supervisor should help by keeping a lookout, making sure it is safe for you to carry out each step of the exercise.

## Changing down whilst slowing down

Remember to grip the steering wheel a little more firmly with your right hand. When safe, ease off the accelerator pedal and begin gentle braking so that the car slows to about 20 mph. Keeping your eyes on the road, cup your left hand over the gear lever ready. Push the clutch down quickly and at the same time move the gear lever from fourth into third. Raise the clutch pedal smoothly and return your right foot to the accelerator pedal or continue braking as appropriate. Bring your left hand back to the steering wheel.

Check the mirror to make sure it is safe and repeat the exercise, slowing to around 10 mph and changing from third to second gear.

## Block gear changes

You don't need to change down through the gears in order. It is preferable when slowing down to brake to the desired speed and then select the appropriate gear. Move off and build up your speed until you are travelling at about 30 mph in fourth gear. Check the mirrors to make sure it is safe and brake gently to slow the car down to about 10 mph. Release the brake and change from fourth gear into second.

**Fourth to second**

If safe, build up your speed, changing up through the gears, until you reach about 30 mph again. Keep practising until you can carry out the exercise smoothly and confidently.

## Changing from third to first gear

To practise this exercise you will need to move off and build up your speed until you are driving along at about 20 mph in third gear. If safe, brake gently to slow the car down until you have almost stopped. Push the clutch down, keep it down and release the brake so the car keeps rolling forwards very slowly. Just before the car stops, change from third gear into first.

When safe, accelerate gently to build up speed again. Change up through the gears until you reach about 20 mph in third so that you can practise again. Keep practising the exercise until you feel confident.

## Changing down under acceleration

Sometimes you need to select a lower gear because you anticipate needing more power. You might need to have a reserve of power to overtake another vehicle, or you could be approaching a hill and need more power for the upward slope.

Cup your left hand on the gear lever ready, push the clutch pedal down fully and at the same time keep a little pressure on the accelerator pedal. Select the appropriate lower gear, and then raise the clutch pedal smoothly as you increase pressure on the accelerator. You will practise this exercise in the next stage.

Knowing when to change gear is just as important as knowing how to change. Listening to the engine will help the driver know when to change. With experience you will learn to anticipate hazards in the road ahead and select appropriate gears for the conditions.

It is inadvisable to drive for prolonged periods with your left foot resting on the clutch pedal. Try to get into the good habit of placing your left foot on the floor away from the clutch pedal after each gear change.

## *Stopping smoothly at a fixed point*

To practise this exercise you must find a fairly straight, quiet road with plenty of distinctive features such as telegraph poles or trees. The object will be to stop with your front bumper level with one of these. You will need lots of practice so that you can consistently bring the car to a smooth stop at the required place.

When safe, move off and build up your speed to about 25–30 mph with third or fourth gear selected. Your supervisor should look ahead and select your stopping place. Check your mirrors and, when safe, cover the brake. This will have a slight braking effect as the engine begins to slow down. Use this to help you judge how much braking pressure you will need. To begin with, squeeze the brake very gently. Gradually press it harder until you seem to be stopping short of the required position.

Gradually ease the braking pressure and push the clutch down. This will allow the car to roll up to the stopping point. Select first gear ready for moving away.

As the car comes to a rest with the front almost level with the stopping point, set the gas and find the biting point ready to move the car off again.

Assessment – moving off, changing gear and stopping

# Choosing a safe place to stop

When stopping at the kerb, choose a safe place, not too close to a junction or bend or near to the brow of a hill, for example. You should also try not to inconvenience other road users, for example by parking too close to, or across, an entrance to property or a driveway.

You also need to think about what is on the opposite side of the road and, if you can, avoid parking opposite a junction or another stationary vehicle or obstruction.

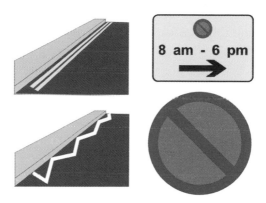

Look out for signs and road markings when choosing a safe place to stop

Find a straight part of the road and, putting the mirrors–signal–manoeuvre routine into practice, stop as close to the kerb as you can without touching it. Of course, you must obey any parking or waiting restrictions in force at the time and place you are stopping. Take heed of road signs and markings. Remember, parking your can in an unsafe place can cause danger by forcely others onto the wrong side of the road.

# More about signalling

Giving appropriate signals at the correct time and place and correctly inter-preting the signals of other road users are important for the safety and convenience of all road users.

## *Purpose of signals*

Signals are used to let other road users know what you intend to do or to warn them of your presence. Signals give advance warning to other road users that you intend to perform a manoeuvre. Remember that your signals are not instructions to other road users and do not give you the right or make it safe to perform your planned manoeuvre.

## *When to signal*

Signal timing is important. Your signals must be given in good time before your manoeuvre and for long enough for their meaning to be clear to other road users. Your signals must not be given too soon or another road user could be confused. Although you should normally follow the MSM routine, there are occasions when the signal may need to be delayed, for example when there are several side roads close together. Take particular care when intending to stop on the left beyond a side road on the left. Signalling too soon may lead an emerging driver to assume you are going to turn.

## *How to signal*

You should normally give signals by direction indicators and/or brake lights. Your signals must be readily recognized by other road users. For this reason, you should only use those signals shown in *The Highway Code*.

Before giving a signal you should ask yourself whether it is necessary, when it should be given and when it will be safe to make your move. You can only answer these questions properly by making proper use of the driving mirrors. Remember the routine: mirrors–signal–manoeuvre.

### Signals by indicator

These can be given when intending to turn left or right, change lane, over-take or stop at the side of the road and will give warning to traffic ahead and behind, providing that their view of your vehicle is not obscured.

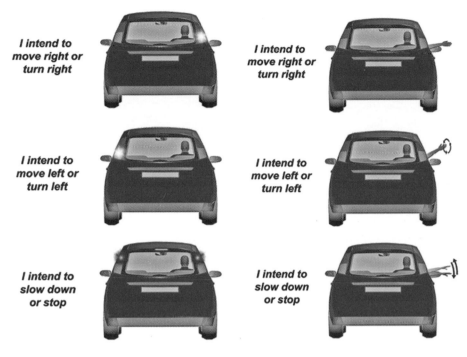

**I intend to move right or turn right**

**I intend to move right or turn right**

**I intend to move left or turn left**

**I intend to move left or turn left**

**I intend to slow down or stop**

**I intend to slow down or stop**

**Signals are normally given by indicators and/or brake lights**

**There are times when you may need to use an arm signal**

## Brake light signals

These illuminate when you have applied a little pressure to the footbrake and warn following traffic of your intention to slow down or stop. Early and progressive braking is important to give following drivers time to react.

## Signals by arm

Arm signals can be given when mechanical signals are not used or have failed and when necessary to reinforce direction indicator and stop light signals. You should not as a routine give both arm and mechanical signals, but there are circumstances where it could be useful to do so, for example when you are the lead vehicle on approach to a zebra crossing.

## *Unnecessary use of signals*

There are good reasons for not giving signals when to do so would not help another road user. Apart from unnecessary wear and tear on your vehicle, you could cause confusion.

When deciding whether a signal is necessary, think about how close you are to junctions and bends, anticipating that another road user could appear just as you are about to make a manoeuvre.

In traffic queues, ask yourself whether it's necessary to keep an indicator signal flashing.

Remember to cancel direction indicators when your manoeuvre is complete – they may not always cancel themselves.

It isn't usually necessary to signal to pass parked vehicles. Take up position in good time to maintain a steady course.

You should not signal carelessly, should not mislead others by giving the wrong signal and should never wave a pedestrian across a road.

## *Warning others of your presence*

**Flashing headlights are a warning of presence**

Flashing headlights and sounding the horn warn other road users of your presence rather than of your intentions. The flashing of headlamps by another driver should not be taken as an invitation for you to proceed. If you see another vehicle flashing headlights you must decide on whether it is safe for you to proceed, and be sure of the other driver's intentions.

The horn is usually operated by a stalk control or a push-switch on the steering wheel. You must NOT sound the horn in a moving vehicle in a built-up area between 11.30 pm and 7.00 am. You must NOT sound your horn in a stationary vehicle unless in danger from another vehicle that is moving nearby. Be considerate; using the horn inappropriately can cause danger or alarm, particularly when there are pedestrians, cyclists or animals nearby. Your instructor will show you how to operate the horn in your vehicle.

### Hazard warning lights

These are activated by the switch in the cockpit and cause the indicator lights on both sides of the car to flash at the same time. They should only be used to inform other road users that you are temporarily blocking the free flow of traffic. You must not use hazard warning lights as an excuse for illegal or inconsiderate parking. They should not be used when the vehicle is moving except briefly on fast

**Don't use hazard warning lights to excuse inconsiderate or illegal parking**

roads such as motorways if you have to slow suddenly for an accident or traffic queue ahead.

## Reversing lights

Reversing light signals warn other road users of your intention to reverse. White reversing lights at the back of your car are activated whenever you select reverse gear. This is particularly important for parking in reverse gear on busier roads. Selecting reverse gear promptly will help other road users anticipate your intention.

## Exercises

These exercises will help you gain confidence with steering.

### Exercise 3.1 – Anticipating when to turn the wheel

Find a quiet road with some sharp bends.

When approaching left bends, move your left hand towards the top of the wheel ready to pull it down to steer round the curve in the road.

When approaching right bends, move your right hand towards the top of the wheel ready to pull it down to steer round the curve in the road.

### Exercise 3.2 – Steering with one hand

Although you should keep both hands on the wheel as much as possible, there are times when you need to change gear or operate the lights, wipers and other controls.

Find a straight, quiet road where you can steer with one hand while you practise using these controls. You can also practise opening and closing the windows.

### Exercise 3.3 – Giving arm signals

Practise giving arm signals for left and right turns and for slowing down.

### Exercise 3.4 – When to check the instruments

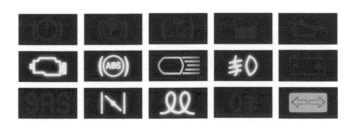

The instruments help to keep you informed of the condition of your car. Ignoring warning lights can result in breakdowns or serious damage.

When checking them, look well ahead and glance quickly at one instrument at a time. Only do this when there is nothing much happening on the road and you can spare the time.

You should stop and get help: if the brake warning light comes on; if the temperature gauge shows the engine is overheating; or if the oil pressure is low.

Find out from your car's handbook what all of the symbols on the dashboard mean.

# Checkpoint 3

**1** Before starting the engine you should ensure that:
*Choose two answers*

   a.   the parking brake is applied
   b.   you have selected first gear
   c.   the gear lever is in neutral
   d.   the hazard lights are on

**2** Starting the engine with the car in gear could:
*Choose one answer*

   a.   waste fuel
   b.   damage the gearbox
   c.   cause the car to move unexpectedly
   d.   ruin the starter motor

**3** You are about to start the engine and see this light on the instrument panel. You should:

*Choose one answer*

   a.   switch off immediately
   b.   check you have enough petrol for your journey
   c.   wait for the light to go out before operating the starter
   d.   start the engine promptly before the light goes out

**4** After starting the engine you see that this warning light doesn't go out. You should:

*Choose one answer*

  a.  drive to the nearest service station for immediate help
  b.  report the fault when your car goes for its next service
  c.  switch off the engine and investigate
  d.  drive to a fuel station and pick up some oil

**5** Before moving off from the left, you must always:
*Choose three answers*

  a.  check the interior mirror
  b.  check the exterior mirrors
  c.  select first gear
  d.  look over your right shoulder
  c.  give a signal

**6** For moving off you should: *Choose two answers*

  a.  always use first gear
  b.  normally use first gear
  c.  use second gear for some down slopes
  d.  never use second gear

**7** When preparing to change gear you should: *Choose two answers*

  a.  look at the gear lever
  b.  put your hand to the gear lever in readiness
  c.  grip the steering wheel more firmly with your right hand
  d.  move your right hand to the top of the steering wheel

**8** To move the gear lever smoothly you should: *Choose one answer*

  a.  'palm' your hand towards the position of the gear you need
  b.  grip the lever as tightly as you can
  c.  push the lever as quickly as you can
  d.  allow the clutch pedal to come up during the gear change

**9** To steer accurately you should look:
*Choose one answer*

    a.   well ahead at where you want the car to go
    b.   towards the kerb to help guide you
    c.   at the central white line
    d.   at the road surface just ahead of the bonnet

**10** When driving along a straight road you should position the car:
*Choose one answer*

    a.   about a metre away from the kerb
    b.   as close to the kerb as you can
    c.   about a metre from the centre line
    d.   as close to the centre line as you can

**11** Parking near bends and hill crests:
*Choose three answers*

    a.   is inconsiderate
    b.   is dangerous
    c.   puts others at risk
    d.   is only advisable on multi-lane roads
    e.   is fine if you use your hazard lights

**12** You are looking for a place to park and see this road marking.
You should:

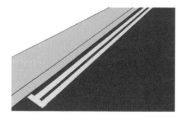

*Choose one answer*

    a.   drive on because no parking is allowed
    b.   check for nearby signs showing when parking restrictions are in force
    c.   park on the lines and switch on your hazard lights
    d.   park on the lines and look for the signs showing when restrictions are in force

**13** Red lines at the edge of a road indicate:

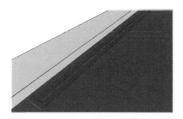

*Choose one answer*

a.  cycle lanes
b.  that parking is allowed
c.  that both parking and loading restrictions are in force
d.  that you are in a congestion charging zone

**14** To stop smoothly and accurately at the left kerb, you should:
*Choose two answers*

a.  brake gently and early
b.  put the clutch pedal down as soon as you start braking
c.  look towards the kerb
d.  ease the pressure on the footbrake just as you are stopping

**15** Before leaving your car, you should always:
*Choose two answers*

a.  apply the parking brake
b.  put on your parking lights
c.  switch off the engine
d.  switch on the hazard lights

**16** If you park near junctions, you will: *Choose three answers*

a.  make other drivers' observations more difficult
b.  make it difficult for pedestrians to cross the road
c.  cause danger and inconvenience
d.  make it easier for you to move off again

**17** Hazard warning lights: *Choose one answer*

a.  must never be used when the vehicle is moving
b.  should only be used on moving vehicles
c.  can be used when broken down and temporarily obstructing traffic
d.  can be used to excuse poor parking

**18** You see the driver ahead giving this signal and should expect
the vehicle to:

*Choose one answer*

a.  slow down
b.  turn left
c.  turn right
d.  stop

**19** An approaching driver flashes his or her headlights. You should take
this to mean: *Choose one answer*

a.  it is safe to proceed
b.  you need to stop
c.  a warning of presence
d.  a fault with your car

**20** You see white lights illuminated at the back of a stationary vehicle
ahead. This means: *Choose one answer*

a.  the vehicle is parked
b.  the driver has left the vehicle unattended
c.  the driver is intending to reverse
d.  it is safe to pass the stationary vehicle

You will find the answers on page 327.

Scores:     First try          Second try          Third try

| | | |
|---|---|---|
| | | |

Record your scores in Appendix 2 (page 330).

# Stage 4
# Learning to plan ahead and gaining more control

Up to now your driving instructor will have been guiding you through most of the things you needed to do. This should have helped you 'get things right first time' and to build up your confidence.

So far during your driving lessons, your ADI will have been checking all around to make sure that everything you do is safe and is not affecting others. When you are practising privately, your supervisor should be doing the same.

Becoming a good driver means taking responsibility for safety by planning your approach to hazards and keeping a safe distance from other vehicles and road users around you. Being able to plan ahead means you will have confidence in yourself and the vehicle. In this stage you will gain confidence by learning how to control the car on hills and how to be able to stop the car quickly and safely in an emergency.

To help you prepare for this stage, you can also:

- Revise *The Official DVSA Guide to Driving: The essential skills*, Section 5 – Starting to drive.
- Read *The Official DVSA Guide to Learning to Drive*, Section 2 Anticipation and planning, Section 2 – Use of speed, Section 2 – Other traffic.

Before going out to practise, read the section of *The Highway Code* dealing with traffic signs and signals, and learn the *Highway Code* rules about:

- Signals.
- Braking.
- Stopping distances.

# Taking responsibility

As your car control skills improve, your instructor or supervisor will be encouraging you to be more aware of what else is happening around you so that you can start dealing with hazards.

In driving terms, a hazard is any road feature or situation that could cause you to change your road speed or position. A hazard is therefore any situation in which there may be a danger to yourself or any other road user, such as:

- road features, for example bends, junctions and hills;
- temporary features, such as parked vehicles and road works;
- moving hazards: pedestrians, cyclists and drivers;
- surface conditions: surface type and weather conditions that affect grip and stability.

# The hazard routine – MSPSL

You already know this routine as mirrors–signal–manoeuvre! A manoeuvre is any change in position or speed, so we expand the MSM routine to:

**Mirrors**
Check the position and speed of following traffic in good time!
Just looking is NOT enough; act sensibly on what you see!

**Signal**
Ask yourself 'Will a signal help another road user?'
If you need a signal, give it in good time.

**Position**
If necessary, steer to a new course or road position.
Position in good time so that others can anticipate what you intend to do.

**Speed**
Slowing down, ease off the accelerator and/or brake. If you need to speed up, accelerate smoothly.
If necessary, change gear for greater control.

**The MPSL routine**

**Look**
Look well ahead. **Assess** the situation. **Decide** on what you need to do. **Act** promptly on your decision to wait or proceed.

You will use the MSPSL routine very often as you drive and adapt to changes going on around you. You must decide whether signals, repositioning and speed changes are necessary for each hazard and may need to repeat the routine as each situation develops or as new hazards arise.

Get into the habit of beginning the routine early when approaching bends, junctions and other hazards such as obstructions in the road. When you look in the mirrors, try to judge the speed and position of vehicles behind. In the early stages, your instructor/supervisor should help you to judge whether your manoeuvre will be safe. Decide whether a signal will help to warn or inform others about your actions. Allow time for them to see and respond to your signals.

Positioning your car early helps to confirm your signals and intentions. The correct position provides you with the best view and safety margins. Others can see you, and you can see them, so your view of any possible danger is improved. Try to get your car into position well before you reach a turn or other hazard. This will cause the least inconvenience to the flow of traffic.

Approach junctions and other hazards slowly enough to look for a safe opportunity to proceed. To do this, you will need to slow down before reaching the junction, giving you time to select an appropriate gear ready to accelerate away.

Remember, the brakes are for slowing and the gears for going. Slow down before changing down. If you need to change gear, do it as you finish braking or after you have released the footbrake.

Approaching hazards too fast will result in frequent and unnecessary stops because you won't have time to look properly on the approach. Start looking early as you approach a junction. Make sure you can see properly before deciding to go forward. Give yourself time!

The MSPSL routine is crucial to **defensive driving**. This means:

- putting safety first;
- always taking effective observation;
- planning ahead and anticipating the actions of other road users;
- not relying on other road users to do the right thing;
- driving responsibly and carefully;
- driving with courtesy and consideration for others.

Defensive driving involves more than control of the car; it involves keeping control of your own feelings and being patient with others on the road. You must not drive in such a way as to give offence to other road users or provoke a hostile response. Think of the risks to yourself of letting situations get out of control.

# Safety margins

Driving too quickly for the conditions and driving too close to a vehicle ahead are major causes of road accidents. Avoiding these faults is simply a matter of applying common sense and realizing your own and your vehicle's limitations.

*The Highway Code* says that you should never drive so fast that you can't stop in the distance you can see to be clear ahead. So what factors affect your stopping distance and how can you judge it?

The stopping distance is the distance travelled between seeing a hazard and stopping the car and is made up of **thinking** and **braking** distances. The diagram shows minimum thinking and braking distances and how these compare to car lengths for an average-sized car.

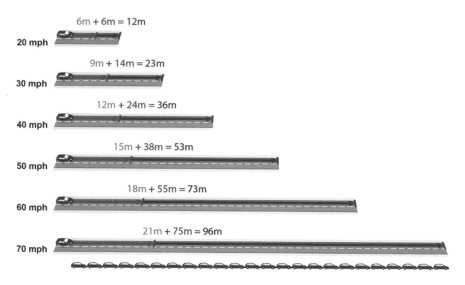

20 mph    6m + 6m = 12m

30 mph    9m + 14m = 23m

40 mph    12m + 24m = 36m

50 mph    15m + 38m = 53m

60 mph    18m + 55m = 73m

70 mph    21m + 75m = 96m

**Your overall stopping distance is made up of 'thinking' and 'braking' distances**

Your thinking distance is the time taken between seeing the hazard and pressing the footbrake. It usually takes just a little over half a second (the time it takes to check your mirrors) for a driver to react to a hazard ahead, and in this time your car will travel about 3 metres per 10 mph of speed.

Braking distance depends on the size and weight of your vehicle and is proportional to the square of road speed. The stopping distances shown are the minimum possible for an alert driver on a level road with good brakes and tyres. Your overall stopping distance will be affected by:

- your health and concentration (thinking distance);
- the condition of your vehicle (brakes, steering and suspension);
- tyres (type, condition and pressure);
- the size and weight of your vehicle and the load it is carrying;
- the gradient of the road – it will take longer to stop going downhill;
- the type and evenness of the road surface;
- the weather conditions – if it is wet your tyres have less grip on the road surface and you need to allow twice the distance. It can take up to 10 times longer to stop on ice!

As a driver you must be able to judge a safe **separation distance** between yourself and the vehicle ahead. The only safe gap is your overall stopping distance; anything less is a risk. However, in heavy traffic it may not be practicable without wasting valuable road space. Therefore your separation distance should NEVER be less than your thinking distance, and much more in poor conditions.

A reasonable rule to apply is a gap of about 1 metre for each mile per hour of speed for good conditions. You can estimate the distance by keeping a two-second time gap from the vehicle ahead.

To judge your separation distance from the vehicle ahead, note when it passes a fixed feature such as a road sign or marking ahead. Count two seconds by saying to yourself either 'One thousand and one, one thousand and two' or 'Only a fool breaks the two-second rule.'

If you reach the fixed feature before the two seconds are up, you are too close and should drop back. Remember to allow at least twice the distance, a four-second time gap, in poor weather conditions when the road surface is wet.

**The 'two second' rule**

**Too close!**

**Keep well back so you can see clearly ahead**

By following other vehicles at a safe distance you can help avoid accidents with vehicles ahead and behind.

Stay even further back from large or slow-moving vehicles. This improves your view of the road and of traffic ahead and helps you to anticipate the actions of the driver in front. You get more time to respond.

When other drivers are following you too closely, drop even further back from the vehicle ahead. This gives you more breathing space and extra time to brake gently. In turn this gives the drivers behind more time to respond.

**Give adequate clearance! What if a car door opens?**

# Passing obstructions

As well as keeping a safe distance when you are following other vehicles, you need to keep clear of parked cars and other obstructions.

When driving along you would normally keep about a metre from the left kerb. When passing parked cars you need to allow the same clearance in case a car door opens or someone steps out. Look well ahead and steer out into position early so you can follow a smooth line past parked cars.

If the road is too narrow or you can't give a metre clearance because of approaching traffic, you need to slow down. The closer you need to get, the slower you should go. As a guide, allow a minimum of a third of a metre clearance for every 10 miles an hour of speed.

Your instructor or supervisor will help you judge separation distances and clearance as you gain driving experience.

**The less clearance you can give, the slower you need to go**

# How to follow and pass cyclists safely

Stay well back from cyclists until you can give them at least 2 metres clearance without endangering oncoming drivers. Following in this position makes passing safer. Remember that cyclists can wobble or move sideways without warning to avoid drain covers and so on. Think of the consequences if a cyclist fell off as you were passing. Allow enough space for this to happen without you running over them.

**It is dangerous to pass too close to a cyclist**

If you must overtake with less clearance, then slow right down.

Notes:

Notes:

Notes:

**Assessment – allowing clearance to other vehicles**

# Dealing with hills

Facing uphill, your vehicle will naturally tend to roll backwards unless you stop it from doing so by means of the brakes or use of **clutch control**. Over-anxiety about rolling back can be a major cause of loss of control on uphill junctions, and it is a good idea to learn to control the car on hills fairly early in your course of lessons. The following exercises should give you confidence with uphill starts.

## Exercises

### Exercise 4.1 – Using the clutch to hold the car on an uphill slope

For this exercise you need to practise on a fairly quiet road with a slight uphill slope. You need plenty of space ahead and behind.

With the engine running, select first gear, set the gas and find the biting point. You will need to set a little more gas than you would for a level road. If there are no other road users nearby, release the parking brake. Keep your feet still and hold the car stationary for a few seconds.

If the car moves forwards, press the clutch down a little. If it rolls back, keep calm and raise the clutch pedal slightly. When the car is still, apply the parking brake, push the clutch pedal down as you come off the gas, select neutral and rest your feet. Practice until you are confident you can use clutch control to hold the car still with the parking brake released.

### Exercise 4.2 – Regaining control when rolling backwards

**Keep tight control of the clutch**

This exercise should help to increase your confidence by showing how easy it is to regain control and stop the car rolling. Make sure the road behind is clear for some way back.

Follow the procedure in Exercise 4.1 so that the car is still; then push the clutch down slightly until the car starts rolling backwards. To regain control, raise the clutch smoothly until you can feel the car stopping.

It is important to control the clutch very gently. If you let the pedal up too far or too quickly it may stall the engine or cause the car to jump forwards. At junctions this could be more dangerous than rolling back a little. Keep tight control of the clutch.

### Exercise 4.3 – Creeping forwards on an uphill slope

Follow the procedure in Exercise 4.1 so that the car is still. Gently raise the clutch pedal a little so that the car begins to move forwards. You may need to add a little more gas as you move. Move forwards 2 or 3 metres; then stop again by dipping the clutch pedal back down to the biting point. If you push the clutch pedal down too far the car will roll back, but you already know how to stop that happening!

Practising Exercises 4.1 to 4.3 on steeper gradients will give you the confidence you need to deal with uphill slopes at junctions.

## *Moving off uphill*

Follow the routine for moving off on a level road that you practised in Stage 3. Remember to check the 'blind areas' before moving off. You will need to allow for a bigger gap in the traffic to move into, because it will take you longer to build up speed going uphill. You may also need to press the accelerator pedal a little more than for a level road. If the car  jerks, you need to let the clutch up more slowly or press the accelerator a little more. If the engine roars, use less pressure on the accelerator or let the clutch up a little further.

The engine has more work to do when driving uphill. This means you will have to accelerate for longer in the lower gears and make upward gear changes promptly so that the car doesn't slow excessively when you push the clutch pedal down.

## *Moving off downhill*

It is easier to move off downhill, because the weight of the car will help move it forward. To practise, park on a quiet road facing downhill. Prepare the car by selecting first gear, or second if on a steep slope. Apply the footbrake to hold the car and release the parking brake. Raise the clutch to just below the biting point. You will have to 'feel' for this, as the change in the engine note will be less noticeable. Use the MSM routine; complete your safety checks and signal if necessary. Ease off the footbrake to let the car roll forwards. Raise the clutch pedal smoothly as the car begins to move and accelerate when safe.

When moving off downhill there are times, such as in heavy traffic, at junctions, or when moving out from behind parked vehicles, when you will need to restrain the speed and move off very slowly. To do this you must keep the clutch just below the biting point and use the footbrake to prevent the car rolling away too quickly.

Practise your clutch control on level roads and on uphill and downhill slopes.

**Assessment – clutch control and hill starts**

## *More about hills*

Now that you know how to move off on a gradient it is time to practise dealing with hills as you drive. A hill is a hazard, so make use of the MSPSL routine described on page 64. Look for road signs that may tell you how steep the slope is.

### Going uphill

On approach, check your mirrors, assess the slope and look out for slow-moving and heavy vehicles. Decide whether you may need to change to a lower gear. If so, it is best to do so before you start to climb.

Remember, in comparison with driving on a level road:

- it is more difficult to increase or maintain your speed;
- your brakes will slow the vehicle sooner;
- you can brake later to stop the car;
- pressing the clutch down will cause your car to slow more;
- releasing the gas pedal will cause your car to slow more;
- you will need to make gear changes more promptly to avoid the car slowing too much.

On the hill, increase your separation distance. The vehicle ahead could slow suddenly. Holding back may mean that you don't have to stop every time the traffic ahead does so.

## Going downhill

On approach, check your mirrors, assess the slope and consider changing to a lower gear. In a lower gear the engine will help control the speed of the car and you will not have to rely so heavily on the brakes.

Remember, in comparison with driving on a level road:

- it is more difficult for the engine to hold the car back;
- your brakes will take longer to slow the vehicle;
- you must brake sooner to stop the car;
- pressing the clutch down will cause your car to gather speed;
- releasing the gas pedal will cause your car to slow less;
- you will need to make gear changes more promptly to avoid the car building up too much speed.

On the hill, increase your separation distance. The vehicle ahead could slow suddenly. Holding back will give you more time to stop, which will give more warning to traffic following you.

## Hazards on hills

Approaching junctions and other hazards on a hill requires extra care. Use the MSPSL routine in good time; position to get the best view without baulking other traffic.

At the brow of a hill, remember that your view of the road ahead will be restricted. Keep well to the left and remember to ease off the gas, as your engine will have less work to do. Beware of oncoming traffic; someone could be trying to overtake.

Parking is more difficult on a slope; you will need more room to manoeuvre. You should leave a bigger gap so that others can manoeuvre safely around you.

Facing uphill:

- With a kerb, leave your front wheels pointing to the right.
- Without a kerb, leave your front wheels pointing to the left.
- Make sure the parking brake is firmly applied.
- Leave your vehicle in first gear (or, in automatic transmission, select park).

Facing downhill:

- With or without a kerb, leave your front wheels pointing to the left.
- Make sure the handbrake is applied.
- Leave your vehicle in reverse gear (or, in automatic transmission, select park).

# How to stop in an emergency

**Quick reactions are important in an emergency**

Anticipation and good forward planning help you to avoid emergencies. The earlier you spot any possible danger, the sooner you can act on it. Taking early precautions, such as slowing down, will make it less likely that you need to brake hard at the last moment. Even experienced drivers sometimes find themselves having to stop quickly because something unexpected happens, for example a child running into the road.

In a real emergency it is vital that you react quickly, and you won't have time to check the mirrors before braking. Make sure you are using them often as you drive along so that you are aware of what is happening behind.

Make sure you know how to stop quickly before you go into heavy traffic. You can practise the emergency stop on quiet, fairly wide and straight roads.

Before you move away, your instructor or supervisor will demonstrate a signal to be given for the stop and, after you move away to practise, will ensure there are no other road users about before giving it.

As soon as you see the danger you need to brake firmly. Follow the rule of progressive braking, but, unlike the case in a normal stop, you will not need to ease off the footbrake as the vehicle stops.

## Exercises

### Exercise 4.4 – Stopping promptly

Your first attempts at stopping promptly should be carried out at fairly low speeds. Just practise stopping with a little more than the pressure needed for a normal stop.

When your instructor gives the signal to stop, respond at once and pivot quickly to the footbrake. Leave the clutch pedal alone until just before stopping. This aids braking and also provides the vehicle with more stability. If you leave the clutch pedal alone until the last moment, the engine will help the car to slow down. You will also reduce the chances of skidding, as the road wheels are less likely to lock if they are still being 'driven' by the engine.

Whilst braking, keep both hands firmly on the steering wheel. In a real situation you may need to steer to avoid injuring another road user. The braking force will throw more weight onto the front wheels and you may find it more difficult to steer.

After coming to a complete stop, apply the parking brake. Remember, you were in your normal driving position on the road before you stopped. Before moving away again, check all around the car that it is safe by looking back over both your right and left shoulders.

### Exercise 4.5 – Stopping quickly as in an emergency

Repeat Exercise 4.4, gradually increasing the speed and the braking pressure until you can stop the car quickly and without skidding or swerving. It may feel as if your car travelled a long way before coming to a stop. If you do cause a skid, use the skid recovery method described in the next section to regain control.

# Skidding

**Always be aware of road surface conditions**

Drivers cause skids; they don't just happen. Keep your car in good mechanical order, drive safely and adjust to the conditions when driving. Always be aware of the road surface; if the surface is loose, wet or icy, your tyres will have less grip. Road signs might tell you that the surface ahead is poor, but you can't rely on road signs to tell you about the weather!

Skids happen when you try to change speed (accelerating or braking) or direction so suddenly that the tyres lose their grip with the road. Uncontrolled braking is one of the main driver faults that result in skidding.

The brakes of a car are most effective when the wheels are almost locked. When braking, the weight of the car is thrown forward, reducing the grip of the rear wheels and making them more likely to lock. This can cause a rear-wheel skid, and the rear of the car may swing round as it tries to catch up with the front.

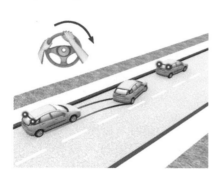

To recover from the skid, remove the cause – release the footbrake to allow the wheels to turn again, and then reapply the brake if necessary, with less pressure. If the rear of the car slides, you will need to steer when you have released the footbrake. Steer to straighten the car. Take care, because over-correction can lead to a skid in the opposite direction.

Very harsh braking, even on a dry road, can cause a four-wheel skid and loss of all control of steering and braking.

## Skids caused by acceleration

Sudden or harsh acceleration can cause wheel spin to the front or rear wheels depending on whether engine power is transmitted to the front (front-wheel drive) or rear (rear-wheel drive).

To recover from the skid, remove the cause – release the accelerator to allow the wheels to grip the road again. If the car slides sideways do not try to steer until some grip has been regained.

Notes:     Notes:     Notes:

Assessment – stopping promptly and avoiding skids

# Planning ahead to avoid danger

Knowing how to stop in an emergency doesn't excuse you from planning sensibly to avoid danger and conflict with others.

Watch out for signals given by the drivers of vehicles in front, and anticipate their actions. When a signal is flashing, the driver is almost sure to slow down for the manoeuvre. Expect this and carry out your MSPSL routine.

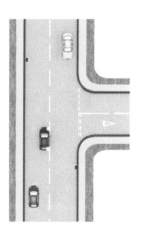

If the vehicle ahead is turning right, position your car well to the left and decide whether or not there is room to pass on the nearside. Remember, the other driver may have to wait for oncoming traffic. Be prepared to slow down and wait if the space is too small to get through safely.

If the driver in front is signalling left, the vehicle may be either stopping or turning. Move into an overtaking position, but hold well back, as drivers waiting in the side road may emerge.

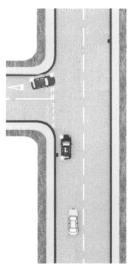

Even when you are sure the driver in front is turning, he or she may still have to stop and wait if the side road is blocked or if there are any pedestrians crossing. Keep well back.

# Checkpoint 4

**1**  At 30 mph your thinking distance is:
*Choose one answer*

    a.  9 m (30 ft)
    b.  14 m (45 ft)
    c.  18 m (60 ft)
    d.  21 m (70 ft)

**2**  At 30 mph your overall stopping distance is:
*Choose one answer*

    a.  9 m (30 ft)
    b.  14 m (45 ft)
    c.  18 m (60 ft)
    d.  23 m (75 ft)

**3**  At 70 mph your overall stopping distance is:
*Choose one answer*

    a.  38 m (125 ft)
    b.  53 m (175 ft)
    c.  75 m (245 ft)
    d.  96 m (315 ft)

**4**  Signs giving orders are normally:
*Choose one answer*

    a.  rectangular
    b.  triangular
    c.  circular
    d.  hexagonal

**5**  Compared to a dry road, on a wet road the gap between you and
the vehicle ahead should:
*Choose one answer*

    a.  remain the same
    b.  be halved
    c.  be at least doubled
    d.  be two seconds

**6** In an emergency you should:
*Choose one answer*

   a. brake gently and quickly

   b. brake immediately

   c. brake harshly and gradually

   d. try to lock the wheels

**7** An anti-lock braking system (ABS):
*Choose two answers*

   a. will always prevent skidding

   b. will help maintain steering control during hard braking

   c. needs you to pump the brake for it to work

   d. will not always prevent skidding

**8** A solid white line across the end of a road means you must:

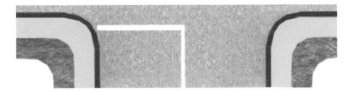

*Choose one answer*

   a. stop at the line

   b. not park in that road

   c. go if the way is clear

   d. apply the parking brake

**9** Double broken lines across the end of a road mean:

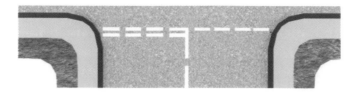

*Choose one answer*

a. stop before you reach the line
b. stop at the line
c. give way to traffic in the major road
d. go if the way is clear

**10** To stop in the shortest possible distance, you should brake:
*Choose one answer*

a. as hard as you can with the clutch down
b. until the wheels lock up
c. firmly and push the clutch down just before you stop
d. gently and then as hard as possible

**11** Braking in an emergency, you should:
*Choose two answers*

a. keep both hands on the wheel
b. brake hard and change down a gear
c. brake but do not touch the clutch
d. brake firmly and push the clutch down at the last moment

**12** Areas of white diagonal stripes on the road are used to:

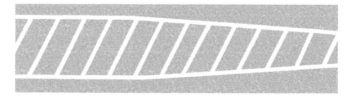

*Choose two answers*

a. separate opposing streams of traffic
b. help speed up the traffic flow
c. protect right-turning traffic
d. show you where to position to turn right

**13** You should drive at a speed:
*Choose two answers*

  a.  dictated by the road signs
  b.  such that you can stop in the distance you can see is clear
  c.  dictated by the road conditions
  d.  to keep up with the other drivers

**14** Coasting is travelling in neutral or with the clutch down. It means:
*Choose two answers*

  a.  engine braking is eliminated
  b.  your speed downhill can increase quickly
  c.  you will achieve more fuel economy
  d.  the appropriate gear may be more difficult to select

**15** Skids may be caused by the driver:
*Choose three answers*

  a.  planning too far ahead
  b.  driving too fast for the conditions
  c.  steering too harshly
  d.  accelerating too harshly
  e.  driving too slowly for the conditions

**16** The correct routine for approaching hazards is:
*Choose one answer*

  a.  MPSL
  b.  MSPSL
  c.  MSMPL
  d.  MSLPS

**17** This sign means:

*Choose one answer*

a. no right turn
b. keep right
c. turn right ahead
d. one-way street ahead

**18** If you saw this sign you would:

*Choose two answers*

a. expect a steep downhill gradient ahead
b. anticipate changing to a lower gear to give more power
c. prepare for an uphill gradient
d. consider selecting a lower gear for speed control

**19** You are the driver of the red car shown.
The broken white centre line means:

*Choose one answer*

a. it is safe to overtake
b. there are no hazards ahead
c. you may park at certain times
d. you may cross the line only if safe

**20** You see this sign ahead and should:

*Choose two answers*

a.   ignore it because it is intended for cyclists
b.   check your mirrors
c.   anticipate cyclists ahead
d.   expect cyclists to keep to their path

You will find the answers on page 328.

| Scores: | First try | Second try | Third try |
|---------|-----------|------------|-----------|
|         |           |            |           |

Record your scores in Appendix 2 (page 330).

# Stage 5
# Road positioning and turning corners

**B**y now you will have had to negotiate some junctions with guidance from your instructor. In this stage you will learn how to correctly approach and turn bends and junctions, putting the MSPSL routine into practice.

Practise in a quiet area with fairly wide roads, rounded corners and not too many parked cars. When you can cope confidently with the simpler junctions, progress to those with sharper corners and roads with a little more traffic.

It is useful at this stage to get some practice driving in and out of built-up areas so that you get used to changes in road and traffic conditions. You will need to adhere to different speed limits, so make sure you know the relevant road signs and speed limit rules from *The Highway Code*. Knowing the speed limits for different types of vehicle will help you anticipate possible problems ahead.

Don't attempt too much too soon. If things go wrong, it will shatter your confidence. Your supervisor must be sure you can cope before taking you on very busy roads, to junctions on hills and to those where your view is restricted.

To help you prepare for this stage, you can also read:

- *The Official DVSA Guide to Driving: The essential skills*, Section 7 – On the road, and Section 8 – Junctions.
- *The Official DVSA Guide to Learning to Drive*, Section 2 – Safe positioning, Section 2 – Junctions.

Before going out to practise, look up and learn the *Highway Code* rules about:

- Speed limits.
- Lines and markings on the road.

- Driving in built-up areas and country roads.
- Moving off and driving along.
- Road junctions.
- Turning right.
- Turning left.

# Road positioning

Unless you intend to overtake or turn right, or road markings, traffic conditions or road layout dictate otherwise, you should observe the rule of keeping well to the left, usually about a metre from the kerb. This will help the free flow of traffic and allow drivers of faster vehicles to overtake if they wish to. Don't weave in and out when passing lines of parked cars or other obstructions. Take a smooth line past a series of obstructions.

You should not drive too close to the left. This could:

- endanger or frighten pedestrians or splash them in wet weather;
- reduce your control of the car, as the surface may be uneven or littered with road hazards;
- result in you hitting the kerb and damaging your tyres;
- mislead other road users into believing you are going to turn left or stop on the left.

You should not drive too close to the middle of the road. This could:

- endanger yourself and approaching traffic;
- mislead other road users into believing you intend to turn right;
- hinder the free flow of traffic and prevent others from overtaking.

# Lane discipline

Lanes are marked to guide the flow of traffic and make best use of the road space available:

- Where lanes are marked, position centrally in your lane.
- Unless road markings, road layout or traffic conditions dictate otherwise, you should normally drive in the left-hand lane.

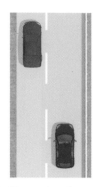

**Keep to the centre of your lane**

- Where the road is wide enough for lanes but they are unmarked, think in terms of lanes and position accordingly.

You should not weave from lane to lane, straddle two lanes or lane lines, change lanes at the last minute or drive in the wrong lane for your intended route.

Judge your position by looking well ahead. With practice, positioning will become second nature and you will find yourself fitting in with other traffic without conscious effort.

# Dealing with bends

**Look out for warning signs that tell you there are bends ahead**

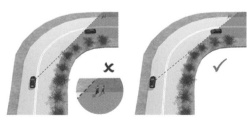

**Positioning towards the left gives you a better view in a right-hand bend**

Apply the MSPSL routine on approach. You will not need an indicator signal to follow a bend, but good positioning will help keep you safe and give you the best view of the road ahead.

Slow down in good time and select a lower gear if needed to give you more control. You should not be braking as you steer round a bend. For best grip, the engine should be 'under acceleration'. This doesn't mean that you should increase speed in the bend; it simply means that the engine should be pulling the car.

In a right-hand bend, position towards the left of your lane. This will:

- increase your zone of vision into the bend;
- keep you out of the path of approaching traffic;
- give you more time to deal with any other hazard in the bend.

In a left-hand bend, keep to the centre of your lane. This will keep you out of the path of approaching traffic.

Do not get too close to the left. This would severely restrict your view of the road ahead and give you little time to deal with hazards in the bend.

As you come out of a bend, check your mirrors again and make progress by building up to a speed appropriate for the road and traffic conditions.

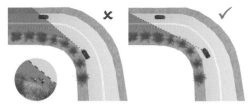

**Positioning too close to the left in a left-hand bend will restrict your view**

Notes:

Notes:

Notes:

**Assessment – positioning and bends**

# Dealing with junctions

A junction is any point where two or more roads meet. Junctions include T-junctions, Y-junctions, crossroads, staggered junctions and roundabouts.

The key to dealing with all junctions safely is to apply the MSPSL routine. Your instructor or supervisor should give you plenty of time to plan your approach. Road signs and markings, traffic flow joining, leaving or crossing the road, a change in the building line, and gaps in lines of parked vehicles will all help you locate a junction ahead.

Assess the junction. The more information you have on approach, the better prepared you will be to make your turn.

Look for the speed, type and density of traffic on the road you are joining, the width and gradient of the road and the presence of other road users, particularly pedestrians. Look out for other road users ahead of you in your own road and in the road you will be joining.

## *Turning left into a side road*

Use the MSPSL routine as follows:

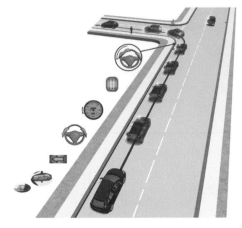

**Turning left**

- **Mirrors:** When you first see the junction you should check the mirrors to assess the speed and position of following traffic.

- **Signal:** Give a left indicator signal to let others know that you intend to turn. Timing the signal is important. If you give your signal too soon, another road user may think you intend to stop or turn into property bordering the road. If there are side roads before the junction you want, take particular care in timing your signal.

- **Position:** Your normal driving position about a metre from the kerb is correct for a left turn. If you do need to change course slightly, first check your exterior mirror in the direction you intend to move.

- **Speed:** Once in position you will need to adjust your speed. Ease off the gas pedal to begin with, but use the footbrake in good time so that following traffic has enough time to react to your stop light signals. When you are travelling slowly enough, select the appropriate gear.

- **Look:** As you are slowing down and changing gear, you should still be watching the corner for more information. Look as far into the new road as you can, and then decide whether or not it is safe to proceed. Look out for any danger from emerging traffic, or obstructions just around the corner. Be particularly careful about pedestrians.

Anticipate the point of turn when the front of your car reaches the corner. You must not turn too soon because of the danger that the rear wheels may take a short cut across the kerb. Neither should you swing out just before turning; you could move into the path of other vehicles.

Steer smoothly so that you follow the line of the corner. Once in the new road, check your mirrors again to make sure it is safe to build up speed again. Remember to check that your indicator signal has cancelled.

# Turning right into a side road

The main danger when turning right is from oncoming traffic. You must normally let approaching vehicles go first. Slow down and hold back until they have passed the junction. If you are going to reach the point of turn first, stop and wait just short of it. Use the MSPSL routine on approach.

Check mirrors and give your right indicator signal in good time.

## Positioning to turn right

Steer to take up a position as close to the middle of the road as is safe. This usually means positioning just left of the centre of the road and may leave room for following traffic to overtake on your left. If there are no markings to guide you, then imagine the centre line for yourself. When turning right, if there are obstructions such as parked cars on the right-hand carriageway, you will need to keep more to the left to give clearance for approaching

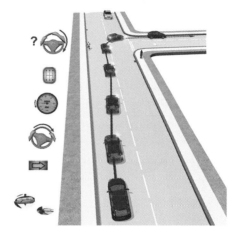

**Turning right**

traffic and any vehicles emerging left at the junction.

When you are travelling slowly enough, select the appropriate gear. Look as far into the new road as you can, and ahead, to decide whether or not it is safe to proceed.

## Priority

Traffic emerging from the side road should give priority to you. If you need to stop for approaching traffic, you must keep to your own side of the road. Stop in position so that the front of your car is just before the centre of the road you intend to turn into. Do not proceed until you are sure it is safe. If in doubt about going, be patient and wait. Your instructor will guide on judging whether or not it is safe to proceed.

**Turning right, if you can't safely cross the path of approaching traffic, wait in position on your side of the road**

When safe, steer smoothly so that you end up in your normal driving position in the new road. Check your mirrors again to make sure it is safe to build up speed, and make sure that your indicator signal has cancelled.

## Point of turn

You should begin turning in good time to avoid the danger of over-steering or clipping the kerb in the new road. How soon you begin turning will depend on the widths of the roads you are leaving and entering and on what else you can see. Move up to the point of turn and make sure you can see into the new road before turning. As a guide, the front of your car should be about level with the centre of the road you are joining before you commence the turn.

## Dangers when turning right

Watch out for vehicles approaching the end of the road, and avoid cutting the corner by turning too soon. This could endanger you and others by putting yourself into the path of an approaching vehicle.

Sometimes obstructions in the side road may force you to turn earlier. If this is the case, don't start your turn until approaching vehicles are clear.

Pay attention when turning right where your view of oncoming traffic is limited.

**Turning right, avoid cutting the corner**

Cross oncoming traffic safely when turning right. Sometimes your view ahead may be restricted near bends and hill crests. There may be an approaching vehicle just out of sight. Try not to rush across.

Before you commit yourself to the turn, stay in your position as close to the middle of the road as is safe until you can see into the new road. Go a little further forward before turning if necessary.

## *Cyclists and pedestrians*

It is dangerous to overtake cyclists as you approach to make a left turn. You would have to cut back in and could hit the cyclist or cause him or her to fall off. Hold back and let the cyclist clear the junction before you start to turn.

**Deal safely with vulnerable road users at junctions**

Give way to pedestrians crossing any road you are turning into. If a pedestrian has started crossing, you should hold back until the pedestrian is safely clear of your path. Watch out particularly for those with their back to you. They may not have seen or heard you and could walk into the road without looking. Be prepared to give way.

## Choosing the correct gear at junctions

Anxiety about which gear to select on approach to junctions can be a distraction. Your instructor may advise that second gear is the most versatile, but this may not always be appropriate. The gear you select will depend on the safe speed for the corner. The safe speed depends on how far ahead the driver can see and the angle through which you need to turn.

A wide, gentle turn with a clear view can be taken at a higher speed than a narrow road with a restricted view, so third gear may be appropriate. You may select first gear if the angle of your turn into the new road is very sharp or your view restricted.

Whichever gear you select, remember it is safe to miss out a gear on approach. You do not need to change through the gears in order.

Once you've selected a gear, make sure you actually use it! You must not 'coast' around the corner with the clutch down. Coasting reduces your control of both braking and steering. When making the turn, the engine should drive your car. This means that you should have enough gas set to be just pulling the car around the corner.

Notes:        Notes:        Notes:

Assessment – approaching and turning into side roads

## Approaching T-junctions at the end of a road

Whilst some T-junctions on quieter roads may be unmarked, most are clearly marked as either 'Give way' or 'Stop'. Look out for signs and road markings as you come up to the end of a road to identify the type of junction.

Give way signs and markings tell you that you must give priority to traffic on the main road and stop if necessary to let it pass.

Stop signs and markings tell you that you must stop before the solid white line to assess the situation before joining the main road.

Your instructor may refer to T-junctions as either 'open' or 'closed'. At an open junction, your line of sight into the major road will be fairly clear of obstructions so that you can see other traffic. At closed junctions, the building line, fences, hedges and so on will restrict your line of sight.

Coming up to a T-junction, use the MSPSL routine you've already learned. Approach the ends of roads slowly enough to give yourself plenty of time to look into the main road. Whether the junction is open or closed, you should scan left and right as you approach it to build up a picture of the traffic flow and other hazards in the main road.

## Emerging

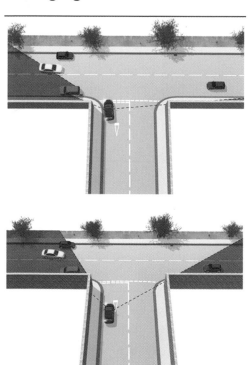

This means leaving the minor road to join the main road. Your zone of vision will get wider as you approach the end of the road. The diagram shows that you will not be able to decide if it is safe to emerge until your eye line is level with any obstructions.

When you are approaching the end of a road, watch out for others who may turn in too soon and cut the corner. Larger vehicles may need more room to turn. Be prepared to hold back for them.

**At a closed T-junction, you can't make a decision to emerge until your eyes are level with the obstructions**

Make sure you have looked both ways before moving into major roads. Be particularly careful turning left that you will not put yourself into the path of any vehicle approaching from the left. The driver may be passing an obstruction and positioned in your intended path. It is very dangerous to emerge left whilst looking right.

**Be prepared to hold back for traffic turning into the minor road**

Parked vehicles and pedestrians standing near a junction can seriously restrict your view of traffic travelling along the main road. Cyclists or motorcyclists can be very difficult to see in these situations.

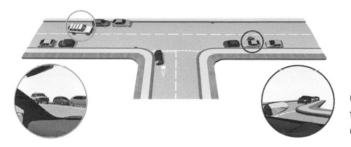

**Check that it is clear to the left and right before emerging**

Sometimes you may need to stop at a 'Give Way' junction. In these situations, and at stop junctions, use clutch control to creep forward into position for the best view. Lean forward in your seat so that the front of your car doesn't need to stick out so far. A good way to remember this is 'peep and creep'.

Whatever the type of junction, you must not cause other traffic to swerve or slow down as you join the major road. Whether you are turning left or right, remember it will take you time to build up speed in the line of traffic you are joining. Turning right, you will be crossing in front of vehicles approaching from your right. Make sure you can clear their path safely.

If an approaching vehicle is signalling to turn left, wait until you are sure the driver is turning before you emerge.

Practise emerging left and right at junctions. As you gain confidence, practise emerging on uphill and downhill junctions.

**If your view is restricted, 'peep and creep'**

At Y-junctions, position to get the best view into the major road

Emerging right from a narrow road, leave enough room for traffic to turn in

## Turning right from different positions

At Y-junctions your view to the left can be severely restricted because of the angle at which the two roads meet. Position so that you are at or near a right angle to the major road. This will give you a wider zone of vision at the junction.

Turning right at the end of a narrow road, you will need to leave enough space for traffic turning in. You may have to keep well to the left to achieve this. You will still be following the rule of *positioning as close to the middle of the road as is safe*.

## Pedestrians at junctions

Pedestrians are very vulnerable at junctions, and you will need to anticipate their movements. Take particular care with infirm, elderly or young people. If a pedestrian has started to cross the road you are entering, you must

Give priority to pedestrians

always give way to him or her. If a pedestrian hesitates after stepping on to the road, try to establish eye contact and allow the pedestrian time to decide whether to proceed or wait. You must not wave a pedestrian to cross; you could be inviting him or her into the path of another vehicle!

When approaching T-junctions, look out for pedestrians and give way to any who may be crossing the end of the road. Be particularly careful when approaching busy shopping streets.

Notes:

Notes:

Notes:

**Assessment – emerging safely at junctions**

# Checkpoint 5

**1**   The correct position to take for turning left is about:
*Choose one answer*

   a.   half a metre from the kerb
   b.   a metre from the kerb
   c.   a metre and a half from the kerb
   d.   2 metres from the kerb

**2**   The correct position for normal driving is:
*Choose one answer*

   a.   as close to the kerb as possible
   b.   in the centre of your side of the road
   c.   half a metre from the kerb
   d.   about a metre from the kerb

**3**   If pedestrians are crossing the road you are turning into you should:
*Choose one answer*

   a.   sound your horn loudly
   b.   hold back and give way to them
   c.   keep moving at the same speed
   d.   wave them across so they know what you are doing

**4** Where there is a stop sign at the end of a road you:
*Choose one answer*

    a.   needn't stop unless pedestrians are crossing
    b.   need only stop if you see other traffic
    c.   must stop at the line until it is safe to proceed
    d.   should keep moving if the road is clear

**5** Approaching a left bend you should take up position:
*Choose one answer*

    a.   half a metre from the kerb
    b.   towards the centre of the road
    c.   in the centre of your lane
    d.   as close to the kerb as possible

**6** In a built-up area with street lights, the speed limit is usually:
*Choose one answer*

    a.   45 mph
    b.   40 mph
    c.   35 mph
    d.   30 mph

**7** When you see a national speed limit sign on a single carriageway road, the limit for cars is:

*Choose one answer*

    a.   40 mph
    b.   50 mph
    c.   60 mph
    d.   70 mph

**8** You must not exceed the maximum speed limits for:
*Choose two answers*

    a.   the type of road you are on
    b.   the type of vehicle you are driving
    c.   your age group
    d.   the age of your vehicle

9 If you are waiting to emerge into a main road and you cannot see because of parked vehicles you should:
*Choose two answers*

   a. wait for several seconds and then go
   b. stop at the line and wait until you can see
   c. creep slowly forwards until you can see past the obstructions
   d. lean forward in your seat if needed to help you see

10 The main danger when turning right from a main road into a side road is:
*Choose one answer*

   a. following traffic
   b. oncoming traffic
   c. traffic ahead of you waiting to turn
   d. traffic emerging from the junction

11 When turning right at the end of a narrow road you should position:
*Choose one answer*

   a. just to the left of the white line
   b. as close to the white line as you can
   c. well over to the left
   d. about a metre from the kerb

12 The speed limit for large goods vehicles travelling in built-up areas is:
*Choose one answer*

   a. 20 mph
   b. 25 mph
   c. 30 mph
   d. 35 mph

13 The speed limit for cars towing trailers on single-carriageway roads outside built-up areas is:
*Choose one answer*

   a. 35 mph
   b. 40 mph
   c. 45 mph
   d. 50 mph

**14** When turning right you should position:
*Choose two answers*

    a.   well over to the left
    b.   well over to the right
    c.   as close to the middle of the road as is safe
    d.   in any space marked for traffic turning

**15** Before turning left you should not:
*Choose two answers*

    a.   position a metre from the kerb
    b.   overtake
    c.   swing out to the right
    d.   pass parked cars without signalling

**16** A sign like this means:

*Choose one answer*

    a.   maximum speed 30 mph
    b.   no vehicles over 30 metres length
    c.   end of minimum speed limit
    d.   maximum speed for cyclists 30 mph

**17** A sign like this means:

*Choose one answer*

    a.   bend to the left ahead
    b.   series of bends ahead
    c.   move left ahead
    d.   junction ahead

**18** White reflective studs mark the: *Choose one answer*

  a.  left edge of the road
  b.  middle of the road
  c.  lanes for traffic
  d.  edge of the carriageway at lay-bys

**19** You are waiting to turn right and your view ahead is restricted by a bend. You should: *Choose two answers*

  a.  move further forward for a better view if needed
  b.  turn in as slowly as possible
  c.  be prepared to cut the corner
  d.  make sure you can see into the new road before turning
  e.  turn in as quickly as possible

**20** Approaching a side road to turn left you see a cyclist ahead and should: *Choose one answer*

  a.  overtake the cyclist quickly before the junction
  b.  sound your horn as you get close to the cyclist
  c.  not overtake the cyclist
  d.  expect the cyclist to dismount so you can pass

You will find the answers on page 328.

Scores:       First try       Second try       Third try

Record your scores in Appendix 2 (page 330).

# Stage 6
# Manoeuvring
# at low speed

This stage explains how to carry out manoeuvring exercises at low speed. Start practising these as soon as you feel confident with your clutch control skills. By the time you reach Stage 8, you should be able to carry out all of these exercises with reasonable accuracy and safety.

In this stage you will be using reverse gear. Only reverse where it is safe, legal and convenient. Remember, when you are manoeuvring, other road users and pedestrians have priority. You must take responsibility for checking all around so that you know you will not be inconveniencing them.

Whilst practising, make sure that you will not inconvenience other road users by blocking driveways and entrances. When choosing a safe place for a manoeuvre, look out for pedestrians, particularly children playing in the road. Whilst reversing, your rear view will be limited and you may not be able to see small children behind your car. You should choose a place where other road users would not have to manoeuvre dangerously to get by. For these reasons you should choose reasonably wide and quiet roads, where visibility is good.

Avoid repeated practice of manoeuvres at the same place. You could annoy local residents, particularly at popular locations for driving school cars.

Initially, your instructor will help by keeping a lookout. When practising with others in the early stages, encourage your supervisor to help with your observations.

To help you prepare for this stage, you can also read:

- *The DVSA Official Guide to Driving: The essential skills*,
  Section 9 – Manoeuvring.
- *The DVSA Official Guide to Learning to Drive*, Section 2 – Turning the vehicle around, Section 2 – Reversing, Section 2 – Parking.

Before going out to practise, look up and learn the *Highway Code* rules about reversing.

## Exercises

### Exercise 6.1 – Revise low-speed clutch control

Revise using the clutch to manoeuvre at slow speed, which you learned in Stage 3 (page 48), and practise again for a few minutes on a quiet road. Begin practising driving slowly forwards and then stopping again by dipping the clutch pedal down.

**Keep tight control of the clutch**

### Exercise 6.2 – How to move out from behind a parked vehicle

When you are confident at controlling the car at low speed, you need to combine this skill with brisk steering so that you can turn the car in a restricted space. To practise, find a vehicle parked on a wide, level road and pull up about 3 metres (10 feet) behind it. You will need to control the clutch to move off more slowly than usual. Take extra observations to the front and rear before you move off, and make a final check of the blind areas before you pull out.

Consider whether you will need a signal to warn oncoming drivers, as well as any approaching from behind. Remember that it will take you longer to move out from behind another vehicle. Make allowance for this so you don't cause other traffic to slow as you move off.

Use a slipping clutch as practised in Exercise 6.1 to keep the car creeping very slowly. Turn the wheel briskly to the right as soon as the car is moving. When sure that the front of your car will clear the parked vehicle, turn it back to straighten the car. Remember to look where you want the car to go.

**Keep the car moving slowly and steer briskly**

When confident, try the manoeuvre starting closer to the parked vehicle as you might have to in a residential street with lots of parked cars. When you have mastered the exercise on a level road, uphill and downhill. Remember to use the footbrake to control your speed when moving off downhill.

*Notes:*          *Notes:*          *Notes:*

**Assessment – moving off at an angle**

# Using reverse gear

Practise on a quiet road. It is important to look where you are going.

When reversing, turn round slightly in your seat until you can see the road clearly through the back window. You may remove your seat belt for reversing if it is restricting you. Remember to put it on again before driving away.

You may place your right hand towards the top of the wheel, at the 12 o'clock position, and your left hand low on the wheel. If you find it difficult or uncomfortable to hold the wheel in this way, place your left arm on the back of your seat or the passenger seat.

When reversing you will find it helpful to steer a little sooner than seems necessary, because the back wheels don't turn. You should always turn the wheel in the direction you want the back of the car to turn. To make the car move towards the kerb, steer towards it. To make it move away from the kerb, steer away from it. It is important to move slowly so that the steering has time to take effect.

## Exercises

Exercise 6.3 – How to reverse in a straight line

**When reversing it is easier to judge whether you are moving towards the kerb or away from it by looking well back down the road**

Choose a wide quiet road for practice. Before starting this exercise, make sure you are parked parallel to the kerb with your front wheels set straight.

Select reverse gear, set the gas and find the biting point. Have a good look round just as you would for moving away.

Keep a special lookout for pedestrians before you start moving backwards.

Use clutch control to move slowly back, and keep checking to the front and rear for approaching traffic.

It is much easier to judge whether you are moving towards the kerb or away from it by looking well back down the road.

Looking at where the kerb intersects the back window doesn't help!

Practise reversing slowly in a straight line, and then experiment by turning the steering wheel a little towards and a little away from the kerb. This will give you a feel for the steering and practice in judging where the back of the car is going.

Notes:

Notes:

Notes:

**Assessment – reversing in a straight line**

## Exercise 6.4 – How to drive into a parking space between two vehicles

Look and plan ahead for a suitable parking space. It will need to be at least two and a half times the length of your car. Remember to put the MSM routine into practice. Slow down almost to a stop just before the space, keeping about a metre (a yard) out from the parked vehicles. Remember to go far enough forward to allow for the back wheels to cut in when you steer left.

Steer briskly into the space until your front wheel nears the kerb; then steer right to bring it into line. When you stop you should be parallel to the kerb with your front wheels set straight.

If necessary, reverse a little to leave yourself enough room to pull out again safely. Don't forget to look through the rear window when you are reversing.

Secure the car with the parking brake and select neutral. Remember to check that your indicator signal has cancelled.

If you are leaving your car, make sure you check it's clear before opening your car door – remember that approaching drivers will find it more difficult to see you if you are parked between other vehicles.

Notes:

Notes:

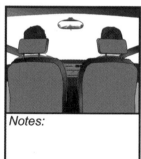

Notes:

**Assessment – driving into a parking space**

## Exercise 6.5 – How to turn the car in the road

This exercise is useful if you need to turn the car round to go back the other way when there are no convenient places for reversing.

Your first attempts at this exercise should be carried out on fairly wide and level roads. Choose a safe place where you can legally make this manoeuvre without causing inconvenience to others. Make sure there are no obstructions such as trees or street lights on the pavement nearby.

Keep away from parked cars and other obstructions in the road that might make it difficult for you to see and be seen.

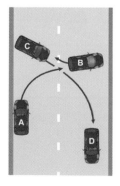

**Turning in the road**

Get the car ready for moving off in the normal manner, with the clutch slightly below the biting point. Check ahead and behind for approaching traffic. Look out for pedestrians nearby. You don't want to cause alarm or danger by driving towards them during the manoeuvre. If necessary, drive on to a safer place.

**A–B:** When you are sure it is clear and safe, look across the road where you intend to go. Bring the clutch pedal up to the biting point so the car begins to

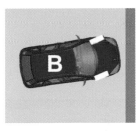

**As you near the right kerb, turn the steering wheel to the left**

creep slowly forwards. As soon as you are moving, steer briskly to the right until it is in 'full lock'. Use the clutch pedal to keep the car moving slowly.

When you are about a metre from the right kerb, start turning the wheel back to the left. As you near the kerb, push the clutch down and brake to stop. You should end up near to the kerb with the front wheels pointing a little left ready for the next part of the manoeuvre. When stopped, you may need to apply the parking brake, depending on the camber (the slope of the road towards the gutter).

**B–C:** Select reverse gear and prepare the car for moving. Check all around. When you're sure it's safe, look over your left shoulder through the rear window. Creep slowly back, turning the wheel briskly to the left. When you have driven over the centre of the road, look over your right shoulder so that you can judge your distance from the kerb and turn the wheel briskly to the right.

**You should end up near to the kerb with the front wheels pointing a little right ready for the next part of the manoeuvre**

Be ready to brake if the car rolls down the camber. Keep turning the wheel to the right and stop just before reaching the kerb. Apply the parking brake if needed to stop the car rolling.

**C–D:** Select first gear and get ready to move. Check all around for others. When you are sure it's safe, look well down the road and creep slowly forward turning the wheel to the right until you are in the normal driving position. Straighten the wheel, carry out the normal MSM routine and pull in and park on the left.

If you don't manage to complete the manoeuvre in three movements, don't worry. Simply repeat the second and third movements.

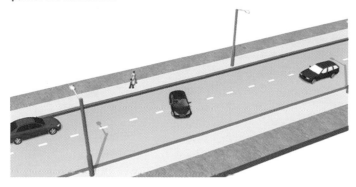

**Give priority to other road users.**

*Dealing with others during the manoeuvre*

As you cross the road, look round at intervals to ensure

**Be prepared for camber. The road will slope towards the gutter.**

that you remain aware of other road users. If you just started moving and you see another vehicle approaching, stop and let it go. If you are already halfway across and see another vehicle approaching it is usually wiser to complete your move to the other side of the road. Otherwise you could be blocking both carriageways.

Practise until you are confident with the 'turn in the road'. With experience you should be able to complete the manoeuvre on narrower roads.

*Notes:*

*Notes:*

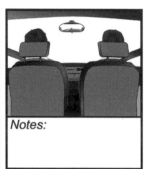

*Notes:*

**Assessment – turning in the road**

## Exercise 6.6 – How to reverse into a side road on the left

This manoeuvre is useful for turning round to travel in the opposite direction or for reversing into your driveway or bays in car parks. It takes practice to master this manoeuvre. Don't worry if you can't get it right first time. Start from a fairly wide road on a corner that isn't too sharp.

**A–B:** With safety in mind, you need to plan this manoeuvre as you approach the side road.

As you drive past the road, check for any parked cars or other obstructions that could make your manoeuvre unsafe. If necessary, move on to another location.

Using the MSM routine, drive past the corner until you can see it in the interior mirror and stop on the left about half a metre from the kerb.

**B–C:** Turn in your seat so that you can see well down the road through the middle of the rear window. You may remove your seat belt if you feel restricted. When you have checked that it's safe all around, use clutch control to creep slowly back.

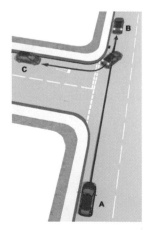

**Reversing into a side road on the left**

As you reverse towards the corner, the kerb will disappear from view in the rear window. You are now close to the point of turn. It is very important to look all around to the front and sides to make sure there will be no danger to other road users. When you steer left the front of your car will swing out!

Look over your left shoulder again and you will see the kerb come into view in the bottom corner of the side window. If sure it is safe, you can begin steering to the left. Keep checking that it's safe and keep steering to the left until you see through the rear window that the car is straight in the new road. The amount of steering you need will depend on how sharp the corner is.

**Anticipate the point of turn when you see the kerb disappear from view in the rear window**

Keep looking well down the road through the middle of the rear window. This will help you judge whether the car is parallel with the kerb. An occasional glance into the nearside door mirror will help you judge your distance from the kerb. If you want the car to go nearer to the kerb, turn the wheel towards it. If you want to take the car away from the kerb a little, turn the wheel away from it. Any

**Follow the line of the kerb when it reappears in the side window**

adjustments in steering at this point should be very slight. If you misjudge and bump the kerb or get too close to it, pull forwards a little and then reverse again to correct your position.

Make sure you finish your reverse in a safe place, far enough away from the junction to allow others to use it properly. As a guide, you need to be far enough back so that when you move off again you can position correctly for turning right at the junction.

If you removed your seat belt for reversing, make sure you put it on again before driving away.

### Dealing with others during the manoeuvre

If your manoeuvre is going to affect other road users, remember they have priority. Be prepared to stop and let them make the decision to proceed or to wait for you.

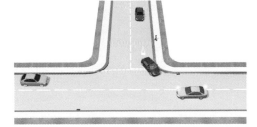

**Be prepared to pull forward to allow emerging traffic to use the junction**

Give priority to pedestrians crossing at the junction. If you have started reversing and a pedestrian approaches, stop and give him or her the opportunity to cross.

If you see another vehicle approaching from behind, you may have to move forward to the start position to allow the vehicle to use the junction safely.

To build up your confidence, practise reversing to the left at different junctions.

Notes:

Notes:

Notes:

**Assessment – left reverse**

## Exercise 6.7 – How to reverse into a road on the right

This exercise is useful for turning the car round where there are no convenient places on the left or for reversing into your driveway or into bays in car parks.

Judging the point of turn in a right reverse is easier because you can see the kerb.

**A–B:** Select a corner where your manoeuvre will be safe, legal and convenient. Use the MSM routine and take up a position as if you were going to turn right. If there are other road users around, you may have to delay your signal, as otherwise they may think you are turning right.

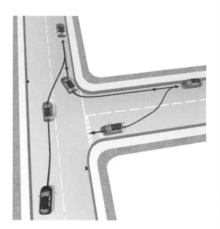

**Reversing into a side road on the right**

**B–C:** Wait for any oncoming traffic at the point of turn and look into the road for any obstructions that would make your manoeuvre unsafe. Steer over to the right and stop a little out from the kerb about two to three car lengths past the corner. Take off your seat belt if you need to. You may want to open your window to see the kerb.

**C–D:** Select reverse gear and prepare to move. Remember, you are manoeuvring on the wrong side of the road. You are more vulnerable; keep looking all around, and respond to others. When you're sure it's clear, move slowly back. You should be looking over your left shoulder as you approach the corner, but look round to the right periodically to check your position and judge when to turn.

Just before turning, look all round again, remembering that the front of your car will swing out as you steer right. Look over your right shoulder as you steer, and follow the kerb. How much steering you need will depend on how sharp the corner is.

When you have turned the corner, look over your left shoulder again. This will help you judge whether or not your car is straight in the new road. You will also be able to see what is happening behind you and to respond to others.

When your car is straight, turn the wheel to the left sufficiently to keep it straight. Remember, any final adjustments should only be slight. Check your distance from the kerb by using your nearside door mirror.

To complete the exercise, drive far enough into the side road so that you have room to get back on to the left side of the road to approach the junction properly. This will also allow others to use the junction safely.

The right reverse manoeuvre is particularly useful when driving a van, because your view to the rear and sides is too restricted to reverse left safely. If the van has no rear windows, you would need to rely more heavily on your side mirrors to look out for others as you manoeuvre.

Just as in the left reverse, you must give priority to other road users when you make this manoeuvre.

Notes:

 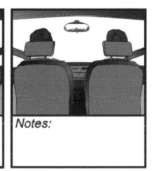

Notes:

Notes:

**Assessment – right reverse**

## Exercise 6.8 – How to reverse into a parking space at the kerb (parallel parking)

Compared to driving forwards into a gap between two other vehicles, you need less space using reverse gear. Start practising this manoeuvre only when you can carry out the previous reversing exercises reasonably well. Choose a quiet area to practise. Make sure you will not be disrupting the traffic and that the place you choose is legal and safe. By the time you master the exercise you should be able to reverse into a space about one and a half times the length of your car.

Use the MSM routine to position your car for the exercise.

**Parallel parking**

Position your vehicle alongside and parallel with the parked car so that the back of your car is slightly forward of the parking space. You should be between half a metre and a metre from the parked car, with your front wheels set straight. Keep your foot on the brake and select reverse gear so that following traffic can see your reversing lights.

Have a good look all round to make sure there is no danger to other road users before you begin to reverse. When you are sure it is safe, reverse slowly, looking back through the rear window until the rear of your vehicle is level with the beginning of the space. This is the point of turn. Look round to check it is safe before steering left – the front of your car will swing out.

**Steer briskly at the point of turn**

Steer briskly to the left to turn the back of your car towards the middle of the parking space. Once you have a good angle, turn the wheels right again enough to straighten them. As a guide you will need to do this when you can line up the right side of your car with the nearside headlamp of the vehicle behind.

Move slowly into the space until you are sure you are clear of the vehicle ahead. As a guide, you ought to be able to see the bumper of this car over the top of your bonnet. At this point, check that you will be reasonably close to the kerb and, if so, steer briskly to the right to bring the front of the car into the space.

**Straighten the wheels when you have a good angle**

When your vehicle is almost parallel with the kerb and still moving very slowly, steer left to bring all the wheels parallel to the kerb.

Carrying out this manoeuvre slowly will allow you more time to see how the car is responding to your steering and will also give you plenty of time to make any necessary adjustments. It also means that you will be able to respond properly if there are other road users about.

Once you are in the space, pull forward so that you are positioned centrally and apply the parking brake.

Notes:

Notes:

Notes:

**Assessment – parallel parking**

## Exercise 6.9 – Reversing into a parking bay

**Bay parking**                    **Angled approach**

In car parks it is usually easier and safer to reverse into a parking bay than to drive forwards into a space. Depending on the layout of the car park and available space you may employ one of two methods to park:

- Reverse turning into the space. Drive past the parking space and then reverse (either left or right) to get into the space. You will probably use this method when the access way to the parking bays is of limited width.

On approach, check that the parking space is clear of obstructions and that it is wide enough for your vehicle. A badly parked car in the next bay might make it difficult for you to park or open your car door. Select reverse gear promptly when positioned for the manoeuvre so that following drivers can anticipate your move. Keep tight control of the clutch and reverse slowly into the space, keeping a good lookout for pedestrians.

Park centrally in the bay. If you misjudge, pull forward a little and then reverse to correct your position. When stopped, apply the parking brake.

- Turning on approach. If space permits you can turn the car as you approach the space so that you are in a better position to reverse into it.

It doesn't matter which method you choose or whether you reverse to the right or left. The important thing is to make sure you complete the manoeuvre safely by keeping a good lookout for other vehicles and pedestrians.

Be considerate when parking in bays. Don't occupy bays set aside for the disabled or parents with children when you are not entitled to use them. Park squarely so that you don't make it difficult for others to enter or exit adjacent bays.

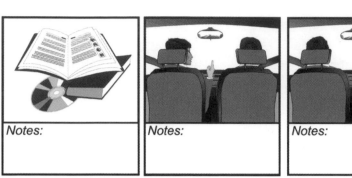

Your instructor will be able to advise where it is safe to practise this exercise.

Notes:

Notes:

Notes:

**Assessment – bay parking**

**A note about technology.** More and more new cars now come with a 'Parking Assist' feature as standard. Using sensors fitted around the car these systems can identify a suitable parking space and take control of the steering to help you manoeuvre the car into a parked position. However, these systems need you to control speed and it remains your responsibility to keep a look out for safety whilst the car manoeuvres.

# Making a U-turn

Turning the car round without any reversing is only possible on wide and quiet roads or in the mouth of a junction. It is not a move that others expect and can be potentially dangerous. Only make this manoeuvre when you can see the road is clear of approaching traffic and you are sure that you have enough room.

**Making a U-turn**

Making a U-turn safely may only be possible at a large roundabout (see Stage 7). You should avoid making a U-turn at mini-roundabouts.

You must not make a U-turn on motorways, in one-way streets or where signs forbid it.

Only make this manoeuvre when you can see the road is clear of approaching traffic and you are sure that you have enough room.

Making a U-turn safely may only be possible at a large roundabout (see Stage 7). You should avoid making a U-turn at mini-roundabouts.

You must not make a U-turn on motorways, in one-way streets or where signs forbid it.

**Making a U-turn in the mouth of a junction**

# Checkpoint 6

**1** Before reversing you should:
*Choose one answer*

   a.  sound the horn
   b.  make sure the road is clear
   c.  switch on the hazard flashers
   d.  switch on the indicator

**2** If you are unable to see when reversing you should:
*Choose one answer*

   a.  sound the horn
   b.  get someone to help
   c.  switch on your lights
   d.  take a walk around the car

**3** When turning the car round in the road you should:
*Choose two answers*

   a.  always complete the exercise in three movements
   b.  keep full control of the vehicle
   c.  take priority over other road users
   d.  give priority to other road users

**4** When turning round in the road you should: *Choose two answers*

    a. keep the car moving slowly

    b. keep the car moving quickly

    c. turn the steering wheel slowly

    d. turn the steering wheel briskly

**5** When parallel parking between two vehicles you should: *Choose one answer*

    a. centre your car in the space

    b. park your car close to the one in front

    c. park your car close to the one behind

    d. finish half a metre from the kerb

**6** When reversing you should normally: *Choose two answers*

    a. take priority over other road users

    b. give priority to other road users

    c. ignore the other road users

    d. let the other road users decide

**7** Reversing into a road on the right is useful when: *Choose two answers*

    a. the road is very wide

    b. you are in an estate car

    c. you are in a van

    d. you can't see through the rear window

**8** Parallel parking between two vehicles will require a space of at least: *Choose one answer*

    a. three times the length of your car

    b. two and a half times the length of your car

    c. twice the length of your car

    d. one and a half times the length of your car

**9** When using a driveway you should: *Choose two answers*

    a. drive across the footpath quickly

    b. drive across the footpath slowly

    c. reverse in so that you can drive out

    d. drive in so that you can reverse out

**10** You must not reverse: *Choose two answers*

    a.  further than is necessary
    b.  less than is necessary
    c.  from a main road into a side street
    d.  from a side street into a main road

**11** When reversing you should: *Choose three answers*

    a.  use your mirrors when necessary
    b.  look out for pedestrians
    c.  only look through the side windows
    d.  mainly look through the rear window
    e.  never use your mirrors

**12** When reversing you should: *Choose one answer*

    a.  look at the kerb as a guide
    b.  use a marker in the rear window
    c.  look where you want the car to go
    d.  mainly use the mirrors

**13** Markings on the kerb like this mean:

*Choose one answer*

    a.  no parking
    b.  no waiting
    c.  loading restrictions in force
    d.  loading and unloading permitted

**14** When reversing into a side road you see a pedestrian about to cross at the junction. You should: *Choose two answers*

    a.  continue and expect the pedestrian to give way
    b.  stop until you are sure of the pedestrian's movements
    c.  allow the pedestrian to decide whether to wait or proceed
    d.  sound your horn as a warning before continuing the manoeuvre

**15** A sign like this means:

*Choose one answer*

a. no U-turns
b. reversing forbidden
c. no right turn ahead
d. restricted turning space ahead

**16** When manoeuvring in a confined space you should:
*Choose two answers*

a. turn the wheel whilst stationary
b. use clutch control to maintain low speed
c. avoid dry steering
d. rely on your mirrors to check it's safe behind

**17** When positioning to reverse round a corner you should:
*Choose two answers*

a. not worry about using the MSM routine
b. be careful when timing your signals
c. position as close to the kerb as possible
d. position a little way from the kerb

**18** A marking like this in a parking bay means:

*Choose one answer*

a. disabled drivers only
b. bay reserved for disabled badge holders
c. space reserved for wheelchairs
d. you can park in the space if no disabled drivers are about

**19** You turn into a side street and see this sign. You realize you have taken the wrong route and should:

*Choose one answer*

a. reverse out of the side road
b. make a turn in the road
c. find a side road to reverse into so you can turn round
d. drive on because it would be illegal to turn round

**20** When deciding on a place to manoeuvre you should:
*Choose two answers*

a. consider the safety of other road users
b. not worry about causing temporary inconvenience to others
c. make sure your intended manoeuvre is legal
d. be more concerned with car control than observation

You will find the answers on page 328.

Scores:   First try        Second try        Third try

Record your scores in Appendix 2 (page 330).

# Stage 7
# Gaining experience and using common sense

**B**y now you should be confident with your car control skills and ready to drive in busier traffic conditions and deal with more complex junctions. In this stage you will also learn more about dealing safely with others on the road.

Build up your confidence and experience by taking things one step at a time. Get plenty of practice on as wide a variety of roads as possible. If you live in a rural area, your instructor may advise you to have longer lessons to incorporate these. If you live in a town you may have to learn to deal with these situations earlier in your course of driving lessons.

To help you prepare for this stage, you can also:

- Revise *The Official DVSA Guide to Driving: The essential skills*, Section 7 – On the road, and Section 8 – Junctions.

- Read *The Official DVSA Guide to Driving: The essential skills*, Section 10 – Defensive driving.

- Read *The Official DVSA Guide to Learning to Drive*, Section 2 – Roundabouts, Section 2 – Dual carriageways, Section 2 – Pedestrian crossings, Section 2 – Independent driving.

Look up and learn the *Highway Code* rules about:

- Lane discipline.
- Road junctions.
- Pedestrian crossings.
- Railway level crossings.
- Tramways.

# Lane discipline at junctions

Where there are two lanes, or room for two lanes that are not marked, unless road markings or signs show otherwise, when intending to:

- turn left – keep to the left-hand lane;
- follow the road ahead – keep to the left-hand lane;
- turn right – move to the right-hand lane in good time.

Where there are three lanes, unless road signs and markings indicate otherwise, when intending to:

- turn left – keep to the left-hand lane;
- follow the road ahead – keep to the left-hand or middle lane;

**Abide by lane markings**

- turn right – move to the right-hand lane in good time.

## *How to choose the most appropriate lane for turning left or right*

**Look and think ahead to get into the correct lane for your route**

Look and plan well ahead, and get into position as soon as you can. At some junctions the road markings do not follow the normal rules. Where there are two or more lanes marked for the direction you wish to take, choose the best for your intended route. To do this you need to know where you should be positioned at the next junction. Look and think ahead. If you don't have knowledge of the local area you should take note of route direction signs that may guide you.

Unless you need the right-hand lane at the next junction it is normally better to select the left lane. This will avoid you having to change lanes after the turn. If you select the right-hand lane for the turn, check carefully to the left after the turn to make sure there is no one in your blind area before returning to the left lane.

Acceleration and deceleration lanes (slip roads) allow you to join or leave a road without hindering the through flow of traffic. Get into position early and use these lanes to build up speed when joining a road or slow down when leaving at a junction.

## *One-way streets*

Look out for signs telling you that you are joining a one-way street or system. Get into position in good time on approach to and once in the one-way street:

**Deceleration lane**

- To enter a one-way street by turning right, turn directly into the right-hand lane.

- To enter a one-way street by turning left, turn directly into the left-hand lane.

In the one-way street, unless road signs and markings say otherwise, when intending to:

- turn left – keep to the left-hand lane;
- follow the road ahead – use any convenient lane;
- turn right – move to the right-hand lane in good time.

Early positioning in one-way streets is important because traffic flows quickly and is permitted to overtake on the left or right. Take particular care and check mirrors well before changing lane.

## *Multi-lane roads*

Unless road signs and markings permit otherwise:

- On three-lane carriageways, drive in the left-hand lane. Use the middle lane only to overtake, and remember that you have no more right to use that lane than traffic approaching from the opposite direction.

Where there are four or more lanes, do not use the lanes on the right-hand half of the road.

## *Dual carriageways*

- Drive in the left-hand lane normally.
- Use the right-hand lane for overtaking or turning right.

On a three-lane dual carriageway you may stay in the middle lane if there are slower vehicles in the left lane, but must return to the left lane when you have passed them.

*Notes:*     *Notes:*     *Notes:*

**Assessment – lane discipline**

# Dealing with pedestrian crossings

There are three main types of pedestrian crossing:

- zebra crossings, which are uncontrolled;
- traffic-light-controlled crossings, which may be at ordinary traffic lights or under the direct control of pedestrians, that is pelican, puffin and toucan crossings;
- supervised crossings, which are controlled by a police officer, traffic warden or school crossing patrol warden with a manual stop sign.

Look and plan well ahead for pedestrian crossings. There may be warning signs if a pedestrian crossing ahead is obscured from a driver's view. The 'Pedestrian crossing'

warning sign is usually placed in advance of a zebra crossing, whilst a 'Traffic signals' warning sign quite often advises of a light-controlled crossing ahead.

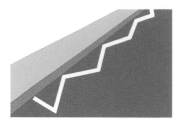

On approach to zebra and pedestrian-controlled crossings, you will notice an area marked by white zigzag markings on the road. You must not park or wait in this area or overtake the lead vehicle approaching the crossing. When driving in lanes of traffic, where there are vehicles in another lane waiting to let someone cross, you may pull level with the lead vehicle but must not proceed in front of it.

In slow-moving traffic and traffic queues, keep pedestrian crossings clear.

## Zebra crossings

**Be ready to slow down and stop on approach to zebra crossings**

Look out for the yellow flashing amber beacons marking zebra crossings. Use the MSPSL routine. Check mirrors when you see the crossing. Look for people standing near or moving towards crossings, and try to work out in advance whether they are likely to cross. Check what is happening behind, and be ready to slow down. You must be travelling at such a speed that you can pull up safely if a pedestrian steps out. Never accelerate towards a pedestrian crossing hoping to beat the pedestrian to it!

If your view of either side of the crossing is blocked, slow down as if people were crossing. Be ready to stop until you can see it is safe to continue.

Where you see pedestrians waiting to cross, check your mirrors and slow down. If you hold back early enough they may have time to go before you reach the crossing. Try to make eye contact with anyone waiting. This helps reassure them that they have been seen.

If you have time, give an arm signal for slowing down. This lets the pedestrian know what you are doing and also warns oncoming drivers that you are stopping. Do not give any kind of invitation for people to cross. Other drivers may not be stopping.

Some pedestrians find it more difficult than others to cross the road. Be patient and allow extra time for the old and infirm. People with prams cannot put a foot on to the crossing to claim priority. They will have to push the pram out. Others with small children also need more time. Young people are often impulsive and may dash out on to the crossing.

If the pedestrians are walking from your right to left, wait until they are on the pavement before moving away. If they are walking from left to right, give precedence to them, but you don't need to wait until they are completely across before you proceed.

Do not startle or try to hurry pedestrians by edging forwards or revving your engine. If you are stopping for more than a couple of seconds, apply the parking brake.

Remember before moving away to check to the sides for other pedestrians in your blind spots.

**Treat a zebra crossing with a central refuge as two separate crossings**

If a zebra crossing has a central reserve, each half is a separate crossing and you only need to give way to people on your side of the road. Beware, however, people running towards the crossing on the right-hand carriageway; you should still be prepared to slow down and stop.

## *Pedestrian light-controlled crossings*

These are recognized by the zig-zag white lines and traffic light signals. A push button mounted on the pole allows pedestrians to operate the crossing.

At pelican crossings, the sequence of lights differs from that

**Pelican crossing**

at other traffic lights. Instead of the red and amber signal, there is a flashing amber phase.

This has the same meaning as the flashing yellow beacon at a zebra crossing – you must give way to people on the crossing. A straight-line pelican crossing that has a central reserve is still one crossing and you must give way to people crossing from your right even during the flashing amber phase.

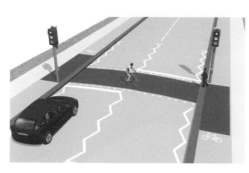

**Toucan crossing**

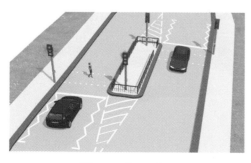

**Equestrian crossing**

At puffin, toucan and equestrian crossings there is no flashing amber phase. Instead, sensors must detect that the crossing is clear before the traffic light signals will change to permit traffic to cross.

At toucan crossings cyclists are allowed to ride across. They are found in places where cycle lanes have to cross busy roads and junctions. On approach to a toucan crossing you may see a cycle lane. Equestrian crossings are similarly designed for use by riders with horses.

At staggered light-controlled crossings you only need to give precedence to users on your side of the road.

When light-controlled crossings are clear and signals permit, you may move on but must make sure that nobody is about to step on to the crossing. Always be ready for the possibility that a pedestrian could rush on to the crossing at the last second. You must still give precedence to pedestrians on the crossing even if traffic control signals indicate that you can proceed.

**Staggered crossing**

## *Supervised crossings*

Near schools these may be preceded by warning signs – look out for the twin flashing light beacon at the beginning and end of the school day. The signs may have supplementary plates to identify the danger ahead. You must obey the manually operated signal given by the school patrol warden. Police or traffic wardens may also use a manually operated stop sign.

**Assessment – pedestrian crossings**

# How to approach traffic lights

Look and plan well ahead and anticipate lights changing. All colours except green mean stop, and you should always be travelling at a speed at which you can pull up safely.

Working things out as you approach will help speed up your reactions. Check your mirrors to see how close following vehicles are and how fast they are travelling. Continually assess what you will do if the lights change.

**Remember the traffic light sequence**

When approaching a red light, check your mirrors and start slowing down. If the light stays red, you will be able to stop comfortably. Apply the parking brake and select neutral. If the light changes to green you may continue, but, remember, green means go only if it is safe. Check for vehicles from all directions and watch for oncoming drivers turning across your path.

A green light can change at any time. When approaching, be aware of what is happening behind, slow down and be ready to stop if the light changes. If the green light stays on, continue, but remember to check in all directions.

Look for pedestrians crossing the road you are taking and be ready to give way to them.

If your exit road is blocked, wait at the stop line – do not drive forward and block the junction.

## What to do at filter lights

Filter lights indicate that you have priority in the direction shown by the arrow. They may be timed to control traffic congestion in peak periods. Arrows may indicate priority to left, right or ahead.

Plan well ahead and look for road markings. Avoid using a filter lane unless you intend to proceed in the direction of the arrow shown. If you find yourself in the wrong lane, continue in that direction to avoid holding other traffic up.

**Where you see a filter arrow to the left, the nearside lane will normally be marked for left-turning traffic only**

At a left filter, when the arrow comes on you may turn left regardless of any other lights that may be showing. Before turning, check for other traffic moving in from your offside.

Where you see a filter arrow to the right, you may turn right regardless of any other lights showing. Remember, however, that green means go only if safe. Check that any oncoming traffic is stopping before you proceed.

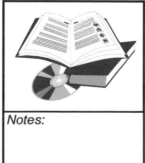

*Notes:*

*Notes:*

*Notes:*

**Assessment – traffic lights**

# How to deal with crossroads

A crossroads is a junction where two roads cross, although not necessarily at right angles to one another. There are basically two types of crossroads, unmarked and marked.

Where a crossroads sign is displayed, the broader line indicates priority through the junction

Treat unmarked crossroads with great care – neither road has priority. To understand this, imagine a junction with traffic lights that have failed – you would be extra careful because no driver would have priority. Approach slowly and be prepared to give way to traffic moving along the other road.

Marked crossroads may have Stop or Give way signs, traffic lights and/or yellow box road markings.

Whether you are approaching on the minor or the major road, use MSPSL on approach and take effective observation before entering the crossroads. You need to look at the road ahead as well as to the right and left. This is particularly important when waiting to emerge on to the major road but applies equally when driving ahead at crossroads on the major road. Remember that a driver in the minor road, in the absence of crossing traffic, may not even realize he or she is about to enter a crossroads and come straight out without looking.

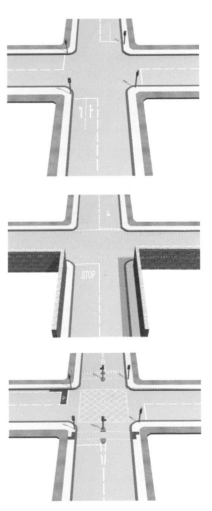

# Choosing the most appropriate lane for going straight ahead

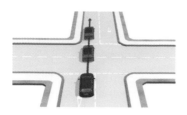

**Use common sense to position for going ahead at crossroads**

You should follow the general rule of keeping to the left to go ahead at crossroads, leaving the right lane clear for traffic wishing to turn right. However, looking and planning ahead will help you select the most appropriate lane for going straight ahead at busy junctions.

If the road ahead narrows at a crossroads, or if the road ahead is offset to the right (staggered junction), you may need to position in the right lane. You must of course obey any road signs or markings that are there to guide the traffic.

Where there is a queue of traffic waiting to turn left and you anticipate being able to proceed safely, you may position in the right-hand lane to follow the road ahead. The same applies where there are parked cars or other obstructions on approach or at the opposite side of the junction. In these situations you need to use your common sense in deciding on the most suitable approach position.

# Turning at crossroads

A crossroads has four entry points, and this can sometimes lead to confusion over priority. The problem here usually occurs when you are waiting to join or cross the major road when there is other traffic on the opposite side of the junction. If you intend to go ahead or turn left and the approaching traffic wishes to do likewise, there is no reason, providing the main road is clear, why you should not both go at the same time.

If one of you wishes to turn right and the other wishes to go ahead, remember that the driver turning right is crossing the path of the approaching vehicle and should give priority to the driver wishing to follow the road ahead. You should try to establish eye contact with the other driver if you are unsure of his or her intentions. Remember, it is unwise to rely on the other driver's signals or lack of them. Consider the other driver's road position, where he or she is looking, and the direction the vehicle's front wheels are facing to help you anticipate the other driver's most likely path.

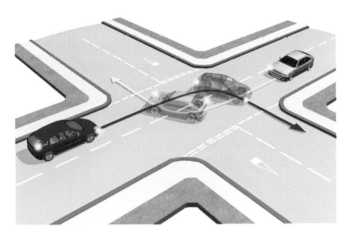

**Both turning right – offside to offside gives a better view of approaching traffic**

If both of you wish to turn right, the main road is clear and there is sufficient space, then you may both proceed at the same time. There are two ways to deal with this situation, regardless of whether you are turning from the major or the minor road.

You can turn offside to offside so that you pass behind the other vehicle. This method gives you a clear view of approaching traffic. You can also turn nearside to nearside, although this method does not give you as good a view of oncoming traffic. Motorcyclists and cyclists are particularly vulnerable in this situation – take care!

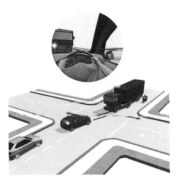

**Turning nearside to nearside can restrict your view of oncoming traffic**

Either method is acceptable and will be determined by the layout of the road, the course that the other driver decides to take and any road markings dictating the position to take. In busy traffic, where space is limited, turning nearside to nearside may have to be the choice to avoid blocking the junction. Whichever method you use, prior to making your turn you should check your mirrors again, especially if you have had to wait for a safe opportunity to proceed.

## *How to deal with box junctions*

If your exit road is not clear, wait at the stop line until you can move through the junction without blocking it.

If you are turning right and the exit road is clear, you may enter the box and wait in the centre for any oncoming traffic to pass.

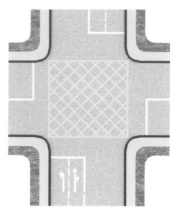

Obey the rules for yellow box junctions to keep the junction clear

## *Be prepared to give way to oncoming traffic*

When turning right at crossroads with traffic lights, oncoming vehicles usually have a green light at the same time. Watch out particularly for traffic that is likely to travel straight through the junction or turn left. You must give way to these vehicles, as they have priority.

Wait just short of the point of turn for a suitable break in the traffic. If it is very busy, you may have to wait for the lights to change before you get an opportunity to turn. When this happens you should normally clear the junction as quickly as you can. Make sure, however, that the oncoming traffic is stopping before you proceed.

Assessment – crossroads

# Dealing with roundabouts

Roundabouts are designed to aid the free flow of traffic at busy junctions, allowing it to cross or merge with traffic from other roads without necessarily stopping. The general rule is to 'give way to traffic from the right'. Long before you reach a roundabout, look for information signs that may show the layout of the roundabout, and make a mental note of the position of your exit road.

## *Procedure on approach to roundabouts*

Use the mirrors–signal–manoeuvre routine. Unless road signs and markings, traffic conditions or the layout of the roundabout dictate otherwise, follow the normal rules for positioning on approach as you would at any junction.

When turning left (blue car 'A' in the diagram), approach in the left lane. Signal left and keep to the left lane through the roundabout. Keep the left signal on until you are into the exit road.

When following the road ahead (green car 'B'), you should normally approach in the left lane and stay in it through the roundabout. As you pass the first exit check the mirrors and give a left signal to indicate you are leaving by the next one.

When turning right (red car 'C'), use the mirror–signal–manoeuvre routine to get into

**It is important to take the correct route on approach and through roundabouts**

the right-hand lane on approach. Keep the right signal on and stay in the right-hand lane into and round the roundabout. As you are passing the exit prior to the one to be taken, check for vehicles in the nearside lane (left mirror) and make sure it is safe to cross it. Change to a left indicator signal and leave by the next exit. You should normally leave in the left lane if it is clear.

If using a roundabout to make a U-turn, approach as if turning right and use MSM before signalling to leave the junction as described above.

## *Helping the free flow of traffic*

The layout of some roundabouts can make it difficult to judge which lane to take on approach. As a guide, imagine the roundabout as a clock face, with you approaching from the six o'clock position. If your exit road is past 12 o'clock and there are no other road markings to guide you, approach in the right-hand lane.

Keep scanning to the right and left as you approach roundabouts. Try to time your arrival to coincide with a gap in the traffic, but give way to any traffic approaching from your right. Look across the roundabout, watching for traffic already moving through it. This will help you anticipate whether traffic on your immediate right will be prevented from joining the roundabout.

Build up and maintain a reasonable speed on roundabouts. Failing to do this, especially when you are in the right-hand lane, may result in other drivers passing on your nearside. Always check for vehicles on your left before leaving a roundabout. If the left-hand lane of the exit road is blocked or there are vehicles in the lane to your nearside, leave in the right-hand lane.

If there are three lanes on approach, use the left to turn left, the right lane to turn right and the left or middle lanes to follow the road ahead. If there are more than three lanes on approach, use the clearest suitable lane. Look well ahead for road markings giving directions that vary from the basic rules. Get into position early and stay in the middle of your lane.

## *Mini-roundabouts*

These are usually road markings, though some may be raised very slightly as a dome on the road surface. Apply the same rules as at any other roundabout. Note, however, limited space means that:

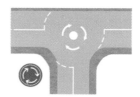

- you have less time to signal to leave the roundabout;
- larger vehicles may not be able to avoid driving over the roundabout road marking;
- you should not enter the roundabout unless certain that other vehicles on it will be able to clear the route you intend to take.

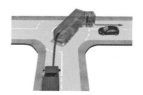

At double mini-roundabouts and multiple roundabouts, follow the normal rules of priority and treat each roundabout separately.

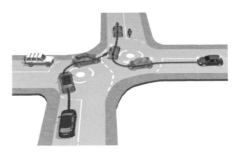

## *Other roundabouts*

**Double mini-roundabout**

**Exceptional roundabout**

Exceptional roundabouts have road markings (give way lines) that indicate that traffic on the roundabout must give priority to traffic entering the roundabout.

Spiral roundabouts may be used at major junctions where there is heavy through-flow of traffic. Lanes within the roundabout are marked in a spiral pattern to help drivers select and stay within the correct lane for their route.

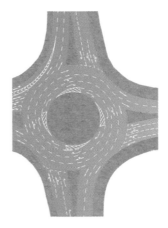

**Spiral roundabout**

Notes:

Notes.

Notes:

**Assessment – roundabouts**

# Driving along dual carriageways

Dual carriageway ahead

As you approach a dual carriageway anticipate that following traffic may rush to overtake you. Check your mirrors! Use mirrors even more frequently driving on dual carriageways.

Look well ahead for problems, and anticipate what may happen. Respond early, giving those behind you time to act. Look for:

- obstructions in your lane;
- vehicles ahead slowing down;
- vehicles turning through central reserves;
- traffic joining the carriageway.

# Turning right on to dual carriageways

When turning right on to dual carriageways, decide if there is enough room in the central reserve to offer your car protection from traffic moving along the new road. If the central reserve is wide enough to wait in, make sure you position correctly to avoid problems for drivers turning right off the dual carriageway.

If the central reserve is too narrow, treat the carriageway as one road

If the central reserve is wide enough you can cross the first carriageway and then wait for a suitable gap in the traffic

# Dealing with level crossings

**Advance warning of a gated level crossing**

At level crossings, the road crosses a railway line. Trains can't stop or give way to road traffic! If you see a sign for a level crossing, use the mirrors–signal–manoeuvre routine on approach. A sign should tell you what kind of crossing it is. There may also be distance count-down markers if the crossing is near a bend.

**Advance warning of a level crossing without gates or barriers**

Most crossings have full or half-barriers and may be controlled by traffic lights and an audible alarm, operated either by an attendant or automatically as the train approaches the crossing. Approach carefully and cross with care.

*At any level crossing you must not:*

- drive on to the crossing unless the road is clear beyond it;

- drive 'nose to tail' over the crossing;

- stop on or just after the crossing;

**Countdown markers to a concealed level crossing**

- park close to the crossing;

- start crossing once the lights, alarm or barriers operate;

- zigzag around half-barrier crossings.

## How to deal with gated level crossings

An amber light and ringing sound will be followed by a flashing red light if a train is approaching. The barriers will then come down. You must stop. The red light will continue flashing whilst the barrier is down. If another train is approaching the lights will continue to flash and the barriers will remain down.

**Don't try to beat the barriers!**

If you have already started crossing and the lights begin to show or the alarm sounds, you *must* keep going.

## How to deal with ungated level crossings

Some level crossings do not have gates or barriers. These will have either traffic lights or 'Give way' signs. Obey the traffic signs. Look both ways, and listen for approaching trains.

**The cross symbol outlined in red is used at all level crossings without a gate or barrier**

## *Railway telephones*

Where provided, you must use the railway telephone to inform the signal operator if:

**Direction to railway telephone**

- you have an accident or break down on the crossing;
- you need to check it is safe to cross;
- you need permission to use the crossing, ie you are:
  - driving a large vehicle;
  - driving a slow-moving vehicle;
  - driving a vehicle with limited ground clearance.

## *Breakdowns and accidents at level crossings*

If you are involved in an accident on a level crossing, or your car breaks down:

- *as your first priority* get everybody out of the car and clear of the crossing;
- if available immediately use the railway telephone to inform the signal operator;
- *obey instructions that you are given*;
- if it is possible and there is time, move the vehicle clear and inform the signal operator on the railway telephone;
- if a train approaches or the lights and audible alarm operate, *get clear*; the train will not be able to stop.

# Dealing with tramways

Tramways or light rapid transport (LRT) systems are becoming more common in British towns and cities. Apart from the tracks on the road surface, warning signs, diamond-shaped signs and traffic lights showing white symbols for tram drivers will all tell you that trams are operating. Where a tramway crosses your road, treat this in the same way as a level crossing. Look out for:

- tram lanes – marked by white lines and/or a different type of road surface;
- traffic lights;
- tracks crossing the road;
- the road narrowing;
- pedestrians running to catch trams.

Do not enter a lane or road reserved for trams. You *must not* drive between trams and the left kerb or park in a way that would obstruct a tram or force other drivers to do so.

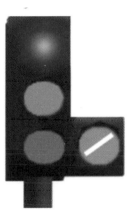

The white symbol at these traffic lights gives instructions to tram drivers only. The instruction given may differ from that given to drivers by the traffic lights

# Checkpoint 7

1 On a multi-laned road you should normally drive:
*Choose two answers*

a. in the centre lane
b. in the left lane
c. in the centre of your lane
d. as close to the lane markings as you can

**2**   When following the road ahead at a roundabout with two lanes, you should normally:
*Choose two answers*

    a.   use the left-hand lane
    b.   use the right-hand lane
    c.   use the lane with least traffic
    d.   look for signs and markings

**3**   For leaving roundabouts you should normally:
*Choose one answer*

    a.   use the left-hand lane
    b.   use the right-hand lane
    c.   check over your right shoulder
    d.   take the lane with least traffic

**4**   If you are in the wrong lane at a junction you should:
*Choose one answer*

    a.   follow the directions for that lane
    b.   stop and wait until you can move over into another lane
    c.   signal and move over quickly
    d.   ask a police officer for instructions

**5**   On one-way streets you should expect:
*Choose one answer*

    a.   pedestrians to be looking the wrong way
    b.   vehicles overtaking on both sides
    c.   fewer road signs and markings
    d.   oncoming vehicles to take priority

**6**   This flashing amber light at a pelican crossing means:

*Choose one answer*

a.   the driver has priority
b.   pedestrians have priority
c.   pedestrians should now start to cross
d.   you should wait for pedestrians within 50 metres of the crossing

7   Following the road ahead at traffic lights, your exit road is blocked.
    You should:
    *Choose one answer*

a.   move into the junction to wait
b.   wait at the line until the exit is clear
c.   move forwards and wait behind the queue
d.   change lanes quickly to avoid waiting

8   When turning right at traffic lights you should:
    *Choose two answers*

a.   give way to oncoming traffic
b.   wait at the stop line for a break in the traffic
c.   proceed because you have a green light
d.   proceed on green only if it is safe

9   A green filter arrow means:

*Choose one answer*

a.   you may proceed only when the main green light shows
b.   you may proceed if safe, regardless of the other lights
c.   all the other lights will be red
d.   it is safe for you to proceed

**10** The first thing to do if you break down on a railway level crossing is:
*Choose one answer*

    a.   get all passengers out of the car
    b.   try to push the car over the crossing
    c.   telephone the signal operator
    d.   try to find out what the problem is

**11** You should treat a zebra crossing with a central refuge:
*Choose one answer*

    a.   as one crossing
    b.   as two crossings
    c.   the same as a single crossing
    d.   the same as a pelican crossing

**12** At level crossings, the flashing red light means:

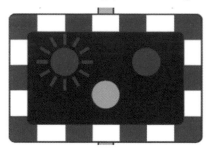

*Choose two answers*

    a.   stop and wait
    b.   another train may be coming
    c.   you have 15 seconds to cross
    d.   the gates will fall in 15 seconds

**13** When turning right on to a dual carriageway you should:
*Choose two answers*

    a.   work out if the central reserve is wide enough to wait in
    b.   check that the road to the right is clear and move to the centre, regardless of the width of the central reserve
    c.   wait until it is safe to cross both carriageways before you move, regardless of the central reserve
    d.   make sure no one is turning through the central reserve

**14** The road used by trams is often marked with:
*Choose one answer*

  a. white dots
  b. white lines
  c. yellow hatch markings
  d. yellow lines

**15** The shape of signs for trams drivers is:
*Choose one answer*

  a. circular
  b. diamond
  c. square
  d. triangular

**16** In areas where there are trams you should:
*Choose two answers*

  a. sometimes give way to trams
  b. always give way to trams
  c. never give way to trams
  d. not try to race or overtake trams

**17** Toucan crossings are shared by:
*Choose one answer*

  a. car drivers and pedestrians
  b. pedestrians and cyclists
  c. cyclists and motorcyclists
  d. motorcyclists and pedestrians

**18** Puffin crossings are designed to:
*Choose two answers*

  a. enable people with animals to cross in safety
  b. improve road safety
  c. reduce unnecessary delays to traffic
  d. stop traffic for longer to allow people with disabilities to cross

**19** At puffin crossings an electronic device:
*Choose two answers*

    a.  detects when cars are approaching
    b.  detects when pedestrians are on the crossing
    c.  can speed up the green light for drivers
    d.  delays the green light for pedestrians

**20** The zigzag lines at all pedestrian crossings mean you must not:

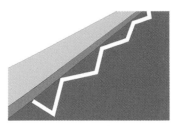

*Choose two answers*

    a.  stop
    b.  park in the marked area
    c.  overtake the lead vehicle in the marked area
    d.  drive over the zigzag lines

You will find the answers on page 328.

Scores:      First try          Second try        Third try

Record your scores in Appendix 2 (page 330).

# Stage 8
# Learning to anticipate problems and avoid accidents

One life lost in an accident is one life too many. Road accidents cost far too many lives, leave a great number of people seriously injured and cost millions of pounds every year.

It has been shown that, by drivers learning how to anticipate and avoid problems, accidents can be reduced by as much as 50 per cent. Your car control skills should now be well developed, and you should have dealt with more types of hazards. You should also have learned from experience that other drivers don't always do what they should do. In this stage you will learn to deal with driving situations that require extra care. This stage shows you how to anticipate what might happen and explains how you can avoid accidents by driving **defensively**.

To help you prepare for this stage, you can also:

- Revise *The Official DVSA Guide to Driving: The essential skills*, Section 10 – Defensive driving.

- Read *The Official DVSA Guide to Driving: The essential skills*, Section 12 – All weather driving, and Section 13 – Driving at night.

- Read *The Official DVSA Guide to Learning to Drive*, Section 2 – Safe positioning, Section 2 – Junctions.

Revise the *Highway Code* rules about:

- Flashing headlights.
- The Horn.
- Speed limits.
- Stopping distances.

Learn the *Highway Code* rules about:

- Adapting your driving and being considerate.
- Mobile phones and in-vehicle technology.
- Traffic calming.
- Country roads.
- Single-track roads.
- Road users requiring extra care.
- Other vehicles.
- Adverse weather conditions.

## Accidents cost lives

Be prepared to give way, even if it may be your priority. No matter who causes an accident, the result is the same:

INJURY      DAMAGE      EXPENSE      INCONVENIENCE      MISERY!

Experience will teach you that other drivers make mistakes.

When you see a possible problem, check your mirrors, adjust your speed and give yourself time to react. Continually look and plan ahead. Near junctions, expect others to move into or across your path.

In areas where your view may be restricted, for example near parked vehicles, expect pedestrians to be walking or even running into the road.

## Concentrate on your driving!

Traffic situations can change very quickly. If you have passengers, keep your eyes on the road when you talk to them.

**In-car radio can keep you up to date with traffic problems ahead**

The use of any in-car entertainment systems or telephones can also be a distraction. Radios can be useful for traffic reports and light background music. Serious listening to plays or other heavy programmes, however, can affect your concentration.

Satellite navigation systems can be an extremely useful aid, but they can also distract. If you are using this technology, make sure any settings are made *before* you start your journey, and don't rely on the navigation system to know when roads are closed or unsuitable for your type of vehicle!

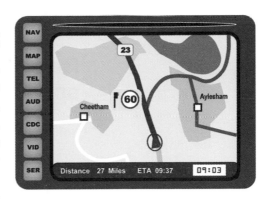

**Don't get distracted by in-vehicle technology**

When you are driving, it is illegal and dangerous to make or receive a call on a hand-held mobile telephone. Even with a hands-free system, any telephone conversation can be a serious distraction. If you must make or receive telephone calls, find somewhere safe to pull in.

**It is illegal and dangerous to use a hand-held mobile phone when driving**

Changing tapes and CDs means looking away from the road and taking a hand from the wheel. It is common sense to avoid this, especially when driving at higher speeds, driving in heavy traffic, and negotiating corners and roundabouts.

Smoking can be dangerous to your health – especially if you do it whilst driving and you drop your cigarette!

# Make good use of the mirrors

Act sensibly on what you see in the mirrors. Simply looking in them is not enough.

Keep regular checks all around on the speed and position of other traffic – particularly on multi-laned roads.

Anticipate traffic joining your road and move over to make room if safe. Be aware when someone has moved out of sight into your blind spots.

**Anticipate traffic joining your road and move over to make room if safe – beware of vehicles that have entered your blind spots**

**Think of the consequences of driving too fast for the conditions – ask yourself 'What if...?'**

**When you double your speed – braking distance increases by four times**

Drive defensively and allow others to overtake. Leave room for them to return to the lane ahead of you.

# Be sensible with your speed

You must keep within the legal speed limits, observing signs. Remember that the speed limit on a road with street lighting is 30 mph unless signs tell you otherwise. If there are no signs or street lighting, the national speed limit of 60 mph on a single carriageway and 70 mph on dual carriageways applies. Look out for national speed limit and maximum and minimum speed limit signs when you approach a new road.

Remember – a speed limit is not a target. It is the highest permitted speed for that area. This means it will not always be safe to travel up to that speed.

The speed at which you drive should depend on the road, the weather and traffic conditions. Think of the consequences of driving too fast for the conditions – ask yourself 'What if...?'

When you double your speed, braking distance increases by four times. Always travel at a speed at which you can stop safely in the distance you can see to be clear ahead!

Within the speed limit for the road you are on, you should be driving at the most appropriate speed for the conditions. Driving too slowly can be just as hazardous as driving too quickly. If you delay following traffic by driving too slowly, you can cause frustration that may tempt a following driver to make a rash move.

# Be patient

In today's volume of traffic you must expect delays in your journeys. You should allow plenty of time, especially if you are driving in peak traffic hours.

Even though you have been taught to drive confidently, there are many others on the road less able than yourself. Be ready to wait patiently. If there are very few gaps in the traffic it's a waste of time losing your patience – there's nothing to be done about it. If you get annoyed it will affect your own safety and you will be tempted to take risks.

If you are driving properly and keeping to the speed limits, don't let drivers behind push you. Keep calm and, if a driver behind seems too close or gets aggressive, drop a little further back from the vehicle ahead of you to increase your braking distance. If you feel threatened, it may even be sensible, when it is safe, to pull in to the left and let the drivers behind get by.

**Assessment – use of speed**

# Dealing with oncoming vehicles

In Stage 4 you learned how to pass parked vehicles safely by slowing down if needed to give adequate clearance. When there isn't enough space for you and an approaching vehicle to pass, one of you will need to hold back. Use the MSPSL routine as you approach the hazard.

You should normally give priority to the approaching driver if the obstruction is on your side of the road, but don't assume priority if the obstruction is on the other side. If you are looking well ahead and anticipate the problem, you should be able to slow down early enough to give the oncoming driver a clear path without you having to stop.

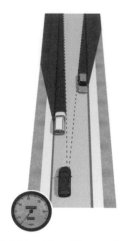

**Give priority to approaching traffic if an obstruction is on your side of the road**

**Choose a 'hold-back' position to give you best view of the road ahead**

If it is necessary to stop, take up a sensible hold-back position well back from the obstruction and not too close to the kerb. This will allow you to see ahead clearly and enable you to change course gradually to steer clear of the obstruction. When the approaching traffic has passed, check your mirrors again before moving on and if necessary give a signal. Take care as you pass the obstacle – pedestrians may step out!

Always be prepared to give way to oncoming drivers, even though it may be your priority. Look well ahead and, when you see a vehicle parked on the other side of the road, expect oncoming drivers to keep coming. Check what is happening behind and ease off the gas. This will give you time to work out whether the other driver is going to make you wait or whether you can keep moving.

Sometimes it is sensible to give priority even when the obstruction is on the other side of the road. Be considerate towards drivers of large vehicles, particularly on hills.

If there are obstructions on both sides of the road, neither you nor the oncoming driver has priority. In these situations the defensive driver would not rely on the oncoming traffic to stop. If you are prepared to give way then you are in charge of the situation.

Where there are lines of parked cars on each side of the road, you may need to pull into a gap between cars or wait opposite a gap so that approaching traffic can pull in to let you pass. In these situations your speed should be kept down and, if there is only room for one vehicle to go through and you can see traffic approaching, always look well ahead for a suitable gap. Remember that there is little point in you pulling into a gap if there is not enough room for traffic following you to do the same. The driver of an approaching vehicle should anticipate this problem, and you can only do likewise if you check your mirrors in good time!

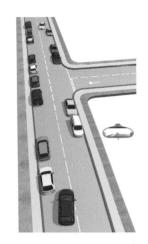

**Using your mirrors may help you anticipate what the approaching driver intends to do!**

Drivers often flash headlights in these situations – make sure you are clear about the other driver's intentions before reacting to a flashing headlight signal!

In towns where traffic-calming measures are in force, you might see signs indicating priority where the road is narrowed. Always be ready for an approaching driver trying to make a dash for the gap!

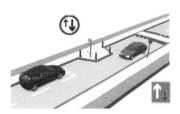

In rural areas, be prepared to meet traffic where the road narrows or where there is a bend ahead – larger vehicles may be forced on to your side of the road.

When you are approaching arch bridges or other height restrictions, remember that larger vehicles may have to move to the centre of the road to pass safely beneath the obstruction – be prepared to give way.

**At arch bridges large vehicles may have to move to the centre of the road**

Notes:    Notes:    Notes:

**Assessment – meeting traffic**

# Overtaking

Overtaking at the wrong place or time can put you on a collision course with oncoming traffic. Before deciding to overtake, ask yourself if the benefit is worth the risk:

- Is it safe?
- Is it lawful?
- Is it necessary?

Think about the distance you will travel and also about the time you will need to overtake and get back in safely. Consider also the distance that will be covered by any oncoming vehicles.

Do not overtake where bends or hill crests restrict your view, or when you are approaching pedestrian crossings and junctions. Take particular care where there is 'dead ground' – a dip in a road that could hide an oncoming vehicle.

There is little point overtaking if you will be turning off shortly, if there is a line of traffic ahead and you will have to slow down, or if the vehicle ahead is driving at the speed limit. Look at the road layout ahead – will there be safer opportunities to get past if you wait a minute or so for example a wider stretch of road or two-lane dual carriageway?

> **Dual carriageway ahead**

Consider what the other driver may be doing:

- Will he or she pull out to pass a parked car or cyclist?
- Is he or she signalling to turn?

Last, but not least:

- Is it safe behind?
- Is someone overtaking you?

## Getting into position to see ahead before overtaking

You will need to use the MSPSL routine several times when overtaking.

To get a good view of the road ahead, stay well back, matching the speed of the vehicle you want to overtake. When possible, particularly with large vehicles, check the mirrors and position so that you can look along the nearside of the vehicle ahead.

**Check along the nearside of the vehicle you intend to overtake**

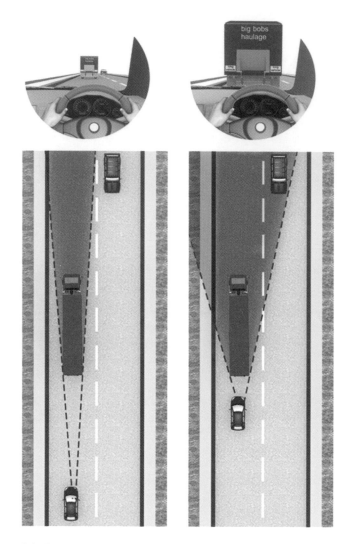

**It is dangerous to keep too close to a vehicle you intend to overtake because you can't see clearly ahead**

Check the mirrors again and, if safe, move over to look along the offside for a long straight stretch of road that is free of oncoming vehicles, obstructions and side turns.

If it appears safe ahead and behind, select a lower gear to give you a reserve of power; be ready to accelerate quickly. Apply MSPSL again – look in the mirrors to check that it is still safe, and signal to let others know of your intentions. Pull out on a smooth line that will give adequate clearance to the vehicle ahead. Overtake as promptly as you can. Try not to stay in the other driver's blind area for too long. As you clear the vehicle, look out for other traffic, or pedestrians in the road ahead hidden from your view before you started to overtake. Use the MSPSL routine again to pull back on to your side as soon as you safely can. Don't cut in too soon – you could force the driver you've just overtaken to brake sharply. Once in your normal road position, check your mirrors again and make progress. Having overtaken, you should not then cause the following driver to slow down, unless some unforeseen danger arises in the road ahead.

**Assessment – overtaking**

# Common dangers at junctions

You shouldn't always expect drivers turning right to wait for you. Be prepared for drivers to make mistakes and turn across your path.

When you see a vehicle approaching with a right indicator signal on, try to work out its speed. If it does not appear to be slowing down enough, check to see what is happening behind and ease off the gas. Hold back if you think it will turn in front of you.

If you're driving ahead at traffic lights, watch for drivers turning across your path. They may not have seen you.

Watch out for drivers emerging from side roads. Even when you're driving along major roads, you should expect drivers to emerge from side roads. As you're driving along, check your mirrors regularly and look ahead for roads to the left and right.

Look for drivers approaching the junctions at high speed. They may not look properly and may pull out in front of you simply because they didn't see you.

Emerging drivers may be distracted by other traffic or respond inappropriately to other driver's signals. Anticipate danger if approaching traffic seems to be inviting emerging drivers to pull out.

When you are approaching side roads, always be aware of what is behind you, particularly before you decide to turn. Follow the mirrors–signal–manoeuvre routine and take a final look in the appropriate door mirror before turning right or left. Remember, if you use your mirrors properly and react to what you see in them, you shouldn't get caught out by vehicles overtaking you.

When you are waiting in traffic, make sure you leave side roads and other main entrances clear for others to drive in and out.

If you are waiting to emerge from a side road, try using eye contact and smiling. This often encourages others to let you in.

## Changing lanes in heavy traffic

Look and plan well ahead, reading the signs and markings. This will help you get into the correct lane in good time. If you do find yourself in the wrong lane in heavy traffic, avoid trying to change lanes quickly.

Use MSPSL and try to make eye contact with a driver already in the lane you wish to take. When you are sure the other driver is letting you in, move over gradually and acknowledge the courtesy. Before you move, however, check in your door mirrors for cyclists and motorcyclists driving between the lanes – they may be able to travel faster than other vehicles in congested conditions.

Take care switching lanes in heavy traffic – check your mirrors for cyclists and motorcyclists who may be moving faster than you

## Avoiding accidents with vehicles to your sides

Make sure other drivers are aware of your presence. Avoid driving in the blind areas to their sides.

Look well ahead for obstructions and anticipate when vehicles ahead will need to change lanes. Check your mirrors regularly and be ready to let people into the lane ahead of you.

Their size makes it difficult for larger vehicles to negotiate some turns. They often need to swing out to the right before turning left, or position well over to the left before turning into narrow roads or entrances on the right. When you see large vehicles signalling to turn, keep well back and allow them plenty of space and time.

Larger vehicles often take unusual courses through bends and round-abouts. Anticipate this, keep out of their blind areas and hold back for them when necessary.

# Dealing with buses

Buses stop frequently, often with little warning. Stay well back from them and watch for:

- last-minute signals for stopping;
- passengers standing on the bus ready to get off;
- people waiting at bus stops ahead.

When you think a bus will be stopping:

- check your mirrors;
- keep well back; and
- position to the offside in case you can get by when it stops.

When passing buses, be aware that passengers may be walking into the road in front of it. Look out for people crossing the road to catch the bus – they may not be paying attention to the traffic! When coming up behind stationary buses, watch for indicator signals. Be prepared to give way when it is safe to do so.

# Dealing with emergency vehicles

Pay attention at all times and stay alert. If you listen to any in-car entertainment, don't have it so loud that it could mask outside noises such as sirens. Use your mirrors regularly, and look and listen. If you hear an emergency vehicle approaching, consider its route. Be ready to take any necessary safe action to let it pass. Think before you act – in busy and narrow roads it may be better to keep moving to create a clear path.

Respond safely and promptly to emergency vehicles – remember that someone's life may be at stake

Whilst emergency vehicles showing blue lights – police, fire and ambulance services – are permitted to break a speed limit or go against a red traffic light, their drivers must give priority to others who are obliged to keep within the law. Don't endanger yourself or others when trying to create a clear path for emergency vehicles.

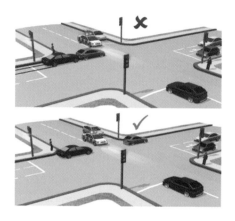

If you see blue lights flashing in your rearview mirror, stay calm and look ahead for a safe place ahead to move over. Remember that when one emergency vehicle comes through there is a good chance another will follow. Stay vigilant!

If a police officer wants you to pull over and stop, he or she will usually flash his or her headlights and/or give a left signal or point to the left. If this happens, pull up when you safely can, switch off your engine and wait for the officer to come to you.

# Vulnerable road users

There could be anything around a bend or over a hill. Wherever you can't see the road ahead, anticipate that there will be some sort of problem and then you will be ready for it when it appears.

When you are approaching bends and hill crests, especially where there are no pavements, expect to meet people walking in the road. Check your mirrors and be prepared to slow down so that you will be able to stop within the distance you can see is clear.

Areas where there are lots of parked vehicles hide all sorts of problems from the driver. Remember, you may have to drive well below the speed limit in built-up areas. You need to:

- look though car windows for signs of movement;
- leave plenty of clearance, allowing for doors opening;
- look out for hidden junctions – others may be emerging;
- watch for pedestrians walking between parked cars;
- allow for the actions of cyclists.

A high proportion of pedestrians killed in road accidents are either under 15 or over 60. They often misjudge the speed and distance of traffic and may step unexpectedly into the road.

Be patient with the elderly and people with disabilities. Give them plenty of time and don't harass them. Watch out at all times for pedestrians in or near the road, particularly when driving:

- in shopping areas;
- near schools;
- near junctions;
- around ice cream vans and other mobile shops;
- near bus stops.

There won't always be signs warning you of pedestrians in the road. Look well ahead and be prepared to slow down, leaving plenty of clearance in case anyone steps into the road. Sometimes a light tap on the horn can draw attention to your presence. Be particularly careful near schools; not all older children feel the need to cross safely with the crossing patrol. Younger children tend to be impulsive,

**There won't always be signs warning you of pedestrians in the road!**

particularly when they've just come out of school. Check the mirrors, slow down and be ready to stop.

**Take a good look for cyclists and motorcyclists when emerging at junctions**

Cyclists and motorcyclists are more difficult to see. When emerging from junctions, watch for cyclists and motorcyclists riding close to the left, particularly when there are lines of parked vehicles close to the junction. Make sure you look properly whatever the conditions, but especially in poor light and bad weather.

When you see a cyclist look round to the right, anticipate that they will move out or turn to the right. Remember though that cyclists don't always check behind before they pull out to pass obstructions. Think ahead. Check your mirrors, slow down and expect them to steer out at the last moment. The closer you get to them, the more cyclists will wobble. Allow them plenty of room. If you can't give them at least 2 metres clearance, then slow right down so that you can stop safely if they cycle into your path for any reason.

When you have been waiting in a traffic queue, check your mirrors for cyclists before moving off. Take particular care if you have been queuing to turn at a junction.

To help air quality and reduce congestion, cycling is now encouraged in cities and towns. Expect to see cycle lanes and priority given to cyclists at junctions. Pay attention to the road markings and signs. Try not to obstruct the free flow of cycle traffic. Horse riders need extra care. Make sure you have enough room before you pass them.

**Horses are easily frightened by vehicle noise**

Check your mirrors, and slow down well before you reach them even if they are on the other side of the road. Drive quietly past, leaving as much room as possible. Expect to see horse riders near riding schools and on rural roads. Take heed of any signals a horse rider may give you.

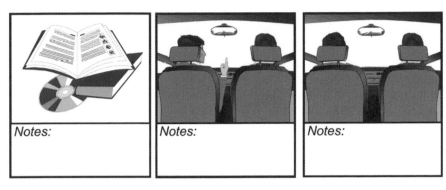

*Notes:* | *Notes:* | *Notes:*

**Assessment – vulnerable road users**

# Avoiding accidents on country roads

Concentrate and plan well ahead. Remember, speed limits are the maximum allowed for the road – not targets! It is a sobering thought that loss of control on country roads is one of the commonest causes of death amongst young and inexperienced drivers. Drive at a speed at which you can stop within the distance you can see is clear.

The countryside holds different dangers from towns and cities. You never know what there may be around the next bend. Drive more slowly on narrow roads, through villages and near farm entrances. Expect to see wild and domestic animals on the road. Expect to meet large and slow-moving farm vehicles.

**The countryside holds different dangers from towns and cities**

Be patient when following slow-moving vehicles. Do not overtake until you are absolutely sure that it will be safe. In rural areas, expect mud in the road and take particular care in wet weather.

Be prepared to give way. On single-track roads there are sometimes pulling-in places. Plan well ahead and work out whether you will need to pull into one on your side or wait opposite one so the approaching vehicle can pull in.

## Make sure you can be seen

Lights should be used, not only when it's too dark or foggy for you to see properly, but to help others see you.

When daylight conditions are poor, or in heavy rain and snow, use your dipped headlights. When visibility falls to below 100 metres, use your fog lights. These should not, however, be used at other times. When used at the wrong time, high-intensity rear lights can mask the brake lights so that following drivers have little or no warning that you may be slowing down. Front fog lights can dazzle and annoy oncoming drivers – use them properly.

Dipped headlights should also be used when glare from a low-angle sun can make it difficult for drivers to see ahead.

## Avoiding accidents at night

It's much harder to see at night. Your view may be masked by shadows, particularly at dusk. Watch out for cyclists riding without lights and pedestrians wearing dark clothing, particularly where there is no footpath or you are approaching a junction.

Use dipped headlights in built-up areas so that you can see and be seen.

Use full headlights where the street lighting is poor. Be ready to dip them for oncoming drivers and when you are following other vehicles so that they don't cause dazzle in the mirrors.

# Fog, snow and ice

Only drive in poor weather conditions if your journey is absolutely necessary.

If you must drive in fog, use dipped headlights. If visibility is really bad, switch on the fog and high-intensity rear lights. To keep down condensation in your car, use the demister and rear screen heater. A slightly open window will not only help this but also help you hear other traffic before you can see it.

**Driving in fog during the hours of darkness requires extra care**

Don't be tempted to follow others too closely in fog – remember, they may brake suddenly. Keep your distance. Drive at a speed at which you can stop safely, and remember that not all other drivers will be using their headlights.

Watch out for obstructions in the road, and drive at a distance at which you can stop safely. Signals for passing parked vehicles and other hazards will become more necessary, as it is more difficult for following drivers to see obstructions.

**Don't use full beam headlights in fog. At night your forward vision would be seriously reduced**

When waiting to turn right into minor roads in fog, it may help to keep your foot on the brake pedal – this will give you an extra set of lights to the rear.

Driving in fog at night is particularly dangerous. Avoid the temptation of clinging to the tail lights of the vehicle ahead. Use dipped headlights in fog at night – if you try to use full beam, reflection from the mist will seriously reduce your forward vision.

In freezing conditions, avoid accelerating or braking on exposed parts of the road such as bridges. There could be black ice, which is almost impossible to detect.

In snow or icy conditions you should:

- slow down early using light pressure on the brake pedal;

- accelerate gently and stay in the highest gear possible;

- when driving uphill try to keep moving steadily by keeping well back from the vehicle ahead;

- remember that road markings may be hidden.

- Ice on the road surface can be difficult to see and takes longer to melt in the shade. Anticipate this and adjust your speed accordingly.

# Avoiding problems by reading the road ahead

Always read the road well ahead and take the weather conditions into consideration.

Check your mirrors and slow down when you can see the road surface deteriorating. Keep off soft verges and look out for mud, gravel or chippings. When it rains after a long spell of dry weather, a combination of oil, dust, rubber and water can make the surface very slippery.

In the autumn, watch for damp patches under trees, where leaves can also make the surface slippery. In the winter, these areas will hold frost longer than the parts of the road the sun has reached.

# Driving in windy conditions

When overtaking high-sided vehicles, expect to feel the wind throwing you off course as you pass by. This will be even worse in high exposed places, such as bridges. Hold the steering wheel firmly to compensate.

When driving in lanes, anticipate other road users being affected.

# Driving through floods and fords

Look well ahead for signs, and always be aware of what is happening behind. At some fords there are gauges to tell you how deep the water may be. Slow down, change into first gear and, using a slipping clutch, keep the engine revs up. Look for any camber in the road, and drive slowly through at the shallowest point.

When you reach the other side you need to make sure the brakes are dry. Drive very slowly and press the brake gently with your left foot.

# Avoiding aquaplaning

Aquaplaning can happen when a cushion of water is built up in front of fast-moving tyres. If the tyres cannot displace the water, they may ride up on to it, losing contact with the road surface. The steering will become light, and you could also lose your braking control.

To avoid aquaplaning:

- keep your tyres in good condition and properly inflated;
- make sure your brakes are well maintained;
- plan well ahead, adapting your speed to suit the conditions;
- take into account the road and weather conditions.

# Checkpoint 8

1    If you must drive in fog:
     *Choose three answers*

     a.   drive nearer to the centre line
     b.   use dipped headlights
     c.   use full beam headlights
     d.   keep your footbrake on when waiting to turn right off a main road
     e.   allow more time for your journey

**2**   When driving near animals you should be ready to:
*Choose two answers*

a.   slow down or stop
b.   sound your horn
c.   drive quickly away
d.   give lots of clearance

**3**   If you park on the road at night, you use your sidelights:
*Choose two answers*

a.   on a road with a speed limit of less than 30 mph
b.   on a road with a speed limit of more than 30 mph
c.   if parking within 10 metres of a junction
d.   if the road is poorly lit

**4**   You should only flash your headlights:
*Choose one answer*

a.   when you want another driver to give way to you
b.   when you are giving way
c.   to let others know you are there
d.   to encourage pedestrians to use zebra crossings

**5**   You should be careful and considerate to other road users.
You should:
*Choose two answers*

a.   expect others to take the correct action
b.   expect others to make mistakes
c.   always be ready to give way
d.   only give priority when you have no choice

**6**   Staying well back from a slower-moving vehicle will:
*Choose three answers*

a.   give you a better view ahead
b.   help you to anticipate its actions
c.   make it more difficult to overtake
d.   make it safer to overtake
e.   waste road space

**7** Wind or side draught can affect your car:
*Choose two answers*

   a.  in high exposed places
   b.  if you drive at high speed with your sunroof open
   c.  mainly in built-up areas
   d.  after overtaking a large vehicle

**8** If a following driver becomes impatient when you are waiting to emerge into a busy road, you should:
*Choose one answer*

   a.  pull out as quickly as you can
   b.  keep calm and wait for a safe gap in the traffic
   c.  take as long as you can to teach the other driver some manners
   d.  put on your high-intensity rear lights to distract the other driver

**9** Driving on a fairly narrow road, you see ahead a large vehicle emerging from a road on the right. You should:
*Choose three answers*

   a.  expect the large vehicle to swing out into the road
   b.  ignore the situation because the other driver should give way
   c.  check your mirrors and steer well in to the left
   d.  hold back and give the other driver plenty of room
   c.  sound your horn and maintain your course

**10** Elderly pedestrians are particularly vulnerable. They:
*Choose two answers*

   a.  should be able to judge your speed
   b.  may not be able to judge your speed
   c.  could step out into the road
   d.  should be encouraged to hurry across the road
   e.  tend to be impulsive and make a dash for it

**11** If you see someone with a white cane with a red band, he or she is:
*Choose one answer*

   a.  deaf and blind
   b.  deaf and mute
   c.  blind and mute
   d.  fitted with a hearing aid

**12** If a pedestrian is hit by a car travelling at 20 mph, the chance of the pedestrian being killed is:
*Choose one answer*

a.  1 in 10
b.  1 in 20
c.  1 in 30
d.  1 in 40

**13** You should only use a hand-held mobile phone when:
*Choose one answer*

a.  driving on motorways
b.  driving in towns
c.  you are stopped in a safe place
d.  you want to answer a call

**14** What does this sign mean?

*Choose one answer*

a.  high-grip surface ahead
b.  slippery road
c.  danger of ice
d.  off-road vehicles only

**15** When an emergency vehicle approaches you should:
*Choose two answers*

  a. try not to panic
  b. stop your car immediately
  c. speed up to get out of the way
  d. pull on to the footpath to get clear
  e. check your mirrors before deciding on the safest course of action

**16** Driving after snowfall, you see this road sign at a junction ahead.
You should:

*Choose one answer*

  a. keep going slowly past the sign
  b. stop and check for traffic on the main road
  c. ignore the sign
  d. report the danger to your local highway authority

**17** Fog lights should be used:
*Choose one answer*

  a. whenever you need to use headlights
  b. when you drive in rural areas at night
  c. only in foggy weather
  d. whenever visibility is less than 100 metres

**18** In wet weather your tyres:
*Choose one answer*

  a. have less grip on the road
  b. have more grip on the road
  c. need to be inflated to a higher pressure
  d. need to be inflated to a lower pressure

**19** Before driving away in icy conditions you should:
*Choose two answers*

a.  clear a patch in the windscreen
b.  clear the front and side windows
c.  clear all of the windows
d.  demist the windows thoroughly

**20** You are driving on a narrow rural road and see this sign. You should:

*Choose three answers*

a.  check your mirrors because of the hazard
b.  not worry, as you are on the road with priority
c.  beware of emerging traffic
d.  be prepared to stop if necessary
e.  position towards the centre of the road
f.  maintain your speed and sound your horn

You will find the answers on page 329.

| Scores: | First try | Second try | Third try |
|---------|-----------|------------|-----------|
|         |           |            |           |

Record your scores in Appendix 2 (page 330).

# Stage 9
# Driving at higher speeds, basic maintenance and dealing with emergencies

By now you should be able to drive confidently in most of the situations covered in the previous eight stages and may have done some driving on higher-speed roads. At this stage your instructor should be making sure you can drive safely and confidently at higher speeds. You may have to take longer lessons to get to areas where there are dual carriageways that carry the national speed limit. Driving on this type of road will prepare you for motorway driving. Although as a learner you are not allowed to drive on motorways, you do need to know the rules. Not only will this prepare you for your theory test, but it will mean that as soon as you have passed the test you will be able to apply those rules.

It is your responsibility as a driver to ensure that the car you are driving is roadworthy. Of course, if you are taking professional tuition in a driving school car you should expect your instructor to take care of it. He or she should show you how to carry out basic safety checks on your vehicle that will be important when you are practising in your own vehicle. You should know how to carry out simple tasks, including:

- checking tyre pressures and tread;
- changing a wheel;
- checking oil and water levels;
- checking and replacing bulbs.

You will be asked questions on these and other vehicle checks in the theory test and may be asked to show or describe how you would perform some of these tasks in your practical test. You should also know what to do in cases of breakdowns and other emergencies.

To help you prepare for this stage, you can also:

- Read *The Official DVSA Guide to Driving: The essential skills*, Section 11 – Driving on motorways, Section 14 – Basic maintenance, Section 15 – Breakdowns, Section 16 – Accidents and emergencies, Section 17 – Eco-safe driving and the environment, and Section 18 – Avoiding and dealing with congestion.

- *Read The Official DVSA Guide to Learning to Drive*, Section 2 – Safety checks, Section 2 – Independent driving, Section 2 – Environmental issues, Section 2 – Passengers and loads, Section 2 – Security.

Look up and learn the *Highway Code* rules about

- Motorways.
- Breakdowns and accidents.
- Road works.

Read the additional advice annexed to *The Highway Code* on: Vehicle maintenance, safety and security, and First aid on the road.

## Planning your journeys

During your final preparation for your practical driving test you should learn how to navigate without prompts from your supervisor or instructor. This should help prepare you for some driving alone after you have passed. Here are some tips for preparing for a journey:

- Allow yourself plenty of time. In today's congested traffic you cannot depend on getting to your destination in the shortest possible time. The later you are, the more frustrated you will become, to the point where you may even be tempted to take risks.

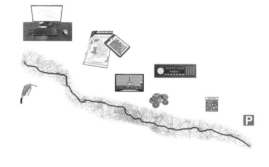

- Plan your journey. Organize yourself with a route plan, noting down all the road numbers and names of towns. Start out early, making sure you allow time for road works and other problems. A route card only takes a few minutes to prepare, and if you have internet access it is easy to download route plans and information. It is worth doing this even if you have satnav technology in your vehicle.

- Learn how to read and follow road signs. Keep up to date with traffic news by tuning your car radio to local stations or having the traffic announcement (TA) system switched on.

- Keep your concentration to a maximum. If you are going a long distance, take plenty of breaks. Keep the temperature comfortable and not too stuffy. Listen only to light programmes on the radio or music centre. Remember, fiddling about with discs and tapes can be a distraction whilst you are driving.

- Mobile phones. In emergencies, mobile phones can be extremely useful (particularly if you are a lone female driver). Remember, however, that they should only be used when you are stationary.

# Lane discipline

When you drive on any type of dual carriageway or motorway, make sure you keep to the correct lane. People not driving in the left lane when it is reasonably clear cause many of the hold-ups that occur on these roads.

Remember, on a three-lane motorway you should:

- use the left lane for normal driving unless there are a number of slower-moving vehicles – you may then use the centre lane;

- use the centre lane as above, but return to the left lane when it is clear;

- use the right lane for overtaking only.

Look and plan well ahead, using your mirrors to keep aware of what is happening all around all of the time. Work out in good time whether the traffic ahead in the left and centre lanes is moving more slowly and you need to consider overtaking. This will allow you more thinking time after checking the mirrors to work out whether or not your manoeuvre will be safe.

Anticipate drivers ahead preparing to overtake, and be prepared to act. You may either slow down a little or, if safe, move over to the next lane on your right. Expect people to be joining the motorway from slip roads and, if you have time and it is safe, be prepared to move over to allow them on to the main carriageway.

When approaching your exits, look for the signs and plan ahead so that you can get over in good time without causing problems for other drivers. You will see advance warnings for motorway exits usually at one mile and half a mile before the turn-off. These may be at the side of the carriageway or they may be overhead gantry signs. By the time you reach the countdown markers you should be in the left lane. Remember that the deceleration lane is for slowing down. Unless there are queues for your exit, try not to slow down drivers on the motorway.

**Get into the left lane in good time for your exit on motorways and dual carriageways**

Speed can be deceiving. Once in the deceleration lane, keep checking your speed and make sure you have full control as you approach the junction. If you have been driving at higher speeds for some time, you will think you are travelling much more slowly than you are when you first leave the motorway.

# Reducing the risk of breakdowns

Your car should be maintained in a road-worthy condition. Before driving at any time, take a look around your vehicle for any obvious defects. You don't need to be a qualified mechanic to make some basic safety checks! These will reduce the chances of your being involved in breakdowns and accidents.

**You don't need to be a mechanic to take care of basic maintenance**

If you are capable of undertaking more than basic maintenance yourself, make sure you use only approved parts and lubricants as recommended by the vehicle manufacturer.

## *Regular checks – at least once a week*

The frequency of these checks will depend on how often and how much you drive. The owner's hand-book will give advice for your car:

- Fuel: Try to avoid running on less than a quarter-tank. Check your fuel as soon as you switch on. Remember, if you are travelling far, it may be a long way to the next service station.

- Oil: Check the engine oil and top up as necessary with the correct type of oil for your vehicle. When you move your car it is worth looking to see if there are telltale oil drips that could indicate a leak. If the oil pressure warning light comes on whilst driving, stop as soon as it is safe and check the problem out. If you run your engine without oil, it could seize up.

- Brake fluid: You should be able to identify the brake fluid reservoir in your engine compartment and check the level against the 'minimum' mark. When topping up the brake fluid level, be careful not to contaminate the reservoir with dust, dirt or water.

- Windscreen wash: Make sure that there is water in the washer bottle and that the windscreen washer jets are functioning. In winter it is worth mixing an additive with water in the wash bottle so that it doesn't freeze.

- When the engine is cold, check the radiator coolant. If it needs topping up, use the correct mixture of water and coolant/ antifreeze. It is best to make fluid checks on a level surface when the engine has been switched off and allowed to stand for at least 30 minutes.

- Electrics: Before driving, check that all the lights and indicators are working. Keep spare bulbs in the car. If you don't have someone to help, reflections in a garage door can be useful. Although many car batteries are now sealed units, yours may be the type that needs checking. Check that the electrolyte fluid level in the battery covers the plates. If necessary, top this up with distilled water.

- Visually check your tyres, looking for any obvious cuts or bulges, and check for uneven tyre wear. Remove any stones from the tread. Use a reliable pressure gauge to check that your tyres are properly inflated. You could get a puncture at any time, so check the spare as well. Check the tyre tread depth against the wear markers on the tyre. You can also use a depth indicator to measure how worn your tyres are.

**Check your tyres for obvious defects and signs of uneven tread wear Use a reliable gauge to check type pressures**

# Changing a wheel

**Hazard warning triangles should be placed at least 45 metres behind the car but you should not use one on a motorway**

**Changing a wheel, you need to loosen the wheel nuts slightly before jacking the car up**

**Refer to the vehicle handbook to locate the correct jacking points and make sure the base of the jack is on firm ground**

You can get a puncture at any time, so it well worth knowing how to deal with it before you start driving by yourself. Read the owner's handbook for your vehicle.

When changing a wheel, as a matter of routine you should park on level, firm ground. Apply the parking brake and leave the car in gear (in an automatic, select Park). If you are on the road, switch on your hazard warning lights. Two items that are worth carrying in the car are a hazard warning triangle and a high-visibility vest. Wear the vest if you have it, and place your warning triangle at least 45 metres behind your car on the same side of the road.

Unfortunately, you never know when or where you will get a puncture. If you are on a slope, position a chock, brick or heavy object at each side of one of the good wheels to prevent movement. Be aware of other traffic, and try not to stand in front of your lights at night.

Place the spare wheel, jack and wheel brace (spanner) near the tyre to be changed. Slightly loosen the wheel nuts of the flat tyre before you jack the car up. If these are difficult to turn you may have to use your foot and bodyweight on the lever. Make sure you support yourself as you do this, so that you are not injured.

Position the jack at a suitable point under the vehicle – refer to the owner's handbook to locate special jacking points. Make sure that the base of the jack is on a firm and level surface so that it can't tilt or collapse when the car is raised. Now raise the vehicle enough to allow room for the properly inflated tyre to be fitted.

Remove the wheel nuts and put them safely to one side where you can find them again! Remove the wheel with the flat tyre and replace it with the spare.

Fit the new wheel, locating two opposite nuts finger tight. Fit the other nuts and tighten them all lightly with the brace. Then lower the jack and tighten the nuts firmly.

Remove the chocks, and remember to replace the tools and the flat tyre in the boot. Check the pressure of the replacement tyre as soon as possible.

**Have everything ready before you jack the car up**

Instead of a full-size spare wheel, some cars have a 'space-saver tyre' or an emergency inflation kit that simultaneously re-inflates and seals the inside of the tyre. These are only intended as temporary repairs. The owner's handbook will advise you on these and may recommend a maximum speed and distance that a space-saver or re-inflated tyre can be used for until you can get a puncture properly repaired.

# If you break down

If possible, try not to inconvenience others, and get your car off the road. Switch on your hazard flashers and place your warning triangle 45 metres behind the car on the same side of the road (but not if you are on a motorway!). At night, be careful not to stand in front of your lights. If you are a lone female, in quieter areas lock yourself in the car and be prepared to speak to others through a slightly open window.

If you don't have a mobile phone and there is no one around, you may have to walk for assistance yourself. Make sure you lock the car, putting any valuables in the boot.

In cases of emergency the police and motoring organizations give priority to lone women.

Before setting out on a long journey, it can be useful to let someone know your route, destination and estimated time of arrival.

## *If you break down on a motorway*

If your car develops a problem, try to get it to the next exit or service area. If you can't do this:

- Get over to the hard shoulder as safely as possible and stop as far to the left as you can.

- Switch on your hazard warning lights.

- Try to stop near one of the emergency telephones.

- If you have a disability and can't get out of the car, display a 'help' sign and wait for the police.

- You and your passengers should exit to the nearside.

- Unless they are in real danger, leave animals in the car.

- Do not try to 'fix it' – you could put yourself in danger even changing a wheel.

- Make sure all passengers get on to the verge as far away from the carriageway and hard shoulder as possible.

- Keep children, and animals, under control.

- Walk to the nearest emergency telephone. An arrow on one of the regular marker posts will tell you which way this is. This is a free service, and you will get a quicker response than by using a mobile.

**Marker posts are at 100 metre intervals and an arrow indicates the direction to the nearest emergency telephone**

- Face the traffic flow when using the telephone.

- Give full details, and inform the operator if you are a lone woman or feel under threat.

- Go back and wait on the verge near your vehicle.

- Should you feel threatened by someone, get in your car from the left and lock the doors. If the danger passes, get out and on to the verge again.

**Emergency telephones are at about one mile intervals on the motorway. Face the traffic flow when using the phone**

# What to do at the scene of an accident

You never know when you're going to arrive at the scene of an accident. Could you do anything to help or would you be one of those who just stands and stares?

Keep a first aid kit in your car where it will be easy to get at if needed – it's no good buried under your luggage!

**Keep a first aid kit in your car**

If you get to the scene before anyone else, keep calm. The first thing to do is warn other traffic – switch on hazard lights and seek assistance. Take charge until someone better qualified arrives. Either call yourself or get someone else to phone for the emergency services.

Impose a smoking ban at the scene! Don't put yourself in danger trying to help a casualty.

People with injuries should be kept warm and calm. Talk to casualties constantly to keep them reassured. Do not give them anything to eat or drink. Only move a casualty if there is the real possibility of further danger to him or her.

Some knowledge of first aid can be very helpful – you could save a life by following some of the simple procedures outlined in Section 16 of *The Official DVSA Guide to Driving: The essential skills* and in the annex of *The Highway Code*. Could you save a life if you found a casualty not breathing?

If you'd like to better equip yourself for dealing with anyone injured in an accident, the St John Ambulance service runs courses all over the country – look in your *Yellow Pages*.

**Are you equipped to save a life?**

# Reducing the risk of fire

**It is worthwhile carrying a small fire extinguisher in your car**

Although the risk of fire in modern cars is minimal, it is sensible to carry a fire extinguisher – and know how to use it!

Pipes can become damaged in accidents, and fuel could leak on to electrical contacts. The engine of any vehicle involved should be switched off immediately.

If no one else has done so, impose a 'no smoking' rule at the scene. If you suspect your car may have electrical problems, get it checked as soon as possible.

If you suspect there is a fire in the engine compartment at any time:

- Pull in as soon as you can and get everyone out and well clear of the vehicle.
- Call the fire services or get someone to do it for you.
- Go back and wait on the verge near your vehicle.
- *Do not* open the bonnet – try to direct a fire extinguisher through the gap created when you operate the bonnet latch release.
- Don't risk injury to yourself if the fire can't be extinguished quickly and easily. Get well clear and wait for the fire brigade. A fire in the engine compartment can completely destroy a vehicle in less than five minutes!

# Breakdowns in tunnels

Tunnels present particular problems if you have a break-down or emergency, because it can be difficult for you to get clear and others to reach you.

If you have a breakdown or accident, switch on hazard warning lights, leave your vehicle and, after dealing with any casualties, get to an emergency refuge point to call for help.

If your vehicle catches fire in a tunnel and you can still drive it, try to get it out of the tunnel before the fire gets out of control. If you can't drive clear, stop and try to put out the fire (there are fire extinguishers in tunnels). If that fails, get to a refuge point as soon as you can and call for assistance.

# Dealing with road works

Delays are inevitable when the carriageway needs to be repaired. You need to take a com-mon-sense approach to these situations and follow some basic safety rules so that accidents and further delays are avoided.

Road works are well signposted, par-ticularly on fast and busy roads. Slow down and get into the correct lane in good time. Remember that there will be workers in the road who might not be concentrating on the traffic. Obey any speed limit that is in force, and keep a good separation distance so that you can avoid braking sharply.

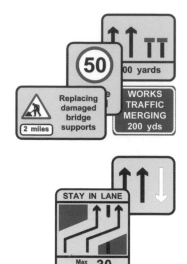

On dual carriageways and motorways it is often the case that a contraflow system is in operation. This permits traffic travelling in the opposite direction to use the same carriageway. This means reduced lane widths and higher traffic density. On motorways, signs may indicate that you should use the hard shoulder as part of the carriageway. Take care in these situations – if a vehicle breaks down, there is nowhere for the driver to pull in!

# Vehicle security

The theft of vehicles and their contents has now become extremely common. To reduce the risks, make sure you secure your car and its contents properly. You should:

- close all windows and sunroofs;
- retract aerials where possible;
- use a steering wheel lock;
- put valuables in the boot;
- remove the keys while in filling stations;
- get your windows etched with the registration number;
- get an immobilizer fitted;
- buy only coded audio equipment;
- use lockable fuel caps and wheel nuts if possible.

Park your car in well-lit areas if possible. If you are leaving a window open for a pet, it is sensible to fit a grille into the gap to deter any would-be thief.

Be alert: if you see anyone acting suspiciously around another vehicle, call the police.

# The driver and the environment

Whilst owning and driving a car are seen by most as an essential part of modern life, you shouldn't forget that the environment suffers in consequence.

Vehicles consume energy and cause pollution. Your choice of vehicle, your style of driving and the times you choose to drive can all contribute to environmental damage and global warming:

- Think before you buy; choose a vehicle with a fuel-efficient engine. Consider alternative fuels such as LPG.

- Think before you drive; short journeys such as the 'school run' contribute to congestion and waste fuel. Wouldn't it be better to walk or use public transport?

- Think about the environment; keep your vehicle well maintained and adopt a driving style that avoids late braking and harsh acceleration. Driving in a fuel-efficient 'eco-safe' way will help the environment and help your pocket!

# Checkpoint 9

1  Red reflective studs mark the:
   *Choose one answer*

   a.  right edge of the road
   b.  left edge of the road
   c.  centre of motorways
   d.  motorway entry slip roads

2  Driving on to a motorway, you should use the slip road to:
   *Choose two answers*

   a.  build up your speed
   b.  look for a gap in the traffic
   c.  change into fifth gear
   d.  check over your left shoulder

**3**   When joining a motorway you should be travelling at:
*Choose one answer*

a.   50 mph
b.   60 mph
c.   70 mph
d.   the speed of the traffic in the left lane of the main carriageway

**4**   To leave a motorway you should:
*Choose two answers*

a.   keep a lookout for the signs
b.   move to the left lane as soon as you see the 300-yard marker
c.   move to the left lane well before reaching the exit markers
d.   slow down as soon as you see the half-mile marker
e.   move on to the hard shoulder as you approach the exit

**5**   If something falls from your car whilst you are on
a motorway you should:
*Choose one answer*

a.   stop on the hard shoulder and retrieve it
b.   stop on the hard shoulder and telephone the police
c.   leave at the next exit and telephone the police
d.   consider it irretrievable and forget about it

**6** If you see this sign above your lane on a motorway you should:
*Choose one answer*

a.   not proceed further in that lane
b.   leave the motorway at the next exit
c.   ignore it, as it is a warning for high vehicles
d.   slow down to less than 50 mph and continue

**7** If you break down on a two-laned road you should first of all:
*Choose one answer*

a.   telephone for the breakdown service
b.   think of other traffic
c.   get your passengers out
d.   call home on your mobile phone

**8** If you are driving on a motorway and think there may be a problem with your car, you should first of all:
*Choose one answer*

a. use your mobile phone to call the police
b. try to get over to the hard shoulder
c. get your passengers out of the car
d. telephone for the breakdown service

**9** Anxiety and frustration when driving can be reduced by:
*Choose two answers*

a. starting your journey earlier
b. keeping the air conditioning on
c. taking anti-depressants
d. accepting that you will sometimes be held up in traffic queues
e. sounding your horn and flashing your headlights

**10** If you break down on a two-lane highway, you should place a warning triangle:

*Choose two answers*

a. at least 45 metres behind your car
b. at least 45 metres ahead of your car
c. on the opposite side of the road
d. on the same side of the road

**11** If you break down on a motorway you should:
*Choose two answers*

a. place a warning triangle at least 100 metres behind your car
b. not use a warning triangle
c. switch on the hazard warning lights
d. switch on the fog lights at night

**12** When wishing to leave a motorway that is carrying freely moving traffic, you should slow down:
*Choose one answer*

a. as soon as you see the half-mile sign
b. as soon as you see the 300-yard marker
c. as soon as you move into the left lane
d. when you move into the slip road

**13** When you see a sign for road works you:
*Choose one answer*

  a.   may exceed any temporary speed limit
  b.   must not exceed any temporary speed limit
  c.   may switch lanes to get into a shorter queue
  d.   may go through a red light at night if there is no oncoming traffic

**14** On a three-lane motorway you see this sign on a slow-moving vehicle ahead that is in the middle lane. The sign displays flashing amber lights. You should:

*Choose two answers*

  a.   approach slowly and overtake on the right
  b.   keep behind the vehicle until it leaves the motorway
  c.   expect that there will be a workforce in the road ahead
  d.   approach cautiously and overtake on the left
  e.   obey the instruction to leave the motorway at the next exit

**15** If you're involved in an accident causing damage to property or injury to someone you must:
*Choose three answers*

  a.   drive straight to a police station to report the incident
  b.   stop
  c.   give your name and address to anyone with grounds for requiring them
  d.   give the registration number and the name of the owner to anyone with grounds for requiring them
  e.   not give your details to anyone until you have spoken with your insurance company

**16** If you cannot produce your insurance certificate at the time of an accident that involves injury, you must produce it for the police within:
*Choose one answer*

a.  24 hours
b.  two days
c.  five days
d.  seven days

**17** You see an accident ahead involving a vehicle displaying this sign. You should:
*Choose two answers*

a.  stop and switch off your engine
b.  stop and leave your engine running
c.  use a mobile phone to call for help
d.  not use a mobile phone close to the vehicle
e.  not stop because of the danger

**18** If you get a puncture in a tyre whilst driving you should:
*Choose two answers*

a.  brake as quickly as you can
b.  not brake suddenly
c.  steer briskly to the left
d.  try to keep the car straight

**19** At the scene of an accident you are treating a casualty who has burns to the arms. You should:
*Choose three answers*

a.  give the casualty plenty to drink
b.  try to cool the burns with clean liquid
c.  talk to the casualty and give reassurance
d.  remove any clothing stuck to the burns
e.  keep the casualty moving to prevent shock setting in
f.  get the casualty to lie down

**20** Someone is injured in an accident and has stopped breathing.
The person's airway is clear, so the first thing you should do is:
*Choose one answer*

a.   tilt the person's head forward
b.   put the person in the recovery position
c.   give chest compressions to maintain circulation
d.   pinch the person's nose and blow into his or her mouth

You will find the answers on page 329.

Scores:       First try           Second try           Third try

Record your scores in Appendix 2 (page 330).

# Stage 10
# The driving test and the Pass Plus scheme

Once you have passed the theory test, you should be able to concentrate on putting all of the rules you have learned into practice in preparation for your practical test.

If you've had sufficient driving lessons and plenty of practice, you should be able to carry out confidently all of the skills listed in *The Official DVSA Guide to Learning to Drive*. Read Section 4 – The test and beyond for information about what to expect on your practical test.

## Applying for the test

You can apply for a driving test appointment by phone, online or by post. Seek guidance from your instructor on completing the booking. If you are going to use a driving school car for your test, your instructor will need to tell you when it is available. If there is a waiting time for tests in your area, get advice from your instructor on when to apply. This will ensure that:

- you can avoid unnecessary delays;
- you don't get an appointment before you're ready;
- your instructor doesn't have another test at the same time.

When booking your test it is important to tell the DSA about any special circumstances or disability that you may have. You will still have to take the same test as anyone else, but more time will be allowed so that the examiner can talk about your disability or any adaptations the vehicle may have. If you need an interpreter to attend with you, ensure you make arrangements in good time.

# Before the test

A few lessons prior to the test, your instructor will probably conduct a couple of mock tests. This will:

- ensure that you can still read a number plate at the prescribed distance;
- demonstrate what it's like to drive totally unaided;
- ensure that you both know you can deal with hazards effectively without any help;
- show up any weaknesses in your knowledge or skills.

If your instructor still has to give you help, you will not be ready to cope on your own, either during or after the test. If this is the case, it is advisable to postpone your test. You must give the DVSA at least three clear working days' notice. Otherwise, you will lose the fee.

# Your vehicle

Take note of the comments in *The Official DVSA Guide to Learning to Drive*, Section 4 – The day of your test. If you are in a driving school vehicle, your instructor should have ensured compliance with all the requirements. If you are taking the test in your own vehicle, make sure that:

**Make sure your vehicle meets the requirements for the driving test**

- your vehicle is taxed;
- L plates (or D plates in Wales) are clearly displayed to the front and rear of the vehicle;
- your seat belts are clean and working properly;
- head restraints are fitted;
- there is an additional rear-view mirror for the examiner to use.
- If your vehicle does not comply, you will not be able to take the test and you will lose your fee.

Note that some makes and models of vehicle (such as convertibles) are considered unsuitable for a driving test because examiners have no clear view to the rear, other than by use of mirrors. Check with your instructor and the DVSA if unsure about the suitability of your vehicle.

# Arriving at the test centre

When your instructor picks you up on the day of your test, make sure that you have:

- the appointment card;
- your theory test pass certificate;
- your provisional driving licence.

If you don't have a photocard licence you must bring your paper licence and your passport as photographic proof of identity.

Your instructor will make sure that you arrive early, leaving plenty of time to park and relax. Tell your instructor in good time if you wish to use the toilet. Some test centres do not have facilities.

It is natural for test candidates to feel a little anxious. Don't worry; your instructor wouldn't let you attempt the test if you were not ready!

**You must have acceptable photographic evidence of identity when you attend for your driving test**

# The test

Your examiner will ask you to sign a form. Your signature will be checked against that on your driving licence and other means of identification.

If you wish your instructor to sit in the car for the test, ask the examiner at this point. You will be asked whether you have any physical disabilities not declared in your application form.

Sometimes senior examiners have to accompany driving examiners on tests. This is to ensure uniformity is maintained. Try to relax, and remember that the examiner, not you, is being checked by this person.

Your examiner will do his or her best to put you at ease, and it is acceptable to chat with the examiner during your test if that helps you relax. Don't be put off if the examiner doesn't say too much – he or she doesn't want to distract you from your driving.

## Your eyesight

**HK55 WES**

*Your eyesight will be tested before you get in the car*

Before you get into the car you will be asked to read a number plate. You will probably feel a little nervous, and this could affect how you see the letters and numbers. Take your time and try not to get flustered.

## Vehicle safety questions

Before the driving part of the test begins, the examiner will ask you two questions related to vehicle safety. Known as 'show me, tell me' questions, these are designed to show that you know basic maintenance and operation procedures for the vehicle you are driving for the test. These checks may require you to open the bonnet of the car and identify fluid reservoirs. You are not asked to touch a hot engine or physically check any fluid levels. There are 19 questions in all, and they are asked in set combinations (see Appendix 1). As a driver, you should recognize the importance of basic vehicle maintenance and safety – do not simply learn the questions and answers by rote.

It can be dangerous to perform these safety checks if you are unsure of what to do. Your instructor will advise you how to make these checks safely on your driving test vehicle. You are recommended to wear disposable vinyl gloves for under-bonnet checks and wear a high-visibility vest when making safety checks outside the vehicle. Your instructor should be able to provide these for you.

Following the show me, tell me questions, you will be asked to seat yourself in your car whilst the examiner takes a look around to make sure it's roadworthy.

## During the test

The examiner will explain the instructions that will be given. Unless you are asked to turn left or right, you should follow the road ahead or go in the direction of any signs or markings. Remember, this is all part of the test. The examiner is checking that you can read and follow signs on your own. If you see a 'Turn left' or 'Turn right' sign, obey it. Don't be tempted to ask which way to go.

During the first few minutes, the examiner should give you time to settle down. Try to relax and concentrate on what is happening on the road all around rather than wondering what the person sitting by your side is thinking.

Put into practice everything you have learned. Show how confident you can be. Don't try to be over-careful, but take all safe opportunities to proceed. However, if you are at all in doubt, hold back.

## Planning ahead

Show how well you can drive by:

- looking and planning well ahead;

- making good use of all of the mirrors;

- showing discrimination in the use and timing of signals;

- concentrating on what is happening all around;

- adjusting your speed well before you reach any hazards by using all of the controls gently – demonstrating eco-safe driving technique;

- allowing adequate clearance and safety margins;

- showing care and consideration to all other road users;

- anticipating and making allowance for others' mistakes.

*Your examiner will expect you to respond appropriately to traffic signs and signals*

Make proper progress: you will not impress your examiner by being over-cautious!

## The manoeuvre exercises

During the test you will be asked to pull in on the left. This is also part of the test. Make sure you stop where it is safe, legal and convenient. If you are asked to pull in behind another vehicle, make sure you leave plenty of room for moving away again.

As well as making normal stops you may be asked to carry out an emergency stop. You may also be asked to carry out one of the following exercises:

- reverse to the left (or right if in a van);

- turn the car round in the road;

- reverse park behind another vehicle;
- park in a bay in the test centre car park.

You should have had plenty of practice at all of these exercises. Remember, the things your examiner will be looking for are good control, accuracy and all-round observations:

- Control: Work out what sort of gradient you are on so that you'll know whether to control the speed with the gas and clutch or with the brake. Keep the speed down so that you have full control of the steering wheel and plenty of time to keep checking for others. Maintain full control throughout and use the parking brake when necessary.

- Accuracy: Keeping the speed down should help you carry out all of the exercises efficiently. Make sure you finish all of the reversing exercises in a safe place.

- Observations: Show that you can respond safely to other road users. Remember, when you are manoeuvring, others have priority.

## The independent driving exercise

For about 10 minutes of your test you will be asked to drive by:

- Following road markings and traffic signs to a destination.
- Following a series of verbal directions such as you might get if you had pulled in to ask your way to a local destination.
- A combination of the above.

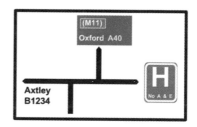

This is so that your examiner can assess how you manage road systems and deal with traffic on your own.

This part of the test will begin with the examiner asking you to pull in at a safe place. He or she will explain what is required. If necessary, the examiner may use a flash card to illustrate the route you need to take. Route cards relate to the local road layout as shown in the examples below.

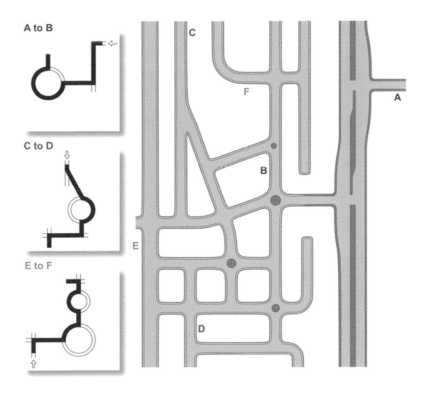

Do not worry if you can't remember all the directions you are given – if you need to just ask the examiner for a reminder. You could simply pull in where safe and ask, just as you would if driving by yourself. You can't fail for taking a wrong turn in this part of the test – your examiner will guide you back to your route.

## At the end of the test

When you return to the test centre, your examiner will complete a driving test report form. This will show those items on which you made mistakes. Not all mistakes result in failure, only those that were serious or dangerous; you will also fail if you accumulate more than 15 driver faults. Your examiner will offer you a verbal explanation. Your instructor may be present for this, providing you give your consent.

Your instructor will probably drive you home. This is normal. You will be either too excited or too disappointed to concentrate properly.

# After passing

You are more likely to pass first time if you have plenty of lessons. Take your instructor's advice and only take your test when you are ready.

Your examiner will ask for your provisional licence and give you a pass certificate in exchange. Your full licence will be issued automatically by post.

In some circumstances, however, the examiner may not be able to take your provisional licence, eg if you've just married and changed your surname. In this case you would have to send your provisional licence and your pass certificate with the appropriate fee directly to DVLA, and they will issue your full licence. Exchange your provisional licence for a full licence as soon as you can – the pass certificate is only valid for two years!

If you try continually to improve your driving skills, you will find that you get many years of enjoyment from your newly acquired freedom of travel.

# If you don't pass

Try not to get too upset if you don't pass first time. The examiner has seen that you are not quite ready to drive unsupervised. Those items for which you have failed will be marked on the driving test report form, and the examiner will explain these to you. Although you may be distracted by your disappointment, try to listen carefully to what the examiner says. Your instructor will advise you on any further training requirements before you take another test. It is important that you keep up with your lessons and practice so that you keep up the standard you have already reached.

# The Pass Plus scheme and advanced driving tests

By passing the practical test you have shown that you can drive to the minimum standard required by law. You are now only at the beginning of your real driving career. You should be prepared to continue learning for a long time to come. To help you with this, your instructor will be able to advise you on the elements in the Pass Plus scheme that will be of benefit and that you may not have covered during your driving lessons. It will also help reduce the risk of your being involved in a road accident.

It is far better to gain experience in different conditions and on different roads, particularly motorways, under the expert and safe guidance of a professional before you try to take on too much too soon.

The subjects covered in the Pass Plus scheme include driving in town, in all weathers, on rural roads, at night, on dual carriageways and on motorways. You can take a Pass Plus course at any time within the first 12 months of passing your practical test. Throughout the course you will be driving with these key factors in mind:

- **attitude:** responsibility for your actions and care and consideration for others;
- **skills:** observation, assessing what you see and taking the right action.

Some insurance companies offer discounts to drivers who have taken extra training under this scheme. Ask your instructor, or visit www.passplus.org.uk for details.

If you are really interested in continually improving your standard of driving you might consider taking an advanced driving test such as that offered by DIAmond Advanced Motorists. You can contact DIAmond on 020 8686 8010 or visit www.driving.org/diamond.

# A final word

The authors hope you have found this book useful and that it has made your driving lessons easier and more enjoyable. We wish you success with your driving theory and practical tests. With good preparation and heeding the advice in this book, you will have made great progress towards a trouble-free driving career.

# Checkpoint 10

By the time you apply for your theory test you should be able to answer the questions in all of the other checkpoints and the theory test section in Part 2 of this book. Your instructor should have been teaching you how to put all of the rules and procedures into practice.

Remember, you are not learning these rules just in order to pass your test! You need to understand them so that you can apply them and enjoy 'safe driving for life'.

This checkpoint includes questions that cover all of the syllabus for learning and also other general rules for all drivers.

1   The main items inspected on an MOT test are: *Choose one answer*
   a.   engine, gearbox, brakes and tyres
   b.   brakes, lights, steering and tyres
   c.   engine, body, brakes and tyres
   d.   paintwork, metal trims, body and tyres

2   You should check your engine oil: *Choose one answer*
   a.   before every journey
   b.   at least once a week
   c.   once a month
   d.   at service intervals

3   Lights and indicators should be checked:
   *Choose one answer*
   a.   before you drive
   b.   once a week
   c.   once a month
   d.   at service intervals

4   The main cause of skidding is:
   *Choose one answer*
   a.   a wet road surface
   b.   icy roads
   c.   high speed
   d.   the driver

**5** If the rear of your car is skidding to the left you should:
*Choose two answers*

  a. brake more firmly
  b. pump the brake on and off
  c. steer to the right
  d. steer to the left

**6** If your wheels lock up during an emergency stop you should:
*Choose one answer*

  a. brake more firmly
  b. use the parking brake to help
  c. release the brake and reapply it
  d. push down the clutch

**7** Car tyres must have a tread depth of:
*Choose one answer*

  a. 1.6 mm across the central three-quarters of the width
  b. 1.6 mm across the entire width
  c. 2.00 mm across the central three-quarters of the width
  d. 2.00 mm across the entire width

**8** At a pelican crossing you may proceed through a flashing amber light if:

*Choose two answers*

  a. there is no one on the crossing
  b. you are sure no one will step out
  c. you use your horn to warn people nearby
  d. a pedestrian beckons you on

**9** On the approach to a zebra crossing you should:
*Choose three answers*

  a. be travelling at a speed at which you can stop safely
  b. not use arm signals
  c. check your mirrors early
  d. only stop when someone steps on to the crossing
  e. be ready to stop

**10** If you see a person with a guide dog waiting to cross the road you should:
*Choose one answer*

a. always wait for him or her
b. proceed carefully
c. wave him or her across
d. sound your horn to warn him or her of your presence

**11** Passing a line of parked cars you see a ball bounce into the road. You should:
*Choose one answer*

a. sound the horn to warn any children and then drive on
b. slow down and be ready to stop
c. stop and wave any children across to get the ball
d. swerve to avoid the ball

**12** So as not to frighten animals you should be ready to:
*Choose two answers*

a. slow down
b. sound the horn to warn them
c. drive past quickly out of danger
d. keep the engine speed low

**13** If you are turning into a road where there are pedestrians you should:
*Choose two answers*

a. sound the horn
b. give way to them
c. wave them across
d. not rush them

**14** You are approaching a T-junction at the end of a road and there are pedestrians crossing. You should:
*Choose one answer*

a. hold back for them
b. expect them to wait
c. sound the horn
d. flash your lights

**15** You may sound the horn when stationary on the road:
*Choose one answer*

a. to test it
b. when in danger from another vehicle moving nearby
c. between 7.00 am and 11.00 pm
d. at no time

**16** You should not sound your horn in built-up areas between the hours of:
*Choose one answer*

a. 10.30 pm and 7.30 pm
b. 7.30 am and 10.30 pm
c. 11.30 pm and 7.00 am
d. 7.00 am and 11.30 pm

**17** If another driver makes a mistake you should:
*Choose one answer*

a. flash your lights
b. sound your horn
c. be ready to compensate
d. shake your head

**18** If there is a solid white line along the centre of your side of the road it means:
*Choose two answers*

a. no overtaking on that road
b. you should not cross the line
c. you should not park on the offside
d. you may only straddle the line to overtake a vehicle travelling at less than 10 mph

**19** Yellow lines along the left edge of the road mean:
*Choose one answer*

a. no waiting at any time
b. there are waiting restrictions in force
c. parking is only permitted at weekends
d. loading is not permitted

**20** You may overtake on the left:
*Choose two answers*

a. in one-way streets
b. when approaching a junction
c. on three-lane motorways
d. in lanes of slow traffic when the queue to your right is moving more slowly than yours

**21** You should not normally overtake:
*Choose three answers*

a. on two-lane highways
b. near junctions
c. near the brow of a hill
d. if there is dead ground ahead
e. on the right

**22** Countdown markers on motorways are:
*Choose one answer*

a. white on black
b. black on white
c. blue on white
d. white on blue

**23** Countdown markers may indicate the distance to a:
*Choose three answers*

a. motorway entrance
b. motorway exit
c. concealed level crossing
d. hazard
e. safety camera

**24** Circular signs usually give:
*Choose one answer*

a. orders
b. warnings
c. information
d. directions

**25** Triangular signs usually give:
*Choose one answer*

a. orders
b. warnings
c. information
d. instructions

**26** At mini-roundabouts you should:
*Choose two answers*

a. give way to traffic from the right
b. give way to all other traffic
c. beware of vehicles making U-turns
d. expect drivers to your left to give way to you

**27** When turning right at a roundabout you should:
*Choose two answers*

a. keep on the right signal throughout the manoeuvre
b. signal left after you have passed the exit before yours
c. signal left before you pass the exit before yours
d. stay in the left lane all the way for safety
e. give a right signal on approach

**28** If you use full beam headlights at the wrong time you could:
*Choose two answers*

a. dazzle oncoming drivers
b. dazzle the driver in front
c. be seen more clearly
d. make better progress

**29** What hazard does this road marking indicate?

*Choose one answer*

a. oncoming traffic
b. traffic merging from the right
c. a pedestrian crossing ahead
d. trams overtaking on the right

**30** It has just started to rain after a long dry spell. When will the road surface be most slippery?
*Choose one answer*

a. when it has rained for an hour or so
b. a few minutes after it starts to rain
c. when puddles have formed on the road
d. about an hour after the rain stops

**31** What hazard do yellow lines across the carriageway indicate?
*Choose one answer*

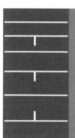

a. cars parked facing the kerb
b. a roundabout
c. a police speed trap
d. a school crossing patrol

**32** What should you do if there is an obstruction on your side of the road?
*Choose one answer*

a. assume priority over oncoming traffic
b. speed up to get past the obstruction
c. give way to oncoming traffic
d. wave approaching vehicles through
e. pull up alongside the obstruction if traffic is approaching

**33** The good driver should always:
*Choose three answers*

a. drive at the speed limit
b. make effective use of the driving mirrors
c. look well ahead
d. anticipate the actions of other road users
e. show off his or her skill

**34** What should you do if you see a sign like this in icy conditions?

*Choose three answers*

a. accelerate
b. gently apply the parking brake
c. use as high a gear as possible
d. slow down well before the bend
e. put on hazard warning lights
f. take care with steering

**35** What does this sign mean?

*Choose one answer*

a. no horse riders permitted
b. no horse-drawn carriages
c. beware of horse riders ahead
d. bridleway ahead, horse riders only

**36** The major cause of 'L' test failure is not: *Choose one answer*

a. being properly prepared
b. passing the theory test first
c. having private practice
d. applying early enough

**37** To make sure there is enough time for your test, when you apply you should declare whether you:
*Choose three answers*

   a.   have severe hearing difficulties
   b.   are restricted in your movements
   c.   have any disabilities that may affect your driving
   d.   have had professional tuition
   e.   have dual controls in the vehicle you will be using for the test

**38** When preparing for your driving test you should practise:
*Choose two answers*

   a.   on test routes only
   b.   on as many types of road as possible
   c.   in all sorts of conditions
   d.   in daylight only

**39** If you pass your test in an automatic car you:
*Choose one answer*

   a.   may only drive automatic cars
   b.   will have to take a test in a manual car within two years
   c.   may drive any type of automatic vehicle
   d.   may not drive any left-hand-drive vehicle

**40** The main purpose of the driving test is:
*Choose one answer*

   a.   to check on the ability of driving instructors
   b.   to see that candidates can safely drive unaided
   c.   to make sure that candidates can carry out reverse manoeuvres
   d.   to restrict the number of drivers on our roads

You will find the answers on page 329.

Scores:        First try        Second try        Third try

Record your scores in Appendix 2 (page 330).

# PART TWO
## DRIVING
## THEORY TEST

# About the theory test

When you have your provisional licence, have had some driving experience and have studied sufficiently you should apply for your driving theory test.

You can apply for a theory test appointment by phone, online or by post. Seek guidance from your instructor on when to make the booking.

If you have special needs or a language or reading difficulty, you need to tell the booking section when you make your appointment. Provision is available to cover these difficulties, and they should not disadvantage you in the theory test.

## What you can be tested on

There are 50 questions in the theory element of the test. Most of these will be multiple-choice, requiring you to select one answer from four. There will also be some multiple-response questions, requiring you to select two or more answers from the choices presented on-screen. Some of the questions will display diagrams or photographic images. The questions are similar in style and content to the checkpoint questions in each stage of this book.

The theory test questions will be selected from 14 different categories relating to road safety and the legal responsibilities of the driver. Examples of the type of question from each category are shown below. Take your time and study the questions carefully. It is very easy to overlook a key word or phrase in the question and arrive at the wrong answer.

### Question categories

#### Accidents

Do you know what to do if you are involved in or witness an accident or incident on the road? What are your legal responsibilities? How would you deal with a casualty?

Example:

Q. At an accident scene you find an adult casualty is not breathing. You should give chest compressions at the rate of:

*Choose one answer*

a.   200 per minute
b.   100 per minute
c.   50 per minute
d.   20 per minute

Correct answer: b.
Knowing basic first aid procedures could save a life.

## Alertness

Do you understand why it is important to be observant, anticipate problems ahead and concentrate on your driving? Do you understand the effects of boredom and distraction on your driving ability?

Example:

Q. Using a mobile telephone when you are driving: *Choose two answers*

a.   could cause you to lose control of your vehicle
b.   may affect your vehicle's electrical system
c.   could take your attention from the road
d.   is fine if the system is hands-free
e.   is acceptable at low speeds

Correct answers: a, c.
Driving needs your full attention all of the time. Even using a hands-free phone will distract you and could cause you to lose control of the vehicle.

## Attitude

Do you understand why it is important to show courtesy and consideration to other road users? Do you understand the rules of priority and the dangers of close following?

Example:

Q. A car driver pulls out in front of you at a junction. You should:
*Choose one answer*

a. accelerate to get past safely
b. flash your headlights and swerve round the other vehicle
c. slow down and be ready to stop if necessary
d. keep close behind the vehicle so the driver knows you are annoyed

Correct answer: c.
If you are driving defensively you should expect others to make mistakes. Being tolerant keeps you and others safe on the roads.

## Documents

Do you know the rules relating to driver licensing, vehicle insurance, MOT test certificates and road tax for your vehicle?

Example:

Q. Your car needs a new MOT certificate. If you drive without a current certificate:
*Choose one answer*

a. you could invalidate the manufacturer's warranty
b. you will have to make a SORN declaration
c. you could invalidate your motor insurance
d. your road tax will be invalidated

Correct answer: c.
If your vehicle MOT certificate has expired, you may not drive it except to a pre-arranged appointment for repairs or a new MOT test. Without an MOT your vehicle insurance will be invalid.

## Hazard awareness

Are you paying attention and planning ahead? Can you relate speed and distance? Are you fit to drive? Do you understand how tiredness, drugs and alcohol can affect your reaction time?

Example:

Q. Which three of the following may result from drinking alcohol?
*Choose three answers*

   a.   a greater sense of self-confidence
   b.   faster reaction times
   c.   poorer coordination
   d.   better judgement of speed
   e.   reduced concentration
   f.   smoother control of the vehicle

Correct answers: a, c, e.
Alcohol can cause a driver to become over-confident and take greater risks. At the same time, driving ability and reaction times are impaired by alcohol. Together these factors greatly increase the risk of a serious accident.

## Motorway rules

Do you know the rules that apply to motorway driving?

Example:

Q. What is the national speed limit for cars on a motorway?
*Choose one answer*

   a.   50 mph
   b.   60 mph
   c.   70 mph
   d.   there is no limit

Correct answer: c.
This does not mean that you should aim to travel at 70 mph all of the time. Drive at a speed that is appropriate for the road and traffic conditions on the motorway.

## Other types of vehicle

Do you understand the handling characteristics and limitations on other types of vehicle so that you can respond safely to their presence on the road?

Example:

Q. In very windy conditions you are about to overtake a motorcyclist. You should: *Choose one answer*

a.   pull out at the last minute
b.   allow extra room as you pass
c.   sound your horn as you start to overtake
d.   pass slowly, keeping close to the motorcyclist

Correct answer: b.
Motorcyclists and cyclists can be easily blown off course by crosswinds and could drift into your path. As you pass, the airflow from around your vehicle could affect these vulnerable road users. Allow plenty of room.

## Road and traffic signs

Do you recognize and respond appropriately to road signs and markings?

Example:

Q. You see a sign like this in a tunnel. It means:

*Choose one answer*

a.   direction to emergency pedestrian exit
b.   pedestrian access prohibited
c.   warning, pedestrians in road
d.   pedestrian crossing ahead

Correct answer: a.
Pedestrian exit points can be found at regular intervals in tunnels. If an incident in the tunnel forces you to leave your vehicle and evacuate, go to the nearest exit marked by this sign.

## Rules of the road

Do you understand the rules and driving procedures outlined in The Highway Code?

Example:

Q. You may only wait in a yellow box junction when:

*Choose one answer*

a.   your exit is blocked
b.   you are in a queue of traffic going ahead
c.   crossing traffic prevents you from turning left
d.   oncoming traffic prevents you from turning right

Correct answer: d.
The yellow box marking is designed to keep junctions clear. Do not enter unless your exit is clear. You can only wait in the box to turn right if your exit is clear but you can't safely cross the path of oncoming traffic.

## Safety and your vehicle

Do you know when and how to use the safety features and equipment in your vehicle? Can you identify vehicle faults and understand the importance of dealing with them? Do you know the consequences of driving a vehicle with defective equipment?

Example:

Q. Tyre pressures need to be checked regularly. What three can result from driving with under-inflated tyres? *Choose three answers*

a.   reduced tyre life
b.   poorer control when braking
c.   increased fuel efficiency
d.   lighter steering
e.   improved cornering
f.   more fuel consumption

Correct answers: a, b, f.

Tyres need to be in good condition and correctly inflated. Driving with under-inflated tyres will affect vehicle stability, increase fuel consumption and reduce the life of the tyres.

## Safety margins

Do you know how long it takes to stop your vehicle at different speeds? Do you understand how road surface conditions can affect your ability to stop your vehicle? Do you know how to avoid skidding and recover from a skid if you caused one?

Example:

Q. You are travelling at 50 mph on a dry road. What is the shortest overall distance you could expect to stop in? *Choose one answer*

  a.  23 metres (75 feet)
  b.  36 metres (118 feet)
  c.  53 metres (175 feet)
  d.  73 metres (240 feet)

Correct answer: c.
As well as knowing the figures you must be able to visualize them.

## Vehicle handling

Can you adapt your driving technique to different weather and lighting conditions? Do you know when to use your vehicle lights? How do you deal with gradients?

Example:

Q. You are driving in daylight but the weather conditions have made visibility poor. Why should you switch on your headlights?

*Choose one answer*

  a.  so that you can see road markings close to your vehicle
  b.  so that others can see you more easily

c.  to warn drivers ahead that you are following

d.  so that you can see further ahead

Correct answer: b.

If you are finding it difficult to see other drivers, they will also find it hard to see you. Using dipped headlights will make it easier for others to see you.

## Vehicle loading

Do you know the rules about vehicle loading and towing? Do you understand how vehicle loading can affect stability?

Example:

Q. Towing a small trailer on a dual carriageway, you realize that it has begun to 'snake'. You should: *Choose one answer*

a.  brake firmly to reduce your speed

b.  ease off the accelerator

c.  accelerate to correct the problem

d.  put on your hazard warning lights and maintain your speed

Correct answer: b.

If you slow down gradually the problem will correct itself. Don't brake harshly – you could cause the trailer to tip over.

## Vulnerable road users

As a car driver, do you understand your responsibilities towards others using the road? Do you recognize that pedestrians, cyclists, motorcyclists, children, the elderly, those with disabilities or animals or those controlling them are vulnerable groups?

Example:

Q. At a pelican crossing you have stopped for an elderly disabled pedestrian. He or she is taking a long time to cross and the lights have changed to green. You should not: *Choose three answers*

a.  wait patiently for the pedestrian to cross

b.  drive round the pedestrian to clear the crossing

c.  edge forward to hurry the pedestrian along

d.   sound your horn
e.   keep your parking brake applied

Correct answers: b, c, d.
Trying to hurry a disabled pedestrian along could cause him or her to
stumble or fall. Be patient – the green light means you can proceed only
if it is safe!

To ensure a broad range of knowledge, you will be tested with questions
from each category. You might notice that some of the questions you are
asked seem quite similar. This doesn't matter, and the test isn't designed
to 'catch you out'. It is simply the case that some subjects can be used to
test knowledge in different categories.

## Case study questions

Some of the questions you will be asked may be presented as part of a 'case
study'. These questions are designed to test whether you have really understood and can apply driving theory. In a 'case study' a driving scenario is
set and you will be asked a number of questions about that scenario and
how you would react as in the example below:

## Case Study

You are going to visit your cousin who lives in the next town. You have
a road atlas in your car although you have been before and know the route
really well. You also have your mobile phone and have promised to call
your cousin if you get delayed. On the way you find that a country lane you
usually travel on is flooded and decide to turn back.

1    You are on a country lane and see that it is flooded ahead. How can
     you judge the depth of the water? *Choose one answer*

     a.   park at the roadside and wait for another vehicle to drive through
     b.   drive through slowly and keep checking through the side window
     c.   look for a depth gauge at the roadside
     d.   get out of your vehicle and wade in

     Correct answer: c.

2    You find that you can't judge the depth of the water so you decide to
     turn round. The road is quite narrow. The best method of turning
     would be: *Choose one answer*

a.   to give a signal and make a quick U-turn

b.   turn around in the road using forward and reverse gears

c.   reverse back down the country lane until you can find a farm
     entrance to turn into

d.   drive slowly forward to a wider section of road to turn round in

Correct answer: b.

3   You have turned round on the narrow country because you can't
    follow you usual route. The best thing to do to find a new route
    would be to: *Choose one answer*

    a.   call your cousin to ask for directions as you drive back towards
         the main road

    b.   drive on slowly whilst checking your road atlas

    c.   find a safe place to pull in and consult your road atlas

    d.   wait until you are back on the main road before calling your
         cousin for help

Correct answer: c.

4   On the way back to the main road you are delayed by a slow-moving
    farm vehicle ahead. You are worried about being late and should:
    *Choose one answer*

    a.   sound your horn so that the driver of the farm vehicle will get out
         of your way

    b.   follow the farm vehicle closely so that you can overtake at
         the earliest opportunity

    c.   pull out to overtake even though the road is very narrow

    d.   keep well back from the farm vehicle so that you can see well ahead

Correct answer: d.

5   You decide to let your cousin know that you will be late. You should:
    *Choose one answer*

    a.   find a safe place to pull in and make a call on your mobile phone

    b.   rely on your hands-free kit to keep you safe whilst you make a call

    c.   stop and get out of your car to make a call

    d.   drive slowly and send a text message to your cousin

Correct answer: a.

You will only be presented with one case study in your car theory test.
Five of your 50 questions will relate to that case study.

# Taking your theory test

When you attend for the test you will need to bring your photocard licence and the paper counterpart with you. If you don't have a photocard licence you must bring your paper licence and passport as photographic proof of identity. If you don't have acceptable identification your appointment will be cancelled and you will lose your fee.

**Make sure you arrive in good time for your appointment and have your photographic identification with you**

The first part of the theory test uses touch-screen technology. You will be able to practise answering the questions using the touch screen for up to 15 minutes before you begin your test. Follow the on-screen instructions to commence.

The computer screen will display the question, the number of answers to be 'marked' and choice of answers. The screen will also display the time remaining to complete the test. There is no need to rush. On-screen buttons will allow you to navigate back and forth through the test. You will be able to 'flag' a question if you are not sure of the answer and come back to it later.

There is also a 'review' button on-screen. If you touch the review button you can:

- view a summary showing the number of the questions you have answered, how many are incomplete and how many you have flagged;

**Follow the on-screen instructions to take the theory test**

- go back through all of the questions;
- have another look at questions you have flagged;
- have another look at questions you haven't completed;
- end the test.

To pass this part of the test you must score at least 43 correct answers out of 50 within 57 minutes.

## Hazard perception test

After completing the theory element you will get a short break before the hazard perception test. You will see a short video tutorial explaining how the test operates and what you need to do in order to pass. The test has 14 animated CG1 clips showing a variety of hazards as seen from the driver's seat of a moving car. Each clip lasts for about a minute, and you will need to click with a computer mouse when you see a potential hazard developing into a moving hazard (a situation in which you would have to change speed or course to deal with it).

Each time you click the mouse a flag symbol will appear on the information bar at the bottom of the screen.

Up to five marks can be scored for each hazard, and the more quickly you respond to the developing hazard the more you will score. Don't try to beat the system by repeating patterns of clicks or clicking continuously; the software will identify what you are doing and award a zero score for that clip.

Remember that one of the 14 clips will feature two developing hazards, allowing you to score up to 10 points. It is important therefore to watch all of the video clips carefully right the way through.

To pass this part of the test, you must score 44 out of the possible 75 marks.

For further reference and for a small charge, there is a DVD *The Complete Theory Test*, available to readers. This comprehensive product features actual DVSA revision questions and hazard perception clips with other learning support material. It can be obtained from Grade Six Supplies Ltd: tel 01353 749807. You can order online at www.g6s.co.uk.

# Theory test practice papers

The remainder of Part 2 contains a series of mock theory tests made up from the authors' bank of theory assessment questions. Like the checkpoint questions, this selection has similar content to the actual questions used in a DVSA theory test and covers all of the question categories listed above.

At first sight some of the questions may appear not to have the correct answer amongst the choices given. In these cases you will need to apply your knowledge to select the best answer from those given. This is not an attempt to catch you out. This material was written to train you in the technique of reading and responding to multiple-choice questions, as well as ensuring that you have read and understood the appropriate literature. To this end, the level of difficulty of the questions in Part 2 is at times higher than you would find in a DVSA theory test examination. Remember also that learning should be both fun and interactive, so some of the questions are designed to promote discussion with your instructor and some are designed to be humorous!

# Paper 1
## Theory test assessment

## Case Study for questions 1–5

You are driving home along a route regularly used by cyclists. The road surface is poor in places and there are a number of potholes. You are going to turn right at a roundabout ahead and you know that shortly after that there is a zebra crossing in the high street just before you enter the housing estate where you live. The road leading to your home has a number of chicanes and speed humps.

1   You should be aware that because of the road surface cyclists ahead might: *Choose one answer*

   a.   speed up
   b.   mount the footpath
   c.   give arm signals
   d.   swerve out in to your path

2   As you approach the roundabout you notice a cyclist in the left lane giving a right turn signal. You should: *Choose one answer*

   a.   keep back from the cyclist and sound your horn
   b.   expect the cyclist to turn left
   c.   expect the cyclist to turn right at the roundabout
   d.   accelerate to overtake the cyclist quickly

3   The high street is busy and there are lots of parked vehicles. You should anticipate: *Choose two answers*

   a.   that pedestrians might step out from between parked vehicles
   b.   that other drivers may warn you of hidden dangers ahead
   c.   no danger from pedestrians as there is a crossing ahead
   d.   pedestrians wanting to cross at the zebra crossing

4    Approaching the zebra crossing you see an elderly person waiting.
     He has a white stick with a red band. You should:
     *Choose one answer*

     a.   assume the person will see you when you stop to let him cross
     b.   stop and be patient because he may be blind and deaf
     c.   stop and wave him across
     d.   stop and gently tap your horn to let him know it is safe to cross

5    What danger will you be particularly concerned about as you turn
     into the road you live on?
     *Choose one answer*

     a.   Speeding vehicles approaching
     b.   Damage to your suspension and steering
     c.   Children playing
     d.   Following traffic trying to overtake

6    You are driving in heavy rain at 30 mph. You are about 25 metres
     (82 feet) from the car ahead. You should consider yourself:
     *Choose one answer*

     a.   to be a safe distance from the car ahead
     b.   to be dangerously close to the car ahead
     c.   able to stop in good time if the driver ahead had to make
          an emergency stop
     d.   to be safe providing your car has an anti-lock braking system

7    Driving at 45 mph in good conditions, what is a safe minimum
     distance to keep between you and a car ahead?
     *Choose one answer*

     a.   75 metres (245 feet)
     b.   45 metres (148 feet)
     c.   35 metres (117 feet)
     d.   23 metres (67 feet)

8 Why is it better to keep to the left when driving in a right-hand bend?
*Choose one answer*

   a.  it improves your view of the road ahead
   b.  it will keep you away from pedestrians in the road
   c.  it allows you take the bend faster
   d.  you needn't worry about the camber

9 Approaching a level crossing you see this sign with the amber light showing and should:

*Choose one answer*

   a.  drive through the crossing quickly
   b.  only drive through if you can see no trains approaching
   c.  drive over the crossing slowly
   d.  stop before the barriers

10 If you need glasses or contact lenses to read a number plate at the distance required for driving you should wear them:
*Choose one answer*

   a.  only when driving in poor weather
   b.  only when driving in heavy traffic
   c.  at all times when driving
   d.  only when driving at night

11 You are about to drive home after a hard day at work but feel very tired. You should: *Choose one answer*

   a.  take some 'pep pills' to stay awake
   b.  not drive
   c.  drive faster to lessen the danger of falling asleep at the wheel
   d.  take a flask of strong coffee with you

12 *The Highway Code* advises that you MUST NOT drive in reverse gear: *Choose one answer*

   a.  for longer than necessary
   b.  into a side road
   c.  unless you are parking
   d.  unless someone is guiding you

**13** How should you signal when you want to go straight ahead at a roundabout?

*Choose one answer*

- a. signal right on approach and then left to leave the roundabout
- b. signal left on approach and through the roundabout
- c. signal left just after passing the exit before the one you want to take
- d. no signal is necessary

**14** On a wet road you see a motorcyclist steer around a drain cover in a right-hand bend. Why would the motorcyclist do this?

*Choose one answer*

- a. to avoid mounting the kerb
- b. to avoid a skid on the metal surface
- c. to annoy following traffic
- d. to avoid splashing passers-by

**15** Where should you position your car before overtaking a long vehicle?

*Choose one answer*

- a. as close as possible to get past quickly
- b. well back to get a clear view ahead
- c. to the centre of the road to get a clear view ahead
- d. well back and well to the left

**16** A bus driver ahead signals to pull out from a bus stop. What should you do?

*Choose one answer*

- a. accelerate to get past quickly
- b. flash your lights and overtake
- c. allow it to pull away if safe
- d. sound your horn if you need to stop

**17** You should switch on rear fog lights when visibility drops below:

*Choose one answer*

- a. 200 metres (660 feet)
- b. 100 metres (330 feet)
- c. 10 metres (33 feet)
- d. your minimum braking distance

18  Bad weather can make road markings difficult to see. When this
    happens you should: *Choose one answer*

    a.  expect other drivers to give way when necessary
    b.  be ready to sound your horn if another driver makes a mistake
    c.  be ready to give way at a junction even if you know you have
        priority
    d.  not worry about traffic joining your road

19  Your car is a dark colour. Towards sunset, you would be advised to
    switch on your lights: *Choose one answer*

    a.  only when other drivers switch on their lights
    b.  only after lighting-up time
    c.  only when you can no longer see clearly ahead without lights
    d.  earlier than drivers of light-coloured cars

20  What does this motorway sign mean?

    *Choose one answer*

    a.  leave the motorway at the next exit
    b.  move to the hard shoulder
    c.  move to the lane on your left
    d.  contraflow, change to the opposite carriageway

21  You see this sign as you approach a junction. You must:

    *Choose one answer*

    a.  stop, even if the road is clear
    b.  stop only if other vehicles are nearby
    c.  stop only if you can't see the road ahead clearly
    d.  be ready to pull up sharply

22  A police officer has asked to see your driving documents but you
don't have them with you. You must produce them at a police station
within: *Choose one answer*

a.  5 days
b.  7 days
c.  10 days
d.  14 days

23  Before driving a friend's car you must make sure that:
*Choose one answer*

a.  your own vehicle has insurance cover
b.  your use of the car is insured
c.  your friend has third-party insurance
d.  you have the insurance documents for your friend's car

24  The Pass Plus scheme is available to all newly qualified drivers and is
designed to: *Choose one answer*

a.  help them supervise a learner driver
b.  help them gain more experience
c.  reduce the cost of vehicle road tax
d.  help them service their own vehicle

25  What type of vehicle would display a flashing green light?

*Choose one answer*

a.  a motorway maintenance vehicle
b.  a slow-moving vehicle
c.  an ambulance or fire engine
d.  a doctor or midwife on an emergency call

26  What is the purpose of the horn? *Choose one answer*

a.  to tell other road users that you intend to come through
b.  to indicate that you have right of way
c.  to warn others of your presence
d.  to show annoyance at other drivers' mistakes

27  Who has responsibility for seeing that a vehicle isn't overloaded?
*Choose one answer*

   a.   the owner of the vehicle
   b.   the driver of the vehicle
   c.   the person who has loaded the vehicle
   d.   the owner of the load

28  You are driving at night in a heavily loaded estate car. What problem should you be aware of? *Choose one answer*

   a.   following drivers will not be able to see your tail lights
   b.   full headlights can't be used
   c.   dipped headlights could dazzle oncoming drivers
   d.   you will be unable to use your mirrors

29  Catalytic converters are designed to: *Choose one answer*

   a.   increase fuel consumption
   b.   reduce harmful emissions
   c.   improve the quality of air circulating in the vehicle
   d.   reduce wear and tear in the engine

30  One of the times you may use hazard warning lights is: *Choose one answer*

   a.   when being towed
   b.   to excuse inconsiderate parking
   c.   when towing another vehicle
   d.   if your car has broken down

31  When may you use the right-hand lane of a motorway? *Choose one answer*

   a.   for turning right
   b.   to drive faster than 70 mph
   c.   to keep away from close-following traffic
   d.   to overtake another vehicle

32  You may ONLY stop on the hard shoulder of a motorway: *Choose one answer*

   a.   when too tired to drive
   b.   in an emergency
   c.   to drop off a passenger
   d.   to answer a call on your mobile phone

33  Signs like these on a motorway are:

*Choose one answer*

a.  lane closure markers
b.  countdown markers to the next exit
c.  distance markers to the next phone
d.  a warning of speed traps ahead

34  A motorcyclist has been injured in an accident. At the scene,
you should:
*Choose one answer*

a.  remove the motorcyclist's helmet
b.  move the motorcyclist off the road
c.  never move the motorcyclist
d.  not remove the motorcyclist's helmet

35  After a breakdown, on a single carriageway road, you should place
your hazard warning triangle:
*Choose one answer*

a.  on top of your vehicle
b.  at least 100 metres (330 feet) behind
    your vehicle
c.  beside your vehicle
d.  at least 45 metres (147 feet) behind your vehicle

36  You may legally drive a car over three years old without
an MOT certificate:
*Choose one answer*

a.  for up to seven days after the old certificate has expired
b.  when driving to an MOT test centre for a pre-arranged
    appointment
c.  if you have just bought the vehicle and it has no MOT certificate
d.  to go and visit an MOT test centre to make an appointment

37  You intend to carry an 11-year-old passenger in the back seat of your car. The child is under 1.35 metres (4 feet 5 inches) in height. You must: *Choose one answer*

a.  make sure that the child can fasten his or her own seat belt
b.  only do so if there is an adult sitting next to the child
c.  ensure that a suitable child restraint is used
d.  not allow the child to use a booster seat

38  You arrive at the scene of an accident. Which of the following should you NOT do? *Choose two answers*

a.  warn other traffic by switching on your hazard warning lights
b.  put yourself in danger to assist casualties
c.  offer casualties something to drink
d.  impose a smoking ban
e.  ask drivers to switch off their engines

39  Which of these signs means overtaking is prohibited?
*Choose one answer*

a.       b.       c.       d.

40  'Coasting' by keeping the clutch pedal down or selecting neutral for long periods of time is not recommended because:
*Choose two answers*

a.  you will use more fuel
b.  you could cause damage to the catalytic converter
c.  you will have less steering control
d.  it will increase tyre wear
e.  it will reduce your control of braking

41  You come up behind a vehicle being driven by an elderly driver. You should: *Choose one answer*

a.  expect the driver to make a lot of mistakes
b.  sound your horn and overtake
c.  anticipate that the elderly driver may have slower reactions than yours
d.  follow closely until the elderly driver lets you pass

42 Which of these are most likely to cause you to lose concentration whilst driving?

*Choose three answers*

   a.  loading a CD into your car audio system
   b.  using a hands-free telephone
   c.  checking your mirrors
   d.  looking at a map
   e.  using the windscreen demisters

43 At an accident a casualty has stopped breathing. Your priorities should be to:

*Choose three answers*

   a.  tilt the head forwards
   b.  remove anything that is blocking the airway
   c.  check for any internal injury
   d.  tilt the head back to keep the airway clear
   e.  call for help

44 What should you do if your vehicle has a puncture on a motorway?

*Choose one answer*

   a.  stop in lane and change the wheel
   b.  drive slowly to the next service area or exit
   c.  pull up on the hard shoulder and change the wheel
   d.  pull up on the hard shoulder and phone for assistance

45 What does this sign mean?

*Choose one answer*

   a.  end of speed limit
   b.  clearway, no waiting
   c.  national speed limit applies
   d.  trams must turn right

46  You intend to turn right on to a dual carriageway with a very narrow central reservation. You should:
*Choose one answer*

   a.  proceed to the central reservation and wait
   b.  wait until the road is clear in both directions and then turn right
   c.  expect approaching traffic to give way as you pull out
   d.  put on your hazard lights and edge into the traffic stream

47  Before driving through a tunnel you should:
*Choose one answer*

   a.  switch your radio off
   b.  switch on your fog lights
   c.  remove sunglasses if you were wearing them
   d.  select a low gear

48  Your car is fitted with anti-lock brakes. This means that the tyres:
*Choose one answer*

   a.  will wear more evenly
   b.  will be less likely to skid
   c.  can't be over-inflated
   d.  are less likely to aquaplane

49  Which of these vehicles is least likely to be affected by crosswinds?
*Choose one answer*

   a.  cyclists
   b.  cars
   c.  high-sided vehicles
   d.  motorcyclists

50  After passing your driving test, you suffer ill health that affects your ability to drive safely. You:
*Choose one answer*

   a.  must report the fact at your local police station
   b.  should avoid driving at higher speeds
   c.  must get a certificate from your GP confirming you can drive
   d.  must inform the licensing authority

# Paper 2
## Theory test assessment

## Case Study for questions 1–5

On your way to work you dropped your car off for an MOT test. Unfortunately, when you go to collect your car after work, you are told it has failed the test and needs a repair which the garage can't do until the following morning. You are worried because you have left everything to the last minute and also need to get the car taxed the following day.

1   When you find out that your car has failed the MOT test you should:
    *Choose one answer*

    a.   drive it home
    b.   consider bribing the mechanic who did the test
    c.   have the vehicle scrapped immediately
    d.   confirm that you would like the repair completed the following day

2   When a vehicle passes an MOT test this means that:
    *Choose one answer*

    a.   it meets the legal minimum standards at the time of the test
    b.   it will be legally roadworthy for the next 12 months
    c.   there will be no need to get it serviced
    d.   it can be driven safely for another three years

3   Your car is repaired the following day and you get the MOT certificate. To get the car taxed you:
    *Choose one answer*

    a.   can apply to the MOT station
    b.   must pay online via the DVLA website
    c.   must drive to Swansea
    d.   can go to a local Post Office

4   Your vehicle insurance cover could be affected if:
*Choose two answers*

a.   you drove your car just before the MOT ran out
b.   you drove your vehicle when it was not legally roadworthy
c.   you did not declare relevant information when applying for
      the insurance
d.   you renewed your car tax online

5   What must you have in order to tax your vehicle over the counter?
*Choose two answers*

a.   your driving licence
b.   a current Certificate of Insurance
c.   proof of 'no claims discount' entitlement
d.   a current MOT certificate

6   If you have to leave valuables in your car, the best thing to do is:
*Choose one answer*

a.   park in a quiet area
b.   park at a bus stop
c.   lock them out of sight in the boot
d.   leave them concealed in a bag on the back seat

7   What does this sign mean?

*Choose one answer*

a.   no overtaking
b.   give priority to approaching vehicles
c.   two-way traffic ahead
d.   you have priority over vehicles from the opposite direction

8   You see this sign at a junction and should:

*Choose one answer*

a.   ignore it and continue on your route
b.   slow down and proceed carefully
c.   stop and report the fault
d.   turn around and find another route

9   Front fog lights may only be used if:
*Choose one answer*

a.   you use rear fog lights at the same time
b.   visibility is seriously reduced
c.   they were fitted by the vehicle manufacturer
d.   you are driving in fog at night

10  As a driver, how can you help improve air quality in city centres?
*Choose one answer*

a.   by only using your car for short journeys
b.   by only using the lower gears in town
c.   by walking, cycling or using public transport
d.   by driving through as quickly as possible

11  If you have just joined a motorway you should:
*Choose two answers*

a.   get into the middle lane as soon as you can
b.   take a little time to get used to the traffic
c.   move into the fast lane
d.   keep to the left-hand lane
e.   set your cruise control to 70 mph

12  As a car driver why is it important to keep these road markings clear?

*Choose one answer*

   a.  so that teachers can enter the school
   b.  so that children can be dropped off
   c.  so that there is a clear view of the crossing area
   d.  so that school buses have a place to park

13  In very windy conditions you need to take extra care when:
*Choose two answers*

   a.  passing large vehicles
   b.  moving off
   c.  passing a cyclist
   d.  parking
   e.  checking your oil

14  At the scene of an accident you are dealing with a casualty with a back injury. You should:
*Choose one answer*

   a.  put him or her in the recovery position
   b.  not move him or her unless there is further danger
   c.  keep the casualty on his or her back and raise his or her legs
   d.  get him or her to sit upright

15  A Statutory Off-Road Notification (SORN) is:
*Choose one answer*

   a.  valid for as long as the vehicle has insurance
   b.  only valid for 12 months
   c.  only required for four-wheel-drive vehicles
   d.  only needed for vehicles over three years old

16  You are about to turn left at this junction and see the pedestrian step into the road. You should:

*Choose one answer*

a.  sound the horn to warn the pedestrian to step back
b.  expect the pedestrian to give way
c.  give way to the pedestrian
d.  stop and wave the pedestrian across

17  You see a pedestrian carrying a white stick with a reflective red band. This indicates that: *Choose one answer*

a.  the person is deaf and dumb
b.  the person is blind and deaf
c.  the person is blind in one eye
d.  the person is blind and dumb

18  You should only use a hand-held mobile telephone in a vehicle: *Choose one answer*

a.  if stopped in a traffic queue
b.  to take an incoming call
c.  when parked in a safe place
d.  if you need to make an urgent call

19 Whilst turning your car in the road you should: *Choose one answer*
   a. keep a close watch on your mirrors
   b. keep a good look out for other road users
   c. use your hazard warning lights
   d. make the most of driveways

20 The last thing to do before moving off from the side of the road is: *Choose one answer*

   a. give a signal
   b. check your door mirror
   c. look over your right shoulder
   d. release the handbrake

21 You are approaching an obstruction on your side of the road and see oncoming traffic. You should: *Choose one answer*

   a. continue as you have priority
   b. hold back so that oncoming traffic can come through
   c. flash your headlights and accelerate through the gap
   d. give a signal and cross to the right-hand side of the road

22 Driving in icy conditions, your car's steering may feel lighter than usual. This is because: *Choose one answer*

   a. your tyres have more grip
   b. cold weather deflates your tyres
   c. your tyres have less grip
   d. your steering mechanism has iced up

23 On a fast road in good conditions, reasonable estimates for a safe distance to keep between you and the car ahead are: *Choose two answers*

   a. about three car lengths
   b. close enough to read the number plate of the car ahead
   c. a time gap of two seconds
   d. 3 metres (10 feet)
   e. at least a metre (3 feet) for every mile per hour of your speed

24  The barriers have just lifted at this level crossing. The driver of the blue car (arrowed) should:

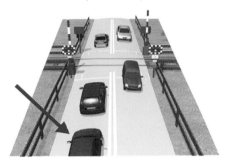

*Choose one answer*

a.  drive across nose to tail with the red car in front
b.  overtake the red car in front
c.  let the car in front clear the track before driving across
d.  drive across very slowly and carefully

25  The national speed limit for cars and motorcycles on a dual carriageway is:
*Choose one answer*

a.  50 mph
b.  60 mph
c.  70 mph
d.  80 mph

26  Leaving a car parked on a road, when can you keep the engine running?
*Choose one answer*

a.  at any time
b.  never
c.  if you have a flat battery
d.  if you leave hazard warning lights on

27  In which of these places are you sometimes allowed to park?
*Choose one answer*

a.  on zigzag lines near a zebra crossing
b.  where there are red or yellow lines at the edge of the road
c.  in the nearside lane of a motorway
d.  on a clearway

28  It is raining and spray from the vehicle ahead affects your vision.
You should:
*Choose one answer*

   a.   move out and overtake
   b.   get closer to the vehicle to avoid the spray
   c.   signal to the driver ahead to pull over
   d.   drop back to get a clearer view

29  In bad weather, which vehicles are least likely to be affected by high
winds?
*Choose one answer*

   a.   motorcycles
   b.   cars
   c.   bicycles
   d.   high-sided lorries

30  Driving in daytime mist, you can see more than 100 metres ahead and
should:
*Choose one answer*

   a.   use fog lights
   b.   keep close to the vehicle ahead
   c.   switch on dipped headlights
   d.   switch on hazard warning lights

31  You need to park at night in fog. The best thing to do is:
*Choose one answer*

   a.   leave on your rear fog lights
   b.   park off the road
   c.   leave on your headlights
   d.   leave on your hazard warning lights

32  For what two reasons would you pull into a passing place on
a narrow country road?
*Choose two answers*

   a.   to pass the time on a peaceful afternoon
   b.   to turn your car in the road
   c.   to allow a following vehicle to overtake
   d.   to give way to another vehicle coming from the opposite direction
   e.   to take a rest when you are too tired to drive

33 Normally, you should not drive with your foot down on the clutch for longer than necessary because it will:

*Choose one answer*

a.  reduce your fuel consumption
b.  wear out the gears
c.  reduce your control of the vehicle
d.  prevent you from changing gear

34 Which type of sign tells you NOT to do something?

*Choose one answer*

a.

b.

c.

d.

35 What does this motorway sign mean?

*Choose one answer*

a.  leave the motorway at the next exit
b.  move to the hard shoulder
c.  move to the lane on your left
d.  contraflow, change to the opposite carriageway

36 At a pedestrian crossing, what do these zigzag lines mean?

*Choose one answer*

a.  parking limited to five minutes or less
b.  slow down and use third gear
c.  no parking at any time
d.  you must not stop

37  To drive on a road, learners MUST:
*Choose one answer*

    a.   not have any penalty points
    b.   have a signed, valid provisional licence
    c.   take professional tuition
    d.   have passed the theory test

38  To supervise a learner driver you MUST:
*Choose two answers*

    a.   not have any penalty points
    b.   have held a full licence for three years or more
    c.   be an approved driving instructor
    d.   be at least 21 years old
    e.   have passed an extended driving test

39  At a pelican crossing, a flashing amber light means that you should:
*Choose one answer*

    a.   drive on
    b.   give way to pedestrians who are waiting to cross
    c.   not stop if following traffic is too close
    d.   give way to pedestrians already on the crossing

40  Driving along a dual carriageway at 70 mph, another driver comes up behind flashing his or her headlights. What should you do?
*Choose one answer*

    a.   switch on your hazard warning lights
    b.   allow the vehicle to overtake
    c.   show your brake lights
    d.   accelerate to keep a safe gap between you

41  You are driving in a one-way street and want to turn right ahead. What road position should you take?
*Choose one answer*

    a.   in the right-hand lane
    b.   just left of the centre line
    c.   as close to the middle of the road as is safe
    d.   in the lane with the fastest-flowing traffic

42 You are loading a caravan ready for a holiday trip. You should place any heavy items: *Choose one answer*

   a.   as close to the front of the caravan as possible
   b.   as near to the back of the caravan as possible
   c.   as high off the floor as possible
   d.   as low to the floor as possible

43 You see a symbol like this flashing on your instrument panel. What does it mean?

   *Choose one answer*

   a.   your hazard warning lights are on
   b.   your brakes need adjustment
   c.   your handbrake is on
   d.   your main headlights are on

44 A child under 14 years and his or her parents are passengers in the car you are driving. Who must ensure that the child wears a seat belt? *Choose one answer*

   a.   the child's parents
   b.   the child
   c.   you
   d.   the front-seat passenger

45 To join a motorway from a slip road you: *Choose one answer*

   a.   must speed up to 70 mph
   b.   should adjust your speed to match the speed of the traffic in the inside lane
   c.   must never stop
   d.   should keep to a steady 40 mph

46 Driving along a three-lane motorway, which general rule applies?
*Choose one answer*

    a.   the right-hand lane is the fast lane
    b.   keep to the middle lane for safety
    c.   keep to the left lane unless you are overtaking
    d.   keep to the lane with the least traffic

47 At the scene of an accident you notice a casualty who seems to be suffering from shock. You should:
*Choose one answer*

    a.   offer the casualty a drink to calm his or her nerves
    b.   talk to the casualty to reassure him or her
    c.   keep the casualty moving to prevent fainting
    d.   leave the casualty alone

48 After a motorway breakdown, your car has been repaired on the hard shoulder. To continue you should:
*Choose one answer*

    a.   wait for a suitable gap in the traffic and then move off into the left lane
    b.   build up speed on the hard shoulder before rejoining the carriageway
    c.   keep your hazard warning lights on as you rejoin the carriageway
    d.   complete your journey on the hard shoulder

49 What is a 'red route'?
*Choose one answer*

    a.   a stretch of road where there have been very few accidents
    b.   a route in a city where parking and waiting are restricted
    c.   a stretch of road with an unusually high number of road signs
    d.   a road with a red tarmac surface

50 Another vehicle overtakes you and cuts in sharply ahead. What should you do?
*Choose two answers*

    a.   keep calm
    b.   flash your lights
    c.   sound your horn
    d.   drop back to leave a safe space between you
    e.   overtake the other driver to show how it should be done

# Paper 3
## Theory test assessment

## Case Study for questions 1–5

You and some friends have tickets for a football match and it is your turn to drive. The journey will take about 3 hours. Your friends are excited about the day out and they have had alcoholic drinks before you set off. You have had a cold recently and are still taking an off-the-shelf remedy for your symptoms. You have a flask of coffee with you for the journey. It is raining and you have the car's demisters on full as you start the motorway section of your journey.

1   What do you need to know about the cold remedy?
    *Choose one answer*

    a.   whether it contains any sweetener
    b.   whether it could cause drowsiness
    c.   how effective the manufacturer says it is
    d.   where you can buy more if you run out on the way to the match

2   Your friends are singing loudly as you get on to the motorway.
    You should: *Choose one answer*

    a.   join in the fun
    b.   not join in as you are feeling unwell
    c.   ask them to keep quiet if the noise is affecting your concentration
    d.   pull up on the hard shoulder to explain your problem to your friends

3   After an hour on the motorway it is warm in the car and your friends have gone quiet. You begin to feel drowsy and should: *Choose one answer*

    a.   ask your friends to start singing to keep you awake
    b.   open a window and get some fresh air
    c.   ask your friends to pour you a coffee
    d.   turn off the demisters to cool the car down

4   You decide to pull in for break. The best plan to keep you alert for
    the rest of your journey is to:
    *Choose one answer*

    a.  stop briefly on the hard shoulder and have some coffee
    b.  pull in at the next services, have a rest and pour a coffee as you
        set off again
    c.  pull in at the next services, drink some coffee and then have a rest
        before continuing
    d.  pull in at the next services and give the coffee to your friends to
        liven them up so that they can keep you awake

5   After resting for twenty minutes you feel drowsy but your friends are
    anxious to continue the journey. You should:
    *Choose one answer*

    a.  not worry as the drowsy feeling will go once you start driving
        again
    b.  not drive until you feel fully alert
    c.  ask one of your friends to take over the driving
    d.  have an alcoholic drink to stimulate your senses

6   What would reduce the chances of a neck injury in a collision?
    *Choose one answer*

    a.  anti-lock brakes
    b.  seat belt pre-tensioners
    c.  a side impact protection system
    d.  a properly adjusted head restraint

7   It has just started to rain after a long dry spell. When will the road
    surface be most slippery?
    *Choose one answer*

    a.  when it has rained for an hour or so
    b.  a few minutes after it starts to rain
    c.  when puddles have formed on the road
    d.  about an hour after the rain stops

8    What is the purpose of these raised red lines on the road surface?

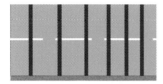

*Choose two answers*

a. they prohibit parking and waiting
b. they alert you to a hazard ahead
c. to encourage you to slow down
d. warning of a school crossing patrol ahead
e. a reminder to check your suspension

9    If you are unsure whether a medicine will affect your driving you should:
*Choose two answers*

a. check the label on the medicine
b. ask a friend to try driving after taking the medicine
c. ask your doctor or pharmacist
d. ask a friend to follow you as you drive
e. stop taking the medicine

10    You see this sign whilst driving your car on a single carriageway road. What does it mean?

*Choose one answer*

a. it is safe to drive at 60 mph
b. the national speed limit applies
c. you may drive at 70 mph if safe
d. you must not exceed 30 mph

11  Where may you overtake in a one-way street? *Choose one answer*

    a.  on the right only
    b.  on the left only
    c.  you may not overtake
    d.  on the left or right

12  To correct a front-wheel skid caused by fierce acceleration you should: *Choose one answer*

    a.  use the choke
    b.  brake sharply
    c.  ease off the accelerator
    d.  apply the parking brake

13  The best way to slow your car on a very icy road is to: *Choose one answer*

    a.  coast to a halt with the clutch down
    b.  use engine braking
    c.  select reverse gear and slip the clutch
    d.  use the parking brake

14  Rear-wheel skids are usually caused by: *Choose one answer*

    a.  harsh braking
    b.  coasting
    c.  steering too gently
    d.  accelerating too late

15  It is more dangerous to overtake a tram than a car because: *Choose one answer*

    a.  trams are quieter
    b.  trams are very slow-moving
    c.  you could get stuck in the tracks
    d.  trams can be very long

16  Cyclists are more vulnerable than car drivers because: *Choose one answer*

    a.  they have less protection in an accident
    b.  they are unable to brake firmly
    c.  they are more prone to mistakes
    d.  they can't accelerate out of danger

17 What danger should you be aware of
when overtaking a car and caravan?
*Choose one answer*

a. the car and caravan may accelerate sharply
b. the driver towing the caravan may have difficulty seeing you
c. caravans are prone to swing wildly from side to side
d. you will need to pull in sharply after you have overtaken

18 What does this sign mean?

*Choose one answer*

a. no horse riders permitted
b. no horse-drawn carriages
c. beware of horse riders ahead
d. bridleway ahead, horse riders only

19 What does this sign mean?

*Choose one answer*

a. priority over approaching traffic
b. one-way street ahead
c. give priority to oncoming vehicles
d. contraflow ahead

20 What does this sign mean?

*Choose one answer*

a. one-way street
b. ahead only
c. bus lane ahead
d. danger overhead

21  You see this pedestrian crossing the road in the zigzag area and should:

*Choose one answer*

a.  show the pedestrian consideration
b.  give a short beep of the horn
c.  accelerate as a warning to the pedestrian
d.  stop and suggest to the pedestrian that he pays more attention in future

22  You need to take extra care when driving near a tramway because:
*Choose one answer*

a.  trams may stop suddenly to let passengers get off
b.  you could get stuck in the tram rails
c.  it is difficult to hear trams approaching
d.  trams can't stop in an emergency

23  Parking illegally on double yellow lines can impede traffic flow and:
*Choose one answer*

a.  reduce air quality for local people
b.  is only permitted if you show hazard warning lights
c.  results in reduced congestion
d.  always results in prosecution

24  An overloaded trailer is:
*Choose one answer*

a.  not dangerous at low speed
b.  a danger at any speed
c.  only dangerous at higher speeds
d.  only dangerous on a motorway or dual carriageway

25 You have a heavy load in your car boot and never seem to have time
to unload it. You should remember that:
*Choose two answers*

   a.  the load is likely to affect your vehicle's handling
   b.  carrying the load will help you when braking
   c.  the load will give you greater stability
   d.  your car will not be so economical to run with the load in it
   e.  your tyres will wear unevenly because of the load

26 Which four of the following could cause uneven tyre wear?
*Choose four answers*

   a.  incorrectly inflated tyres
   b.  faulty suspension
   c.  hydrolastic suspension
   d.  power steering
   e.  misaligned front wheels
   f.  a faulty braking system

27 How would a police officer that was following you indicate that he or
she wanted you to pull in?

*Choose one answer*

   a.  by using a flashing blue light only
   b.  by indicating and pointing to the left
   c.  by overtaking you and braking sharply
   d.  by using both a siren and flashing blue lights

28 On a three-lane motorway this gantry sign indicates that:

*Choose two answers*

   a.  you may use any lane except the hard shoulder
   b.  you may use all lanes including the hard shoulder
   c.  there is a temporary advisory speed limit of 50 mph
   d.  there is a temporary mandatory speed limit of 50 mph
   e.  there is a queue of traffic 50 metres ahead

29 Which of these types of vehicle may not use motorways?
*Choose one answer*

a. farm tractors
b. motorcyclists
c. buses
d. learner lorry drivers

30 Reflective amber studs on a two-lane motorway separate the:
*Choose one answer*

a. lanes
b. hard shoulder and slip roads
c. hard shoulder and left-hand lane
d. right-hand lane and central reserve

31 If involved in a traffic accident you: *Choose one answer*

a. must stop
b. need only stop if a person is injured
c. must show your licence to any other person involved
d. must always report it to the police

32 How should you deal with a traffic accident casualty who is bleeding heavily from a severe cut to his or her forearm?
*Choose two answers*

a. keep the casualty standing
b. apply firm pressure to the wound
c. apply a tourniquet
d. put the casualty's head between his or her legs
e. raise the arm to reduce blood flow

33 If you suspect a spill of flammable liquid at the scene of an accident you should first: *Choose one answer*

a. test the liquid with a lighted match
b. impose a smoking ban
c. call the fire brigade
d. go and find a fire extinguisher

34  A cover note is a document which may be issued before you receive:
*Choose one answer*

a.  your MOT test certificate
b.  your driving licence
c.  your insurance certificate
d.  your vehicle logbook

35  Winter conditions can affect the distance it takes you to come to
a stop. On an icy road you should expect stopping distances to
increase by up to:
*Choose one answer*

a.  2 times
b.  3 times
c.  5 times
d.  10 times

36  You should update your Vehicle Registration document (V5C) when:
*Choose one answer*

a.  your insurance is due for renewal
b.  you move to a new address
c.  your next service is due
d.  you are involved in an accident

37  The light sequence seen by drivers at a puffin crossing is:
*Choose one answer*

a.  green – flashing amber – red – steady amber – green
b.  red – flashing amber – green – steady amber – red
c.  red – red and amber – green – steady amber – red
d.  green – red and amber – red – flashing amber – green

38  You may park on the right-hand side of a road at night:
*Choose one answer*

a.  provided you leave sidelights on
b.  in a one-way street
c.  only if you are more than 10 metres from a junction
d.  under a street light

39  Your vehicle catches fire whilst you are driving through a tunnel.
    You should:
    *Choose one answer*

    a.  turn your vehicle around and drive back out of the tunnel
    b.  continue through the tunnel if you can
    c.  stop and then reverse out of the tunnel
    d.  stop and wait behind your vehicle until help arrives

40  The driver ahead gives this arm signal. It means:

    *Choose one answer*

    a.  the driver intends to turn right
    b.  the driver intends to turn left
    c.  the driver intends to slow down
    d.  the driver wants you to overtake

41  You are waiting to turn left at a T-junction. A vehicle is coming
    from the right showing a left indicator signal. You should:
    *Choose one answer*

    a.  emerge before the vehicle reaches the junction
    b.  emerge and accelerate quickly
    c.  wait until the vehicle starts to turn before pulling out
    d.  creep forward to see but not pull out

42  Whilst driving you see this sign at the roadside and should:

    *Choose one answer*

    a.  ignore it as it is intended for cyclists
    b.  drive on knowing there will be no cyclists ahead
    c.  be aware that there may be cyclists in the road
        ahead
    d.  stop because you have driven into a cycle lane

43  Before starting a long holiday journey it is a good idea to:
    *Choose two answers*

    a.  look at a map
    b.  have a heavy meal
    c.  plan for rest stops
    d.  fit new tyres
    e.  overload your car

44  In which of these places would parking be inconsiderate to others?
    *Choose three answers*

    a.  in a lay-by
    b.  near the brow of a hill
    c.  where the road narrows
    d.  where there is tactile paving at the kerb
    e.  in a multi-storey car park

45  You are approaching a roundabout and
    see a cyclist signalling to turn right. You should:
    *Choose one answer*

    a.  sound your horn to warn of your presence
    b.  hold back and wave the cyclist across
    c.  accelerate to get past the cyclist before the junction
    d.  allow the cyclist plenty of room

46  You are following a large and slow-moving vehicle on a narrow road.
    The road is straight and there is a junction just ahead. You should:
    *Choose one answer*

    a.  use the MSM routine and overtake
    b.  wait until past the junction before attempting to overtake
    c.  sound your horn and then overtake quickly
    d.  follow the vehicle until you reach a dual carriageway

47　You see someone waiting on the footpath to cross
　　at a zebra crossing. You should:
　　*Choose two answers*

　　a.　accelerate to get past before the pedestrian steps on to
　　　　the crossing
　　b.　check your mirrors
　　c.　stop and wave the pedestrian across
　　d.　ignore the pedestrian as he or she is still on the pavement
　　e.　stop and let the pedestrian cross the road

48　You are carrying a child using a rear-facing baby seat and only have
　　room in the front passenger seat. Before setting off you must make sure:
　　*Choose one answer*

　　a.　that the seat is in the fully forward position
　　b.　that you deactivate any front passenger airbag
　　c.　that all passenger airbags are deactivated
　　d.　that the child has been fed and sedated

49　You are driving on a well-lit motorway at night. You must:
　　*Choose one answer*

　　a.　use only your sidelights
　　b.　use front and rear fog lights
　　c.　use your headlights
　　d.　only use headlights in poor weather conditions

50　You are on a single-track road and see another vehicle coming
　　towards you. You should:
　　*Choose one answer*

　　a.　pull into a passing place on your right
　　b.　expect the other driver to reverse out of your way
　　c.　reverse so that the approaching driver can come through
　　d.　wait before a passing place on your right

# Paper 4
## Theory test assessment

## Case Study for questions 1–5

James arrives at the scene of an accident involving a motorcyclist and a number of cars. James stops and puts on his hazard warning lights before going to check on those involved. There are a number of casualties with minor injuries, a motorcyclist is conscious but lying down in the road, and another casualty is at the roadside who isn't moving or making any sound. A witness is talking to the motorcyclist.

1   Apart from putting on his hazard lights, how else could James have warned other traffic about the accident? *Choose one answer*

    a.  by setting off his car alarm
    b.  by parking at right angles to the kerb to block traffic movement
    c.  by placing a hazard warning triangle on the road
    d.  by standing in the middle of the road to flag down other motorists

2   What should James have done before checking on the casualties? *Choose one answer*

    a.  called the emergency services
    b.  made sure that he wasn't putting himself or anyone else in danger
    c.  got the names and addresses of any witnesses
    d.  asked the casualties if they had any infectious diseases

3   Who should James first give his attention to? *Choose one answer*

    a.  the motorcyclist
    b.  the casualties with minor injuries
    c.  the casualty at the roadside who isn't moving or making any sound
    d.  any witnesses who may have had a shock

4    James sees the witness trying to unfasten the motorcyclist's helmet.
     He should: *Choose one answer*

    a.   shout instructions on how to do this safely
    b.   not worry about the motorcyclist since he is talking to the witness
    c.   tell the witness to get away from the motorcyclist
    d.   tell the witness to leave the helmet in place

5    James finds that the unconscious casualty isn't breathing and decides
     to give chest compressions to maintain circulation. With what
     frequency should he push down on the casualty's chest?
     *Choose one answer*

    a.   about 10 times per minute
    b.   about 20 times per minute
    c.   about 50 times per minute
    d.   about 100 times per minute

6    The driver of the car in front is giving this arm signal. It means:

    *Choose one answer*

    a.   the driver is slowing down
    b.   the driver intends to turn right
    c.   the driver wants you to overtake
    d.   the driver intends to turn left

7    Which of the following should not be kept in your vehicle?
     *Choose two answers*

    a.   a fire extinguisher
    b.   the MOT certificate
    c.   a first aid kit
    d.   the vehicle registration document (logbook)
    e.   the owner's handbook

8   You are trying to move off on snow. You should:
*Choose one answer*

   a.   use the lowest gear you can
   b.   keep the engine revs high to prevent stalling
   c.   use the highest gear you can for the conditions
   d.   put on your hazard warning lights

9   You break down on a motorway. To call for help it may be
    better to use an emergency roadside telephone rather than
    a mobile phone because:
    *Choose one answer*

   a.   it will connect you directly to a national breakdown service
   b.   it would be illegal to use the mobile phone
   c.   the emergency services will be able to locate you more easily
   d.   it will connect you directly to a local garage

10  At an accident you are treating a burn victim. The shortest time you
    should cool the burn for is:
    *Choose one answer*

   a.   5 minutes
   b.   10 minutes
   c.   15 minutes
   d.   20 minutes

11  Where would you see this sign?

    *Choose one answer*

   a.   in the window of a car taking children to school
   b.   at the side of the road
   c.   at playground areas
   d.   on the rear of a school bus or coach

12  Driving along this country road you see a horse and rider ahead. You should:

*Choose two answers*

a.  give plenty of room
b.  give a light tap of your horn
c.  flash your headlights
d.  drive past slowly and carefully
e.  speed up to get past the danger promptly
f.  select a low gear and keep your engine speed high as you pass

13  As a new driver, how likely are you to have an accident compared to more experienced drivers? *Choose one answer*

a.  less likely
b.  more likely
c.  about the same
d.  it depends on your age

14  Why is it good planning to take regular stops on a long journey? *Choose one answer*

a.  to reduce engine wear, particularly on fast roads
b.  to avoid losing concentration
c.  to check your route
d.  to adjust the driving seat and mirrors

15  Approaching a sharp bend on an icy road, what two things should you do for safety? *Choose two answers*

a.  keep the clutch pedal down
b.  accelerate to keep the wheels gripping
c.  use as high a gear as you can
d.  slow down well before the bend
e.  put on hazard warning lights

16 Which of the following affect your thinking distance?
*Choose three answers*

   a.  the weather conditions
   b.  your health
   c.  your distance from the vehicle ahead
   d.  your concentration
   e.  the speed of your vehicle

17 In England, what is the maximum LEGAL level of alcohol you can
have in your breath when driving?
*Choose one answer*

   a.  50 micrograms per 100 ml
   b.  35 micrograms per 100 ml
   c.  100 micrograms per 100 ml
   d.  80 micrograms per 100 ml

18 On a busy road you realize you are going the wrong way. You should:
*Choose one answer*

   a.  pull into a side road and reverse out into the main road to turn
round
   b.  do a 'three-point turn'
   c.  find a quiet road to turn round in
   d.  make a quick U-turn

19 You see this sign ahead and should:

*Choose one answer*

   a.  slow down to 30 mph or less after you pass the sign
   b.  keep to about 35 mph after the sign
   c.  make sure you are travelling at 30 mph or less as you reach
the sign
   d.  assume it is safe to drive at 30 mph after the sign

20  What is the closest you should park your car to a junction?
*Choose one answer*

    a.   5 metres (16 feet)
    b.   10 metres (33 feet)
    c.   15 metres (50 feet)
    d.   20 metres (65 feet)

21  What will happen if you push the clutch pedal down when travelling down a steep hill? *Choose one answer*

    a.   your brakes will not work
    b.   the clutch plate will wear unevenly
    c.   the vehicle will slow down
    d.   the vehicle will speed up

22  If you have to park your car on a road in fog, what should you do?
*Choose one answer*

    a.   leave on your headlights and rear fog lights
    b.   leave on your sidelights
    c.   leave on your rear fog lights and sidelights
    d.   leave on your hazard warning lights

23  You are following a long vehicle towards a mini-roundabout.
You wish to turn right and should:

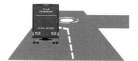

*Choose one answer*

    a.   pull alongside the long vehicle
    b.   keep back until the long vehicle has cleared the mini-roundabout
    c.   drive on the white roundabout marking
    d.   expect the driver ahead to keep left

24  You are about to overtake a cyclist. Which one of these signs would make you take special care? *Choose one answer*

a.
b.
c.
d.

25 You are driving up a steep hill on a narrow road. A lorry is coming from the opposite direction and will need to pass a parked car. You should: *Choose one answer*

   a.  expect the lorry to give way to you
   b.  accelerate to clear the hazard
   c.  be ready to give way to the lorry
   d.  flash your lights to beckon the lorry driver through

26 After you give a signal to make a right turn at a junction, why is it important to get into position in good time? *Choose one answer*

   a.  to stop any other drivers from getting to the junction before you
   b.  to help other road users anticipate what you intend to do
   c.  to hold up following traffic if necessary
   d.  to get a better view into the junction you are approaching

27 You are driving at the speed limit and a following driver wants to overtake. There is a slower vehicle ahead. What should you do? *Choose one answer*

   a.  allow the following driver to overtake
   b.  move to the right to prevent the following driver from overtaking
   c.  ignore the following driver and concentrate on the vehicle ahead
   d.  give a signal and pull out to overtake the slow vehicle ahead of you

28 Carrying a heavy load in your car will: *Choose one answer*

   a.  not affect your steering
   b.  not affect your steering or braking
   c.  affect your braking only in a bend
   d.  affect your braking only
   e.  affect your car's handling, particularly in a bend

29 A breakaway cable on a caravan is designed so that: *Choose one answer*

   a.  overloaded caravans can be towed more safely
   b.  the caravan will slow if the towing hitch comes loose
   c.  the caravan can be released when driving
   d.  the caravan can be released more quickly in an emergency

30  You notice a strong smell of petrol when driving. You should:
*Choose one answer*

    a.  speed up to increase the airflow through your car
    b.  stop and investigate the problem
    c.  mention it when you next have your vehicle serviced
    d.  look out for a nearby fuel station

31  You are in a slow-moving traffic queue on a motorway. You may:
*Choose one answer*

    a.  move left to overtake
    b.  overtake slower queuing traffic on the right or left
    c.  only overtake by moving to a lane on your right
    d.  use the hard shoulder to overtake

32  Whilst driving you realize there is a fire in
your engine compartment. You:
*Choose one answer*

    a.  should drive to the nearest petrol station
    b.  must drive to the nearest fire station
    c.  must increase speed to blow out the fire
    d.  should pull in and get everyone out of the car

33  Within two years of passing your driving test you get six penalty
points on your licence. What are the consequences?
*Choose two answers*

    a.  you would be limited to six more penalty points before losing
       your licence
    b.  you would revert to provisional status
    c.  you would have to retake your theory and practical tests
    d.  you would be banned from driving for 12 months
    e.  you would be restricted to driving a three-wheeled car

34  What does this sign mean?

*Choose one answer*

a.  end of two-way traffic
b.  no low bridges ahead
c.  end of motorway
d.  no motorway traffic allowed

35  What does this sign mean?

*Choose one answer*

a.  two-way traffic ahead
b.  end of dual carriageway
c.  two-way traffic crosses one-way road
d.  T-junction ahead

36  You are waiting in the left-hand lane at traffic lights to turn left.
    At which signals can you proceed if safe?
    *Choose two answers*

a.     b.

c.     d.

37  You hold a provisional licence for cars and want to ride a motorcycle.
    You: *Choose one answer*

    a.  may start riding immediately
    b.  must apply for motorcycle entitlement
    c.  must not ride until you have passed a driving test for a car
    d.  must apply for a motorcycle licence but can start riding
        immediately

38  Where should you normally expect other drivers to overtake you on
    the left? *Choose one answer*

    a.  on a motorway
    b.  in a contraflow system
    c.  in a one-way system
    d.  nowhere

39  Driving in heavy rain you realize that your steering suddenly feels
    very light. You should: *Choose one answer*

    a.  steer towards the middle of the road
    b.  gently increase pressure on the accelerator pedal
    c.  brake firmly to reduce speed
    d.  ease off the accelerator pedal

40  When should you use hazard warning lights?
    *Choose one answer*

    a.  when stopping briefly in a restricted parking zone
    b.  when your vehicle has broken down and is causing an obstruction
    c.  when warning approaching traffic that you intend to stop
    d.  when being towed

41  You are driving on the motorway when a suitcase falls from your
    vehicle roof rack. You should:
    *Choose one answer*

    a.  stop at the next emergency telephone and contact the police
    b.  stop in lane, put on hazard warning lights and reverse back for
        the suitcase
    c.  walk back up the motorway to pick the suitcase up
    d.  pull in at the next service area and report the incident

42  What would you expect to find at a motorway contraflow system?
*Choose two answers*

a. temporary traffic lights
b. lower speed limits
c. narrower lanes than normal
d. an extra-wide hard shoulder
e. faster-moving traffic

43  Planning ahead and making smooth use of the controls can:
*Choose two answers*

a. reduce journey times by about 15 per cent
b. increase your journey times by an unacceptable amount
c. increase fuel consumption by about 15 per cent
d. reduce fuel consumption by about 15 per cent
e. reduce the environmental impact of your driving

44  Where would you see these red and white markers?

*Choose one answer*

a. on approach to a ford or flood
b. at the end of a motorway
c. on approach to a concealed level crossing
d. on approach to a slip road leaving a dual carriageway

45  What could be caused by having too much oil in your engine?
*Choose one answer*

a. low oil pressure
b. the engine running at a higher temperature than normal
c. oil leaks
d. reduced fuel consumption

46 You are driving at night in fog. The fog clears but you forget to switch off your rear fog lights. This:
*Choose two answers*

a. will warn approaching traffic that there is fog ahead
b. could make other drivers think you are braking
c. will save you putting them on again later
d. could dazzle following drivers
e. may drain your battery

47 You see a cyclist in the road ahead look back over his or her right shoulder. You should anticipate that the cyclist:
*Choose one answer*

a. is going to dismount
b. intends to move right
c. will turn left ahead
d. will accelerate sharply

48 If disqualified from driving for being over the alcohol limit, the minimum period of disqualification a court must impose is:
*Choose one answer*

a. 1 week
b. 1 month
c. 6 months
d. 12 months

49 When following the road ahead at a roundabout you should:
*Choose one answer*

a. not use any indicator signal
b. indicate left before leaving the roundabout
c. indicate left when approaching the roundabout
d. indicate right on approach and then left to leave the roundabout

50 Active Traffic Management (ATM) areas on motorways may allow drivers to use the hard shoulder as a running lane. This:
*Choose one answer*

a. only applies to emergency vehicles
b. allows you to stop on the hard shoulder for a rest break
c. is to help ease congestion
d. is risky if there are police vehicles about

# Paper 5
## Theory test assessment

## Case Study for questions 1–5

Nicole is a specialist nurse who must start her shift at 6.00am. This winter morning it is bitterly cold and raining as she gets into her car. On the way to work she turns right on to a main road and feels the back of her car sliding to the left. Traffic seems to be heavier and slower than usual on the main road.

1  What danger should Nicole be particularly wary of given the rain and bitter cold conditions? *Choose one answer*

   a.  snow drifts
   b.  high winds developing
   c.  rain freezing on the roads as it falls
   d.  hailstones developing

2  What could tell Nicole she was driving on black ice?
*Choose two answers*

   a.  roadside signs
   b.  there would be very little road noise
   c.  the car's steering would feel very light
   d.  the car would pull to one side when braking

3  How should Nicole react to recover from the skid as she turns right? *Choose one answer*

   a.  by easing off the accelerator and steering gently left to straighten the car
   b.  by gently applying the brakes and steering to the right
   c.  by braking firmly and holding the steering wheel straight
   d.  by accelerating gently and steering more to the right

4  As there seems to be more traffic than usual, what precaution
   should Nicole take given the weather and surface conditions?
   *Choose one answer*

   a.  drive in as low a gear as possible for better control
   b.  allow less room between her and the vehicle ahead because of the
       traffic volume
   c.  leave a bigger gap ahead because it could take longer to brake to
       a stop
   d.  use hazard warning lights to stop following drivers from getting
       too close

5  Given the road and surface conditions, how should Nicole use
   the accelerator and footbrake? *Choose one answer*

   a.  firmly and promptly
   b.  firmly and slowly
   c.  gently and slowly
   d.  gently and promptly

6  What is the THINKING distance at 50 mph? *Choose one answer*

   a.  6 metres (20 feet)
   b.  9 metres (30 feet)
   c.  15 metres (50 feet)
   d.  21 metres (70 feet)

7  Which of the following affect your overall stopping distance?
   *Choose three answers*

   a.  the weather conditions
   b.  how soon you react
   c.  your distance from the vehicle ahead
   d.  the condition of your tyres
   e.  the gear you are in

8  Emerging at a junction with poor visibility, you should:
   *Choose one answer*

   a.  creep forward, looking to the right
   b.  creep forward looking to the left
   c.  creep forward looking both ways
   d.  sound your horn and pull out after a quick glance both ways

9   In heavy slow traffic, how can you lessen the risk of hitting a cyclist
or motorcyclist? *Choose one answer*

   a.   by making regular use of your exterior mirrors
   b.   by keeping close to the car ahead
   c.   by relying on cyclists and motorcyclists to take care
   d.   by regularly looking over both shoulders as you are driving

10  Having just less than half the maximum legal level of alcohol in your
blood when driving is: *Choose two answers*

   a.   safe enough in any circumstance
   b.   no guarantee that you can drive safely
   c.   unlikely to affect your driving
   d.   very likely to affect your driving ability

11  You have had a lot of alcohol at a party in the evening.
The next morning you: *Choose one answer*

   a.   should be perfectly safe to drive
   b.   could still be over the legal alcohol limit for driving
   c.   may feel 'hung over' but should be within the legal alcohol limit
   d.   will be safe to drive after a good breakfast

12  In a narrow road you notice an oncoming vehicle and a parked car on
your left ahead. Who has priority? *Choose one answer*

   a.   you do if you can reach the parked car before the approaching driver
   b.   the driver of the wider vehicle
   c.   the driver of the oncoming vehicle
   d.   the driver who is going faster or who has the larger vehicle
   e.   you do unless the owner of the parked car signals to move off

13  What would you need to do after passing a sign like this?

*Choose one answer*

   a.   gently try your brakes
   b.   rev the engine to clear the carburettor
   c.   perform an emergency stop
   d.   consider changing your make of car

14 Front fog lights should only be used when:
*Choose one answer*

    a.   your rear fog lights don't work
    b.   it is foggy
    c.   visibility drops below 200 metres
    d.   visibility drops below 100 metres

15 After heavy rain you notice that water hasn't drained from the road ahead. What should you do?
*Choose one answer*

    a.   drive in second gear, slipping the clutch
    b.   use acceleration to keep the wheels gripping
    c.   drive with one foot on the brake
    d.   slow down and keep engine speed low

16 Approaching a mini-roundabout to turn right, you see ahead a large vehicle in the left-hand lane showing a right indicator signal. You should:
*Choose one answer*

    a.   assume the driver has signalled incorrectly and overtake
    b.   keep back until the long vehicle has cleared the mini-roundabout
    c.   flash your lights and take a short cut across the mini-roundabout
    d.   expect the driver of the large vehicle to keep left

17 How often do you need to check that the horn is working properly?
*Choose one answer*

    a.   every night
    b.   daily
    c.   only if you need the horn
    d.   before an MOT test

18 You are approaching traffic light signals to go ahead. Which signals mean you can proceed if safe? *Choose two answers*

a.    b.    c.    d.

19  The reason for giving signals is to:
    *Choose one answer*

    a.  give instructions to other road users
    b.  help other road users anticipate what you intend to do
    c.  warn other road users to give way
    d.  ensure that you have priority

20  You live half a mile from your child's school and own a car.
    You should:
    *Choose two answers*

    a.  use your car to collect your child if other parents do the same
    b.  try to avoid using your car to collect your child from school
    c.  instruct your child to walk home alone
    d.  be aware that very short journeys are wasteful of fuel
    e.  only use your car if it has a catalytic converter

21  What is the best way to load a caravan you intend to tow with your
    family car?
    *Choose one answer*

    a.  so that the caravan is loaded front heavy
    b.  so that the caravan is underloaded
    c.  so that the caravan has a high a centre of gravity as possible
    d.  so that the caravan has a low centre of gravity

22  You give an indicator signal when driving and notice the repeater light
    on the dashboard flashing faster than usual. What does this mean?
    *Choose one answer*

    a.  you are taking corners too quickly
    b.  your car's battery is overcharged
    c.  one of your indicator bulbs may have blown
    d.  the fuse has blown on the indicator circuit

23  You notice oil leaking from your car and should:
    *Choose one answer*

    a.  keep adding more oil to the engine
    b.  investigate and have the leak repaired
    c.  mention it when you next have your car serviced
    d.  not worry unless the oil warning light comes on when driving

24  You are in a slow-moving traffic queue on a motorway. You may:
*Choose one answer*

a.  move left to overtake
b.  not overtake
c.  pass on the left if your traffic queue is moving faster than traffic in the lane on your right
d.  use the hard shoulder to overtake

25  What is the purpose of this post at the side of a motorway?

*Choose one answer*

a.  it advises police of the direction to the nearest speed trap point
b.  it advises the direction to the nearest emergency telephone
c.  it advises the distance to the nearest service station
d.  it advises the direction to the next motorway exit

26  Whilst driving on a busy road, you realize that your car is losing power. You should:
*Choose one answer*

a.  drive to the nearest petrol station
b.  drive faster to complete your journey
c.  pull in as soon as you safely can
d.  slow down to a crawl and hope that your car will make it home

27  In what circumstance would you try to move a traffic accident casualty?
*Choose one answer*

a.  only if the casualty was awake
b.  only if the casualty was unconscious
c.  only if the casualty was in further danger
d.  only if you had a first aid qualification

28 At a T-junction your view to the right is partly blocked by parked cars. You should:

*Choose one answer*

a. open the window and shout to see if there is any danger
b. just pull out and hope for the best
c. lean forward in your seat and edge out to get a better view
d. sound your horn before you emerge

29 What does this sign mean?

*Choose one answer*

a. minimum speed 30 mph
b. distance to next services
c. maximum speed 30 mph
d. waiting limited to 30 minutes

30 Where would you most expect to see this type of sign?

*Choose one answer*

a. on motorways
b. in a one-way street
c. in tourist areas
d. on minor roads

31 A driver behind you is very close and flashing his or her headlights. You should: *Choose one answer*

a. keep to the speed limit
b. pull in and wave the driver through
c. slow down and allow the driver to overtake you
d. touch the brakes to show your stop lights as a warning

32 Driving too slowly for the road and traffic conditions is:
*Choose two answers*

    a. not likely to cause a hazard
    b. potentially dangerous
    c. safe in wet conditions
    d. likely to irritate other drivers
    e. not likely to affect other road users

33 Any load carried on a roof rack on your car must be:
*Choose one answer*

    a. as light as possible
    b. covered with a tarpaulin
    c. as heavy as possible
    d. properly secured

34 You are going on holiday and wish to take the family pet.
You should only carry the pet in your car if: *Choose one answer*

    a. it can't be secured on a roof rack
    b. you can keep it tied up
    c. it is in a box
    d. you can keep it from roaming freely in the car
    e. it is trained to sit quietly

35 Which of the following MUST be in good working order for your car
to be legally roadworthy? *Choose four answers*

    a. speedometer
    b. rev counter, if fitted
    c. brakes
    d. horn
    e. temperature gauge
    f. oil warning light
    g. windscreen washers

36 How should you carry spare fuel in your vehicle?
*Choose one answer*

    a. in an old oil can
    b. in a plastic bottle
    c. in an approved container
    d. in a thick glass container

37　What could cause your tyre tread to wear excessively in the centre?
*Choose one answer*

   a.　power steering
   b.　driving for short distances in very cold conditions
   c.　driving at high speed for long periods
   d.　having too little pressure in the tyre
   e.　having the tyre over-inflated

38　Why should you check the condition of your vehicle before a motorway journey?
*Choose one answer*

   a.　you will be braking more often
   b.　breakdowns are expensive
   c.　you will be changing gear more often
   d.　high speeds increase the risk of breakdowns

39　In an accident involving a tanker, what should you do before dialling 999?
*Choose one answer*

   a.　get the tanker off the road
   b.　plug up any leaks from the tanker
   c.　wash away any liquid that has been spilled
   d.　try to identify what the tanker was carrying by reading the hazard information plate

40　What is the correct thing to do if you injure someone when driving?
*Choose one answer*

   a.　nothing
   b.　leave it to the injured person to report the accident
   c.　inform the police as soon as possible
   d.　inform the police within 14 days

41　You see horse riders ahead riding side by side. You should:
*Choose one answer*

   a.　ask yourself whether both riders are experienced
   b.　sound your horn in annoyance
   c.　accelerate promptly to pass safely
   d.　shout at the riders as you pass

42 Which of the following should you show particular concern for?
*Choose two answers*

   a.  elderly drivers
   b.  learner drivers
   c.  drivers of your own age
   d.  more experienced drivers

43 What can help you to keep your concentration on a long journey?
*Choose one answer*

   a.  driving only on long straight roads
   b.  driving slowly
   c.  fast driving
   d.  regular rest stops
   e.  listening to the radio

44 The good driver should always:
*Choose three answers*

   a.  drive at the speed limit
   b.  make effective use of the driving mirrors
   c.  look well ahead
   d.  anticipate the actions of other road users
   e.  show off his or her skill

45 What can happen to a road surface in very hot weather?
*Choose one answer*

   a.  nothing
   b.  it will become firmer
   c.  it could get softer
   d.  it will become safer to drive on

46 Compared to a dry road, in wet conditions you should allow:
*Choose one answer*

   a.  twice your usual braking distance
   b.  four times your usual braking distance
   c.  10 times your usual braking distance
   d.  six times your usual braking distance

47 Why should you always check the label of any prescribed medicine you take before driving?
*Choose one answer*

   a.  in case the medicine is out of date
   b.  to make sure the medicine is legal
   c.  some medicines can cause drowsiness
   d.  in case the medicine increases your level of concentration

48 Where should you not park?
*Choose four answers*

   a.  near the brow of a hill
   b.  at a bus stop
   c.  near a police station
   d.  across a driveway
   e.  opposite a traffic island
   f.  in a recognized parking place

49 When overtaking at night you should:
*Choose one answer*

   a.  wait until you can see oncoming headlights
   b.  take care because you can see less
   c.  put your headlights on full beam
   d.  sound your horn

50 What lights must you leave on if parked at night on a 40 mph road?
*Choose one answer*

   a.  none
   b.  sidelights
   c.  dipped headlights
   d.  hazard warning lights

# Paper 6
## Theory test assessment

## Case Study for questions 1–5

Harry has a busy morning ahead. He is going to deliver some unwanted pieces of furniture to a friend's house in the next town. Harry's friend has given him a roof rack for his estate car in exchange, helped him load the furniture and will be travelling with Harry to give him directions. On the way, Harry has to take the family pet cat to the vet for a small operation, and drop his children Tom aged 15 and Sarah aged 12 at school. He will pick the cat and the children up again later on return from his day's work.

1   Who is responsible for ensuring that the vehicle and roof rack are safely loaded?
    *Choose one answer*

    a.   Harry
    b.   Harry's friend
    c.   the police
    d.   the local authority

2   What effects will the loaded roof rack have on the vehicle?
    *Choose two answers*

    a.   it will increase stability, especially in bends
    b.   it will reduce stability
    c.   it will cause the car to handle differently
    d.   it will reduce fuel consumption

3   Who is responsible for ensuring that Sarah wears her seatbelt?
    *Choose one answer*

    a.  Sarah
    b.  Harry's friend
    c.  Tom
    d.  Harry

4   How should the cat be carried in the car? *Choose one answer*

    a.  in a cardboard box
    b.  one of the children should hold it
    c.  in a suitable pet carrier
    d.  tied to the rear seat

5   With the furniture unloaded at his friend's house, Harry sets off for
    work. What will he notice about carrying the empty roof rack on his car?
    *Choose one answer*

    a.  it will make the car unstable
    b.  it will reduce noise levels
    c.  it will cause increased fuel consumption
    d.  it will be noisy and increase fuel economy

6   On a single carriageway the speed limit for goods vehicles over
    7.5 tonnes is: *Choose one answer*

    a.  60 mph
    b.  70 mph
    c.  50 mph
    d.  55 mph

7   You are driving on a multi-lane road and see these overhead gantry
    signs. What do they mean?

    *Choose one answer*

    a.  traffic in the right lanes should stop
    b.  the two right lanes are open
    c.  the two left lanes are open
    d.  traffic in the middle lane should leave the road

8  You are driving in daylight when it is raining.
   Which lights should you use?
   *Choose one answer*

   a.  full headlights
   b.  dipped headlights
   c.  sidelights only
   d.  hazard warning lights

9  How can you dry your brakes after driving through a flood?
   *Choose one answer*

   a.  with tissue paper
   b.  by practising emergency stops
   c.  by driving slowly with your left foot gently on the brake pedal
   d.  by driving with one foot on the brake and one foot on the clutch

10  When driving, you press the accelerator pedal on your car and notice
    the engine speed increase but the car doesn't accelerate very well.
    This means that:
    *Choose one answer*

    a.  the accelerator cable has snapped
    b.  the clutch is worn
    c.  the brakes have seized
    d.  your exhaust system needs replacing

11  Which shape of sign is used to indicate a 'Give way' junction?
    *Choose one answer*

    a.           b.

    c.           d.

12  Your car has a six-speed gear box. When would you use sixth gear?
*Choose one answer*

   a.  only at low speed
   b.  for greatest acceleration
   c.  when cruising at high speed
   d.  in slow-moving traffic

13  When parked at the left kerb, facing uphill, you should leave your car:
*Choose three answers*

   a.  in top gear
   b.  with the parking brake firmly applied
   c.  with the front wheels turned to the right
   d.  in first gear
   e.  with the front wheels turned to the left

14  What is the best way to control your speed when driving down
a steep hill? *Choose one answer*

   a.  constant use of the footbrake
   b.  using the parking brake
   c.  using a low gear to avoid constant pressure on the footbrake
   d.  switching off the engine and coasting

15  Your car pulls sharply to the right when braking. What is likely to be
wrong? *Choose one answer*

   a.  your steering mechanism has seized
   b.  you are not braking hard enough
   c.  your brakes need adjusting
   d.  your brakes have faded

16  What does this sign mean?

*Choose one answer*

   a.  be ready for a surprise
   b.  warning of danger ahead
   c.  overhead cables
   d.  hospital ahead

17  Approaching a junction you should:
    *Choose one answer*

    a.   look out for pedestrians only as you begin to turn
    b.   look out for pedestrians well before and during the turn
    c.   only be concerned with pedestrians in the road
    d.   always sound your horn to warn any pedestrians who are
        out of sight

18  Where would you see a sign like this?

*Choose one answer*

    a.   at a junction
    b.   on a long vehicle
    c.   on a vehicle with an overhanging load
    d.   at a level crossing

19  The purpose of the compulsory MOT test is to ensure that:
    *Choose one answer*

    a.   drivers are competent
    b.   vehicles reach a minimum safety standard
    c.   vehicles are mechanically sound
    d.   vehicles are unlikely to break down

20  What are the three most important things to think about when
    deciding on a safe speed at which to drive?
    *Choose three answers*

    a.   the engine size of your car
    b.   the weather conditions
    c.   the road surface conditions
    d.   the national speed limit
    e.   how far you can see ahead
    f.   your level of high-speed driving skill

21  A fire engine showing flashing blue lights is following your car in
a very narrow residential road with a lot of parked cars. You should:

*Choose one answer*

a.  stop immediately
b.  concentrate on looking for the fire
c.  pull in at a suitable passing place when you can do so safely
d.  speed up if there is no suitable place for the fire engine to pass

22  You need to park and see a space marked with these red lines.
You should:
*Choose one answer*

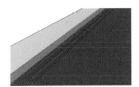

a.  assume that parking is never permitted
b.  park and use your hazard warning lights
c.  check for information signs to find out if parking restrictions are
in force
d.  park but leave your engine running

23  Driving on a motorway, you see a large package fall from a lorry head.
The lorry driver doesn't appear to notice, so you should:
*Choose one answer*

a.  stop on the carriageway and retrieve the package
b.  swerve to avoid the package and then drive on
c.  stop on the hard shoulder and contact the police on an emergency
phone
d.  pull in on the hard shoulder and pick up the package when safe

24 You switch on your lights as night falls and notice this symbol light up on your instrument panel. This means:

*Choose one answer*

   a.   your front fog lights are on
   b.   your headlights are on main beam
   c.   you need to put on full headlights
   d.   it isn't dark enough for headlights yet

25 Your car has an anti-lock braking system (ABS). This is designed to: *Choose one answer*

   a.   make it is impossible to skid
   b.   prevent your car being broken into
   c.   help you with car control
   d.   stop you having to use the footbrake early

26 If your car has a catalytic converter, you should remember that: *Choose one answer*

   a.   unleaded petrol can damage it
   b.   it is most efficient on short journeys
   c.   it is only for use with diesel fuel
   d.   it could cause more pollution than ordinary exhaust systems on short journeys

27 When may you overtake on the left? *Choose two answers*

   a.   in a one-way system
   b.   at any time
   c.   if a vehicle ahead is signalling to turn right and positioned to do so
   d.   in fast-moving traffic when the right lane is blocked

28 After a motorway breakdown you have stopped on the hard shoulder and should: *Choose two answers*

   a.   get out of your car on the left side and leave it unlocked
   b.   get out of your car and lock it
   c.   put on your hazard warning lights
   d.   wait in your car for assistance

29  Towing a trailer on a three-lane motorway, you are not permitted to:
*Choose two answers*

   a.  use the left-hand lane
   b.  exceed 60 mph
   c.  use the middle or third lanes
   d.  use the right-hand lane
   e.  exceed 50 mph

30  In an emergency, you have to stop the car suddenly and should:
*Choose two answers*

   a.  grip the steering wheel firmly
   b.  not brake before checking the mirrors
   c.  brake firmly
   d.  use the parking brake to help stop the car

31  After a frosty morning, the sun has begun to thaw ice on the road.
Where in particular would you expect the road to remain slippery?
*Choose one answer*

   a.  where there has been a steady flow of early morning traffic
   b.  where the road has had plenty of sunlight but little traffic
   c.  where the road surface is in the shade
   d.  where the road has been treated with salt and grit

32  You wish to overtake the vehicle ahead and see this sign. You should
be aware that:

*Choose one answer*

   a.  it will be easier since the vehicle ahead will be slowing down
   b.  you will be safer because you can pick up speed more quickly
       on the hill
   c.  you will not be able to accelerate so well on the hill
   d.  it could take longer than you expect

33  Your car needs a new battery. How should you dispose of the old one?
*Choose one answer*

    a.   take it to a local authority recycling site
    b.   break it up and bury it in your garden
    c.   leave it at the roadside
    d.   burn it

34  In areas where there are 'traffic calming' measures you should:
*Choose one answer*

    a.   travel at a reduced speed
    b.   always travel at the speed limit
    c.   position in the centre of the road
    d.   only slow down if pedestrians are near

35  Which four of these must not use motorways?
*Choose four answers*

    a.   learner car drivers
    b.   motorcycles over 50 cc
    c.   double-deck buses
    d.   farm tractors
    e.   horse riders
    f.   cyclists

36  Why would this temporary speed limit sign be shown?

*Choose one answer*

    a.   to warn of the end of the motorway
    b.   to warn you of a low bridge
    c.   to warn you of a junction ahead
    d.   to warn of road works ahead

37 What do these yellow markings on the kerb indicate?

*Choose one answer*

a. no parking except for loading
b. passenger set-down prohibited
c. loading restrictions in force
d. loading bay, no waiting permitted

38 You have third-party-only insurance. What does this cover?
*Choose three answers*

a. collision damage to your own vehicle
b. theft of your vehicle
c. injury to another road user
d. damage you cause to someone's property
e. damage you cause to other vehicles
f. any injury you suffer in an accident that you cause

39 Signals to other road users should normally be given by direction indicators and: *Choose one answer*

a. fog lights
b. the horn
c. brake lights
d. flashing headlights

40 You are on a road that has street lights. Unless traffic signs tell you otherwise, the speed limit is: *Choose one answer*

a. 20 mph
b. 30 mph
c. 40 mph
d. 60 mph

41 What is meant by 'tailgating'? *Choose one answer*

a. a way to keep pets in the rear of an estate car
b. reversing into a driveway
c. following another vehicle too closely
d. reversing out of a driveway

42  By taking a Pass Plus course after passing your driving test you will:
*Choose one answer*

   a.  get a discount on your MOT
   b.  learn how to tune your engine
   c.  gain more experience and improve your driving skills
   d.  be exempt from the 'new driver' regulations

43  What does this sign mean?

*Choose one answer*

   a.  dual carriageway ahead
   b.  no entry
   c.  vehicles may pass either side to reach the same destination
   d.  go back

44  You wish to turn right at a crossroads where an oncoming driver is
    also turning right. It will normally be safer to:
    *Choose one answer*

   a.  keep the other vehicle to your right and turn behind it (offside to
       offside)
   b.  keep the other vehicle to your left and turn in front of it (nearside
       to nearside)
   c.  hold back so the oncoming driver can turn ahead of you
   d.  turn left and find another route to your destination

45  At an accident scene you are dealing with a casualty who is bleeding
    from a cut on his or her arm. The wound seems clean so you should:
    *Choose two answers*

   a.  apply firm pressure over the wound
   b.  lower the arm to keep the circulation stable
   c.  give the casualty plenty of fluids
   d.  raise the arm to reduce blood flow
   e.  keep the casualty moving to prevent a faint

46  Powered wheelchairs driven by the disabled have a maximum speed of:
*Choose one answer*

a.  8 mph
b.  12 mph
c.  22 mph
d.  30 mph

47  When might it be useful to look at the reflections of vehicles in shop windows? *Choose one answer*

a.  to pass the time when waiting in a traffic queue
b.  when emerging at a junction and your view of approaching traffic is restricted
c.  when trying to avoid eye contact with others after you have made a mistake
d.  when deciding whether it is time to switch on your headlights

48  Snow is falling heavily and the weather forecast suggests it will continue for some time. You had planned a long journey and should: *Choose one answer*

a.  follow a snow plough or road gritter
b.  not drive unless the journey is essential
c.  make sure your fuel tank is full because you won't have time to stop
d.  only drive in a low gear

49  When driving a car with automatic transmission, what would you use 'kick-down' for? *Choose one answer*

a.  an emergency stop
b.  quick acceleration
c.  to control speed going downhill
d.  to reduce fuel consumption

50  The left-hand lane of a motorway should be used for:
*Choose one answer*

a.  rest breaks
b.  normal driving
c.  overtaking
d.  emergencies only

# Paper 7
## Theory test assessment

## Case Study for questions 1–5

You work in the city centre and are driving in from your village home. You notice there is a side wind as you drive along a section of dual carriageway. After overtaking some large vehicles you see ahead a motorcyclist riding quite slowly as you near the end of the dual carriageway. Later, as you enter town your view ahead is restricted by a delivery truck. The truck turns off your route but traffic seems to be very slow and heavy making you anxious about being late for work.

1    What should you anticipate as you overtake the large vehicles? *Choose one answer*

   a.   that your car may pull sharply to one side as you pass
   b.   that your speed will increase suddenly as you pass
   c.   that the large vehicles will be pushed to one side as you pass
   d.   that the large vehicle drivers will slow down for you as you pass

2    What should you do as you approach the end of the dual carriageway? *Choose one answer*

   a.   speed up to get past the motorcyclist before the road narrows
   b.   check your speed
   c.   sound your horn to warn the motorcyclist of your presence
   d.   pull in close behind the motorcyclist

3    How can you improve your view ahead when you are behind the delivery truck? *Choose one answer*

   a.   by straddling the centre line of the carriageway
   b.   by keeping well back
   c.   by signalling the delivery truck driver to pull over
   d.   by driving well to the left of your lane

4   The truck driver gives a left signal but moves towards the centre of the road. You should: *Choose two answers*

   a.   assume the driver will turn right and pass on the left
   b.   assume the driver wants to turn into a narrow road on the left
   c.   sound your horn and pass on the right
   d.   keep back until the truck driver has turned off your route

5   You see a bus stop ahead and the bus driver gives a right signal as you get near. You should: *Choose one answer*

   a.   accelerate to get past the bus quickly
   b.   sound your horn as a warning of your presence
   c.   expect the bus driver to wait for you to pass
   d.   give way and let the bus pull out if you can do so safely

6   On approach to a speed hump you should:

   *Choose one answer*

   a.   try to avoid it
   b.   accelerate in readiness
   c.   slow down
   d.   coast over it with the clutch down

7   When you are turning left on a slippery road, the back of your car slides to the right. What should you do? *Choose one answer*

   a.   brake firmly
   b.   steer more to the left
   c.   accelerate for stability
   d.   steer gently to the right

8   When you are not using the clutch pedal, your left foot should be: *Choose one answer*

   a.   resting on the clutch pedal
   b.   tucked under your seat
   c.   over the footbrake
   d.   within easy reach of the clutch pedal

9  You see this sign on a busy road. What hazard should you expect?

*Choose one answer*

a.  the road will narrow ahead
b.  merging traffic ahead
c.  traffic joining from your left
d.  a difficult Y-junction

10  Whilst driving on a motorway you feel tired. What should you do?
*Choose one answer*

a.  keep to 50 mph
b.  drive more quickly to shorten your journey
c.  stop on the hard shoulder for a rest
d.  leave the motorway at the next exit or service station

11  What does this sign mean?

*Choose one answer*

a.  no sharp bends ahead
b.  you must not turn left at the next junction
c.  you are in a one-way street
d.  you must drive on the right

12  What is the first thing you should do when you see a hazard in
the road ahead?
*Choose one answer*

a.  show your brake lights
b.  change gear
c.  check your mirrors
d.  ease off the accelerator pedal

13  Why must you not enter a box junction if your exit isn't clear?

*Choose one answer*

a.  traffic lights could force you to reverse
b.  you could block the junction
c.  you are never permitted to wait in a box junction
d.  to give cyclists a chance in heavy traffic conditions

14  Why do you need to try your brakes after passing through a flood?
*Choose one answer*

a.  your brakes may be wet and not work
b.  to shake any water from the brake linings
c.  to dry out the brake linings
d.  because the road may be wet

15  Why should you check your lights before driving in thick daytime fog?
*Choose one answer*

a.  to avoid dazzling other drivers
b.  to make sure you can be seen
c.  you will need your main beam
d.  it will probably be very dark on the road

16  What should you avoid doing when driving in a bend?
*Choose two answers*

a.  using full headlights
b.  braking sharply
c.  making sudden steering movements
d.  keeping light pressure on the accelerator pedal
e.  checking your mirrors

17  What does the road marking along the centre of the road tell drivers?

*Choose one answer*

a.  give way to oncoming traffic
b.  end of dual carriageway
c.  not to cross the lines
d.  parking permitted

18  What does this sign mean?

*Choose one answer*

a.  holiday route
b.  hot spot for accidents and emergencies
c.  hospital with accident and emergency unit
d.  high vehicles use A and E roads

19  What does this sign mean?

*Choose one answer*

a.  motorways merging
b.  no hard shoulder ahead
c.  motorway widening
d.  motorway contraflow

20  Who must ensure that a vehicle has a valid MOT certificate if needed?
*Choose one answer*

a.  the owner of the vehicle
b.  the person who intends to drive it
c.  the police
d.  the registered keeper of the vehicle

21  You see a slow vehicle ahead. The car in front of you overtakes. You:
*Choose one answer*

a.  can overtake safely if you follow the other car through
b.  shouldn't rely on the other car to protect you
c.  must wait until the show vehicle moves left
d.  should get very close to the lorry first

22  At a puffin crossing, red and amber lights mean that you should:

*Choose one answer*

a.  drive on
b.  wave on pedestrians who are waiting to cross
c.  not stop if following traffic is too close
d.  stop

23  Which statement is true about lane discipline on a motorway?
*Choose one answer*

a.  it isn't important because all the lanes are very wide
b.  you should keep to the middle lane for a long journey
c.  you should keep to the centre of your lane
d.  you should be safest keeping to the left of your lane

24  Why should you not keep loose items on the shelf behind your car's rear seats:
*Choose two answers*

a.  they will be difficult to reach when you are driving
b.  they could fly forward and cause injury if the car stopped suddenly
c.  they will interfere with your rear view
d.  they will distract following drivers

25 You are loading a caravan ready for a holiday trip. Heavier items should be placed:

*Choose one answer*

   a.  higher off the floor than lighter items

   b.  closer to the back of the caravan than lighter items

   c.  nearer to the floor than lighter items

   d.  as high off the floor as possible

   e.  on the offside of the caravan and lighter items on the nearside

26 Which of the following should you never do at a petrol station forecourt?

*Choose two answers*

   a.  put diesel in your car

   b.  light a match or smoke

   c.  use a catalytic converter

   d.  clean your windscreen and lights

   e.  top up your washer bottle

   f.  use a mobile phone

27 On a motorway, a sign like this advises you:

*Choose one answer*

   a.  that road works are complete

   b.  to move to the opposite carriageway

   c.  to drive at 70 mph

   d.  that the lane layout changes ahead

28 Which of these may not use motorways?

*Choose one answer*

   a.  disabled drivers

   b.  riders of mopeds under 50 cc

   c.  buses

   d.  learner lorry drivers

29  In thick motorway fog you see reflective red studs on your right.
This means:
*Choose one answer*

a.  you are in the right-hand lane
b.  you are on a slip road
c.  there is a service area ahead
d.  you are on the hard shoulder

30  If involved in a traffic accident you:
*Choose one answer*

a.  must stop, even if the accident is slight
b.  need only stop if a person is injured
c.  need not stop if the accident is slight
d.  must show your insurance details at the scene

31  What may happen if you don't replace your car's air filter at the
interval recommended by the manufacturer?
*Choose one answer*

a.  You will use less fuel
b.  You will get fewer miles to the gallon
c.  Your engine will run too cold
d.  Your car's demister will fail

32  How should you find out if a liquid spill from a tanker involved in
an accident was dangerous?
*Choose one answer*

a.  test the liquid with a lighted match and touch it gingerly
b.  by asking the tanker driver
c.  by waiting for the fire brigade
d.  by looking for a plate on the tanker that displays information
    about the liquid

33  You are towing a trailer when it begins to swerve or snake.
What should you do?
*Choose one answer*

a.  steer with the snaking motion
b.  brake sharply to regain control
c.  ease off the accelerator until the trailer stabilizes
d.  gently apply the parking brake

34 If the wheels on your car aren't properly balanced:
*Choose one answer*

   a.   the steering may pull to one side
   b.   the steering may shudder
   c.   the brakes could fail
   d.   the tyres could deflate

35 Which of these signs means that no motor vehicles are allowed?
*Choose one answer*

a.     b.     c.     d.

36 You are travelling on a motorway. Unless signs show a lower speed limit you must not exceed:
*Choose one answer*

   a.   55 mph
   b.   60 mph
   c.   70 mph
   d.   77 mph

37 Your car insurance policy has an excess of £250. What does this mean?
*Choose one answer*

   a.   the insurance company will pay the first £250 of any claim
   b.   you will be paid a £250 bonus if you don't make a claim
   c.   your policy will pay a maximum of £250 in a claim
   d.   you will have to pay the first £250 of the cost of any claim

38 You are approaching traffic lights. They have been on green for some time. You should:
*Choose one answer*

   a.   speed up in case they change
   b.   slow down to a crawl
   c.   be ready to stop
   d.   pull in and wait for following traffic to deal with the problem

39  You are parking on a two-way road at night. There is a 40 mph speed limit on the road. You should park:
*Choose one answer*

a.  on the left with parking lights on
b.  on the right with parking lights on
c.  on the left without lights
d.  on the right without lights

40  Which of the following are most likely to waste fuel?
*Choose four answers*

a.  driving defensively
b.  carrying unnecessary weight in the car
c.  harsh braking
d.  under-inflated tyres
e.  gentle acceleration
f.  carrying a roof rack with no load

41  What does this motorway sign mean?

*Choose one answer*

a.  minimum speed 50 mph
b.  maintain a gap of 50 metres between vehicles
c.  50 miles to the next services
d.  temporary maximum speed 50 mph

42  Your car has broken down on an automatic railway level crossing. What should you do first?
*Choose one answer*

a.  get everyone out of the car and clear of the crossing
b.  phone the signal operator
c.  try to repair the car but keep a lookout for trains
d.  ask your passengers to push the car clear of the crossing

43 You are taking medicines that are likely to affect your driving.
What should you do?
*Choose one answer*

a.  seek medical advice before driving
b.  only drive for essential journeys
c.  only drive for short distances
d.  ask a friend to accompany you when driving

44 You intend to turn left into a minor road. On the approach you should:
*Choose one answer*

a.  keep just left of the centre of the road
b.  keep to the middle of the road before turning
c.  keep left and swing out before turning
d.  keep to the left of the road

45 You are driving on a motorway and need to use your mobile phone.
You should:
*Choose one answer*

a.  find a safe place to stop on the hard shoulder
b.  leave the motorway and stop in a safe place to make your call
c.  leave at the next exit and park on the slip road to make the call
d.  drive in the slow lane whilst making your call

46 You should use the right-hand lane of a motorway to:
*Choose one answer*

a.  keep clear of goods vehicles
b.  turn right
c.  overtake slower vehicles
d.  avoid safety cameras

47 You are turning right on to a dual carriageway. Before pulling out you
should:
*Choose two answers*

a.  assess the speed of the traffic
b.  position your car to the left of the side road
c.  check the width of the central reservation
d.  sound your horn to warn of the danger

48 Driving up a steep hill you need to be aware that:
*Choose two answers*

a. higher gears will give better acceleration
b. you will slow down sooner if you ease off the accelerator
c. overtaking will be much easier
d. there will be more work for the engine to do
e. lower gears should be avoided

49 You have just passed your driving test and will need to drive on motorways for your job. To reduce your risk of having an accident you should:
*Choose one answer*

a. take further training
b. use L plates on your car
c. keep to a maximum of 50 mph for the first few weeks
d. only drive in the left-hand lane

50 Diamond-shaped signs give instructions to:

*Choose one answer*

a. bus drivers
b. cyclists
c. tram drivers
d. taxi drivers

# Paper 8
## Theory test assessment

## Case Study for questions 1–5

Jeff has just got a new job and will be driving to work the following morning. He hasn't driven his car for a few weeks and knows it is overdue for a service. He gives it a quick check over and notices one of the tyres has a bit of a cut in the wall. He decides to change the wheel and finds the spare seems a bit flat. He drives to the nearest garage to check the tyre pressures. On the way home he notices the steering seems to be pulling to one side when he presses the footbrake.

1   What should Jeff do about the tyre with the cut in the wall?
    *Choose one answer*
    a.   check the tyre pressure and keep it as the spare
    b.   deal with it when the car is next serviced
    c.   have it replaced with a new tyre as soon as possible
    d.   let some of the pressure out and keep it as a spare

2   What could be badly affected by under-inflated tyres?
    *Choose two answers*
    a.   braking
    b.   steering
    c.   gear changing
    d.   manoeuvring at low speed

3   Why would Jeff be better to keep his car serviced at the correct intervals?
    *Choose two answers*
    a.   it will reduce the cost of his road tax
    b.   it will help to lower pollution
    c.   it help improve fuel economy
    d.   it will guarantee the car passes its next MOT test

4    What is the most likely cause of the car pulling to one side?
     *Choose one answer*

     a.  the tyres being correctly inflated
     b.  the tyres being over-inflated
     c.  a fault with the brakes
     d.  a fault with the steering

5    What should Jeff do about the problem he experiences when braking?
     *Choose one answer*

     a.  seek qualified help from a garage as soon as possible
     b.  not worry about it until he takes the car for a service
     c.  try changing the wheels round to see if it makes a difference
     d.  top up the brake fluid and avoid heavy braking

6    You are driving towards an unmarked crossroads intending to go
     ahead. You can see another vehicle approaching from the left.
     You should:
     *Choose one answer*

     a.  be ready to give way to the other driver
     b.  assume the other driver has seen you
     c.  assume the other driver will give way because you are on his or
         her right
     d.  flash your headlights and drive through

7    You buy a non-prescription medicine from your pharmacist. How can
     you tell if the medicine will affect your driving?
     *Choose two answers*

     a.  check the label on the medicine
     b.  try a short journey after taking it
     c.  ask the pharmacist
     d.  ask another driver to try it

8  Which type of sign tells you that parking is always forbidden:
*Choose one answer*

a.

b.

c.

d.

9  Where are you not allowed to park?
*Choose two answers*

a.  at a bus stop
b.  on a pedestrian crossing
c.  near a police station
d.  in a one-way street

10  Where are you permitted to overtake on a one-way street?
*Choose one answer*

a.  on the right only
b.  on the left only
c.  on the right or left
d.  you are not permitted to overtake on a one-way street

11  When should you signal to leave a roundabout?
*Choose one answer*

a.  there is no need to signal
b.  you should signal left throughout the roundabout
c.  you should signal left after passing the exit before the one you want
d.  you should only give a signal if there is traffic behind you

12  To overtake a long vehicle you should make sure that you:
*Choose one answer*

a.  are far enough back to get a clear view of the road ahead
b.  get as close to the vehicle as possible
c.  flash your headlights before signalling
d.  change to a high gear before moving out to look ahead

13  Where are traffic accidents most likely to happen?
*Choose one answer*

   a.  on motorways
   b.  near junctions
   c.  in car parks
   d.  on busy dual carriageways

14  A driver who sees a bus parked on the opposite side of the road needs
    to be particularly aware of what dangers?
*Choose two answers*

   a.  the bus pulling out without warning
   b.  pedestrians stepping out from behind the bus
   c.  people running for the bus
   d.  sudden gusts of diesel fumes

15  You should only use rear fog lights in falling snow if:
*Choose one answer*

   a.  your brake lights are not working
   b.  visibility is less than 100 metres
   c.  the driver ahead uses his or her fog lights
   d.  your minimum braking distance is more than the distance you can
       see to be clear ahead

16  What does this sign mean?

*Choose one answer*

   a   narrow right lanes ahead
   b.  end of dual carriageway
   c.  no overtaking
   d.  right lanes closed ahead

17  Where would you see a sign like this?

*Choose one answer*

a.  at a junction
b.  on a long vehicle
c.  on a vehicle that has an overhanging load
d.  on approach to a level crossing

18  What is a 'cover note'? *Choose one answer*

a.  a temporary insurance certificate
b.  a letter from your GP excusing you from using a seat belt
c.  a temporary parking permit
d.  the note you should display on your windscreen if you've
    forgotten to renew your tax disc

19  Which of these types of insurance would cover damage to your own
    vehicle if you caused an accident? *Choose one answer*

a.  third-party-only insurance
b.  third-party, fire and theft insurance
c.  fully comprehensive insurance
d.  public liability insurance
e.  term insurance

20  When driving past parked cars or other stationary obstructions you
    should allow enough room. This means that: *Choose one answer*

a.  you should always allow 1 metre (3 feet) of clearance
b.  you should never leave more than 1 metre (3 feet) of clearance
c.  the faster you are going, the bigger the gap should be
d.  you must never get closer than an open car door's width from
    the obstruction

21  A flashing amber light on a vehicle means that: *Choose one answer*

a.  the vehicle belongs to the emergency services
b.  the vehicle is slow moving
c.  the vehicle is dangerously overloaded
d.  the vehicle is carrying a wide load

22  If you can't see properly to reverse, you should: *Choose one answer*

    a.   open your car door to see behind you as you reverse

    b.   ask someone to guide you

    c.   reverse so slowly that you are not likely to injure anyone

    d.   rely on your door mirrors

    e.   use hazard warning lights and look out of your side windows

23  The only time you may use hazard warning lights on a moving vehicle is: *Choose one answer*

    a.   when being towed

    b.   briefly, when on a motorway or unrestricted dual carriageway and you need to warn following traffic of a problem ahead

    c.   when towing another vehicle

    d.   when driving slowly because your vehicle has a mechanical fault

24  When should you use the left-hand lane of a motorway? *Choose one answer*

    a.   only when driving at less than 60 mph

    b.   whenever it is clear

    c.   only to leave the motorway

    d.   to undertake another vehicle

25  You may ONLY stop on the hard shoulder of a motorway: *Choose one answer*

    a.   when too tired to drive

    b.   in an emergency

    c.   to drop off a passenger

    d.   to answer a call on your mobile phone

26  What does this motorway sign mean?

*Choose one answer*

    a.   end of speed limit

    b.   end of motorway

    c.   end of restriction

    d.   the road ahead is clear

27  How should you dispose of waste engine oil? *Choose one answer*

    a.   burn it

    b.   pour into the ground or a drain

    c.   wash it into a drain with plenty of hot water and detergent

    d.   take it to a local authority site or garage for recycling

28  You have a breakdown on a motorway and have stopped on the hard shoulder. You have a hazard warning triangle in your car. You should: *Choose one answer*

    a.   place it at least 100 metres behind your vehicle

    b.   not use it on the motorway

    c.   put it on top of your vehicle

    d.   place it at least 45 metres behind your vehicle

29  The best advice when leaving your vehicle is to: *Choose one answer*

    a.   hide any valuables under the seats

    b.   take all valuables with you

    c.   cover up any valuables with a coat

    d.   put any valuables in the boot

30  Which of these signs means turn left ahead? *Choose one answer*

a.
    b.

c.
    d.

31  Which of these are likely to make you lose concentration when driving? *Choose three answers*

    a.   looking at a map

    b.   changing a CD in your car audio system

    c.   using cruise control

    d.   looking in your mirrors

    e.   using a mobile phone

    f.   using the air conditioning system

32  Which of these would help you stay alert during a long journey?
*Choose two answers*

a.  driving as fast as you can
b.  taking regular rest stops
c.  making sure that there is plenty of fresh air in the car
d.  playing loud music

33  You notice that an ambulance is following you. It is showing its flashing blue lights. You should:

*Choose one answer*

a.  pull over as soon as it is safely possible to let it pass
b.  speed up to get out of its path
c.  maintain your speed and let the ambulance driver take the risks
d.  brake to an immediate stop

34  What does this sign mean?

*Choose one answer*

a.  direction to park-and-ride car park
b.  parking and service area for buses or coaches
c.  direction to coach park
d.  combined parking for cars and coaches

35  You are following a cyclist on approach to a roundabout. The cyclist is in the left-hand lane. Which direction should you expect the cyclist to go?
*Choose one answer*

a.  left
b.  right
c.  ahead
d.  any direction

36 At an accident a casualty is unconscious. As a matter of urgency you should check the victim's:
*Choose three answers*

   a.  circulation
   b.  airway
   c.  limbs for sign of fracture
   d.  breathing
   e.  address
   f.  identity

37 What is the main benefit of having four-wheel drive?
*Choose one answer*

   a.  to impress your friends
   b.  to reduce fuel consumption
   c.  to improve road holding
   d.  to lower your carbon emissions

38 Which of these will help lessen the environmental damage caused by driving?
*Choose three answers*

   a.  keeping your vehicle properly serviced and maintained
   b.  inappropriate use of the gears
   c.  removing any roof rack when it is not in use
   d.  using public transport when possible
   e.  keeping the tyres at less than the recommended pressure

39 You intend to reverse into a side road. When would you present the greatest hazard to passing traffic?
*Choose one answer*

   a.  before you start the manoeuvre
   b.  just as you begin to move
   c.  when the front of your vehicle swings out from the kerb
   d.  when you've entered the side road and continue back in a straight line

40  What does this sign mean?

*Choose one answer*

a.  route for trams only
b.  buses only
c.  pedestrian route to tram station
d.  tram manoeuvring area only

41  Anti-lock brakes are of most benefit when you are: *Choose one answer*

a.  driving on ice
b.  braking hard in an emergency
c.  skidding
d.  aquaplaning

42  You are on a motorway and see lights flashing from side to side above every lane. You must: *Choose one answer*

a.  pull on to the hard shoulder and report the fault
b.  slow down to 30 mph or less and proceed cautiously
c.  stop in lane and wait before the signs
d.  leave the motorway at the next exit

43  What does this sign mean?

*Choose one answer*

a.  queuing traffic ahead
b.  no overtaking
c.  priority to oncoming vehicles
d.  keep to the left-hand lane

44 When is it permitted to reverse from a side road into a main road?
*Choose one answer*

a. at any time
b. not at any time
c. only if the side road is clear of traffic
d. only if the main road is wide enough

45 You are driving at night with your headlights on full beam. There is no approaching traffic, but a following driver begins to overtake. You should:
*Choose one answer*

a. switch your lights off until the driver has passed you
b. dip your headlights when the driver is ahead of you
c. dip your headlights as the driver gets alongside you
d. switch on rear fog lights to assist the other driver

46 You are testing the suspension on your car and notice that it keeps bouncing when you press down on the front wing.
What is this likely to mean?
*Choose one answer*

a. Your tyres are over-inflated
b. You are parked on soft tarmac
c. Your shock absorbers are worn
d. There is a fault with the braking system

47 Where should drivers be particularly careful to look out for motorcyclists?
*Choose one answer*

a. on motorways
b. in traffic-calmed areas
c. when emerging at junctions
d. when parking

48  Unless it is essential, why should you usually not attempt to remove the helmet of a motorcyclist who is an accident casualty?
*Choose one answer*

a.  it could take you a long time if you are unfamiliar with the straps
b.  you could cause more serious injury
c.  it will protect the rider's head in the ambulance
d.  the rider could forget to take the helmet with him or her when he or she leaves

49  Whilst driving you notice an instrument panel warning light come on. You should:
*Choose one answer*

a.  have the problem checked out at the next service
b.  ignore the light if the engine sounds fine
c.  stop and investigate as soon as you safely can
d.  consult the vehicle owner's handbook whilst you drive to the nearest garage

50  What might indicate that you were driving on black ice?
*Choose one answer*

a.  there would be skid marks on the road surface
b.  road noise would seem to increase
c.  the steering would feel very light
d.  the road surface would appear very dry

# Answers to theory test assessment papers

## Assessment paper 1

| | | | | |
|---|---|---|---|---|
| 1. d | 11. b | 21. a | 31. d | 41. c |
| 2. c | 12. a | 22. b | 32. b | 42. a, b, d |
| 3. a, d | 13. c | 23. b | 33. b | 43. b, d, e |
| 4. b | 14. b | 24. b | 34. d | 44. d |
| 5. c | 15. b | 25. d | 35. d | 45. c |
| 6. b | 16. c | 26. c | 36. b | 46. b |
| 7. b | 17. b | 27. b | 37. c | 47. c |
| 8. a | 18. c | 28. c | 38. b, c | 48. b |
| 9. d | 19. d | 29. b | 39. b | 49. b |
| 10. c | 20. c | 30. d | 40. c, e | 50. d |

# Assessment paper 2

| | | | | |
|---|---|---|---|---|
| 1. d | 11. b, d | 21. b | 31. b | 41. a |
| 2. a | 12. c | 22. c | 32. c, d | 42. d |
| 3. d | 13. a, c | 23. c, e | 33. c | 43. a |
| 4. b, c | 14. b | 24. c | 34. d | 44. c |
| 5. b, d | 15. b | 25. c | 35. a | 45. b |
| 6. c | 16. c | 26. b | 36. c | 46. c |
| 7. d | 17. b | 27. b | 37. b | 47. b |
| 8. b | 18. c | 28. d | 38. b, d | 48. b |
| 9. b | 19. b | 29. b | 39. d | 49. b |
| 10. c | 20. c | 30. c | 40. b | 50. a, d |

# Assessment paper 3

| | | | | |
|---|---|---|---|---|
| 1. b | 11. d | 21. a | 31. a | 41. c |
| 2. c | 12. c | 22. c | 32. b, e | 42. c |
| 3. b | 13. b | 23. a | 33. b | 43. a, c |
| 4. c | 14. a | 24. b | 34. c | 44. b, c, d |
| 5. b | 15. d | 25. a, d | 35. d | 45. d |
| 6. d | 16. a | 26. a, b, e, f | 36. b | 46. b |
| 7. b | 17. b | 27. b | 37. c | 47. b, e |
| 8. b, c | 18. c | 28. b, d | 38. b | 48. b |
| 9. a, c | 19. c | 29. a | 39. b | 49. c |
| 10. b | 20. a | 30. d | 40. b | 50. d |

## Assessment paper 4

| | | | | |
|---|---|---|---|---|
| 1. c | 11. d | 21. d | 31. b | 41. a |
| 2. b | 12. a, d | 22. b | 32. d | 42. b, c |
| 3. c | 13. b | 23. b | 33. b, c | 43. d, e |
| 4. d | 14. b | 24. b | 34. c | 44. c |
| 5. d | 15. c, d | 25. c | 35. a | 45. c |
| 6. a | 16. b, d, e | 26. b | 36. a, d | 46. b, d |
| 7. b, d | 17. b | 27. a | 37. b | 47. b |
| 8. c | 18. c | 28. e | 38. c | 48. d |
| 9. c | 19. c | 29. b | 39. d | 49. b |
| 10. b | 20. b | 30. b | 40. b | 50. c |

## Assessment paper 5

| | | | | |
|---|---|---|---|---|
| 1. c | 11. b | 21. d | 31. c | 41. a |
| 2. b, c | 12. c | 22. c | 32. b, d | 42. a, b |
| 3. a | 13. a | 23. b | 33. d | 43. d |
| 4. c | 14. d | 24. c | 34. d | 44. b, c, d |
| 5. c | 15. d | 25. b | 35. a, c, d, g | 45. c |
| 6. c | 16. b | 26. c | 36. c | 46. a |
| 7. a, b, d | 17. b | 27. c | 37. e | 47. c |
| 8. c | 18. a, c | 28. c | 38. d | 48. a, b, d, e |
| 9. a | 19. b | 29. a | 39. d | 49. b |
| 10. b, d | 20. b, d | 30. c | 40. c | 50. b |

# Assessment paper 6

| | | | | |
|---|---|---|---|---|
| 1. a | 11. b | 21. c | 31. c | 41. c |
| 2. b, c | 12. c | 22. a | 32. d | 42. c |
| 3. d | 13. b, c, d | 23. c | 33. a | 43. c |
| 4. c | 14. c | 24. b | 34. a | 44. a |
| 5. c | 15. c | 25. c | 35. a, d, c, f | 45. a, d |
| 6. c | 16. b | 26. d | 36. d | 46. a |
| 7. c | 17. b | 27. a, c | 37. c | 47. b |
| 8. b | 18. d | 28. a, c | 38. c, d, e | 48. b |
| 9. c | 19. b | 29. b, d | 39. c | 49. b |
| 10. b | 20. b, c, e | 30. a, c | 40. b | 50. b |

# Assessment paper 7

| | | | | |
|---|---|---|---|---|
| 1. a | 11. b | 21. b | 31. b | 41. d |
| 2. b | 12. c | 22. d | 32. d | 42. a |
| 3. b | 13. b | 23. c | 33. c | 43. a |
| 4. b, d | 14. a | 24. b, c | 34. b | 44. d |
| 5. d | 15. b | 25. c | 35. d | 45. b |
| 6. c | 16. b, c | 26. b, f | 36. c | 46. c |
| 7. d | 17. c | 27. d | 37. d | 47. a, c |
| 8. d | 18. c | 28. b | 38. c | 48. b, d |
| 9. b | 19. a | 29. d | 39. a | 49. a |
| 10. d | 20. b | 30. a | 40. b, c, d, f | 50. c |

# Assessment paper 8

| | | | | |
|---|---|---|---|---|
| 1. c | 11. c | 21. b | 31. a, b, e | 41. b |
| 2. a, b | 12. a | 22. b | 32. b, c | 42. c |
| 3. b, c | 13. b | 23. b | 33. a | 43. b |
| 4. c | 14. b, c | 24. b | 34. a | 44. b |
| 5. a | 15. b | 25. b | 35. d | 45. c |
| 6. a | 16. d | 26. c | 36. a, b, d | 46. c |
| 7. a, c | 17. c | 27. d | 37. c | 47. c |
| 8. d | 18. a | 28. b | 38. a, c, d | 48. b |
| 9. a, b | 19. c | 29. b | 39. c | 49. c |
| 10. c | 20. c | 30. c | 40. a | 50. c |

# PART THREE
## APPENDICES

# Appendix 1
## Show me, tell me questions for car drivers

Driving test candidates are required to answer two vehicle safety questions at the beginning of their practical driving test. Known as 'Show me, tell me', these questions cover basic maintenance and operation procedures for the vehicle being used in the driving test. These checks may require you to open the bonnet of the car and identify fluid reservoirs. You are not asked to touch a hot engine or physically check any fluid levels. There are 19 questions in all, and they are asked in set combinations (shown in the table at the end of this appendix). As a driver you should recognize the importance of basic vehicle maintenance and safety – do not simply learn the questions and answers by rote.

WARNING: It can be dangerous to perform these safety checks if you are unsure of what to do. Your instructor will advise you how to make these checks safely on your driving test vehicle. You are recommended to wear disposable vinyl gloves for under-bonnet checks and to wear a high-visibility vest when making safety checks outside the vehicle.

## 'Show me' questions

These questions require you to demonstrate how to perform basic safety checks. These are the questions you may be asked and the minimum required for a correct answer.

Question S1: Open the bonnet, identify where you would check the engine oil level and tell me how you would check that the engine has sufficient oil.

Answer: *Identify the dipstick/oil level indicator; describe check of oil level against the minimum and maximum markers.*

**Supplementary:** *The dipstick is usually brightly coloured for easy identification. The engine should have been off for several minutes and the car parked on a level surface before checking the oil.*

**Question S2:** Show me/explain how you would check that the power-assisted steering is working before starting a journey.

**Answer:** *If the steering becomes heavy the system may not be working properly. Before starting a journey two simple checks can be made. Gentle pressure on the steering wheel, maintained while the engine is started, should result in a slight but noticeable movement as the system begins to operate. Alternatively turning the steering wheel just after moving off will give an immediate indication that the power assistance is functioning.*

**Supplementary:** *A warning light on the instrument panel may indicate a fault with power-assisted steering.*

**Question S3:** Open the bonnet, identify where you would check the engine coolant level and tell me how you would check that the engine has the correct level.

**Answer:** *Identify high/low level markings on header tank where fitted or identify the radiator filler cap, and describe how to top up to the correct level.*

**Supplementary:** *The coolant system is pressurized and it can be dangerous to unscrew the filler cap when the engine is hot! It is safest to check the coolant level when the engine is cold.*

**Question S4:** Show me how you would check the parking brake (handbrake) for excessive wear; make sure you keep safe control of the vehicle.

**Answer:** *Apply the footbrake firmly. Demonstrate by applying parking brake so that when it is fully applied it secures itself, and is not at the end of the working travel.*

**Question S6:** Show me how you would check that the horn is working (off road only).

**Answer:** *Check is carried out by using the control (turn on ignition if necessary).*

**Supplementary:** *Take care not to alarm other road users when making this check.*

**Question S7:** Open the bonnet, identify where the brake fluid reservoir is and tell me how you would check that you have a safe level of hydraulic brake fluid.

**Answer:** Identify the reservoir and check fluid level against high/low markings.

**Supplementary:** When checking the brake fluid level, be careful not to contaminate the reservoir with dust, dirt or water.

**Question S8:** Show me how you would check that the direction indicators are working.

**Answer:** *Operate the indicators or hazard warning switch and check functioning of all indicator lights.*

**Supplementary:** *You may need to switch the ignition on to answer this question, but there is no need to start the engine.*

**Question S9:** Show me how you would check that the brake lights are working on this car.

**Answer:** *Operate the brake pedal, make use of reflections in windows, garage doors, etc, or ask someone to help (the examiner will offer to help).*

**Supplementary:** *You may need to switch the ignition on to answer this question, but there is no need to start the engine.*

**Question S14:** Show me how you would clean the windscreen using the windscreen washer and wipers.

**Answer:** *Operate the control to wash and wipe the windscreen.*

**Supplementary:** *You may need to switch the ignition on to answer this question, but there is no need to start the engine.*

**Question S15:** Show me how you would set the demister controls to clear all the windows effectively; this should include both front and rear screens.

**Answer:** *Set all relevant controls including: fan, temperature, air direction/ source and heated screen to clear the windscreen and windows.*

**Supplementary:** *You may need to switch the ignition on to answer this question, but there is no need to start the engine. Opening a window should help screens clear more quickly.*

**Question S16:** Show me how you would switch on the rear fog light(s) and explain when you would use it/them. (There is no need to exit the vehicle.)

**Answer:** *Operate the switch (turn on dipped headlights and ignition if necessary). Check that the warning light is on. Explain use.*

**Supplementary:** *Remember that these high-intensity lamps can dazzle following drivers. Fog lights should only be used when visibility is seriously reduced (less than 100 metres).*

**Question S17:** Show me how you switch your headlight from dipped to main beam and explain how you would know the main beam is on whilst inside the car.

**Answer:** *Operate switch (with ignition or engine on if necessary) and check with the main beam warning light.*

**Supplementary:** *Remember that you can dazzle approaching drivers and those you are following if you don't dip headlights in good time.*

# 'Tell me' questions

These may require you to open the bonnet. Usually you need to identify the relevant part of the car or engine and describe how you would make the safety check. These are the questions you may be asked and the minimum required for a correct answer.

**Question T5:** Identify where the windscreen washer reservoir is and tell me how you would check the windscreen washer level.

**Answer:** *Identify the reservoir and explain how to check the level.*

**Supplementary:** *You may need to open the bonnet to answer this question. The reservoir may display the windscreen wiper symbol. Check the reservoir regularly.*

**Question T10:** Tell me how you would check that the brakes are working before starting a journey.

**Answer:** *Explain that the brakes should not feel spongy or slack. Brakes should be tested as you set off. The vehicle should not pull to one side.*

**Supplementary:** *To test the brakes, drive forwards slowly as you set off and when safe (mirrors!) apply the footbrake.*

**Question T11:** Tell me how you would check that the headlights and tail lights are working.

**Answer:** *Explain that you would operate the switch (turning on the ignition if necessary for your vehicle) and then walk round the vehicle. (As this is a 'Tell me' question, you don't need to exit vehicle to physically check the lights.)*

**Supplementary:** *Drivers must check that lights and indicators are working before using the car. Some cars have sensors that tell you when a light has failed. It is a good idea to keep a spare bulb kit in the car.*

**Question T12:** Tell me where you would find the information for the recommended tyre pressures for this car and how tyre pressures should be checked.

**Answer:** *Explain that you would refer to the manufacturer's guide, use a reliable pressure gauge, and check and adjust pressures when tyres are cold. Don't forget the spare tyre, and remember to refit the valve caps.*

**Supplementary:** *Information on tyre pressures will be found in the vehicle handbook and is often prominently displayed on the vehicle, eg behind the fuel cap door.*

**Question T13:** Tell me how you would check the tyres to ensure that they have sufficient tread depth and that their general condition is safe to use on the road.

**Answer:** *There should be no cuts and bulges in the tyre. There must be 1.6 millimetres of tread depth across the central three-quarters of the breadth of the tyre and around the entire outer circumference.*

**Supplementary:** *Get into the habit of checking tyre condition and pressures at least once a week. Good tyres are essential for road holding and controlled braking. Replace badly worn or damaged tyres immediately.*

**Question T18:** Tell me how you make sure your head restraint is correctly adjusted so it provides the best protection in the event of a crash.

**Answer:** *The head restraint should be adjusted so the rigid part of the head restraint is at least as high as the eye or top of the ears, and as close to the back of the head as is comfortable.*

**Supplementary:** *NB: Some restraints might not be adjustable.*

**Question T19:** Tell me how you would know if there was a problem with your anti-lock braking system.

**Answer:** *A warning light should illuminate if there is a fault with the anti-lock braking system.*

**Supplementary:** *You should know the meaning of all warning lights on the instrument panel and the appropriate action to take if they come on. Refer to the vehicle owner's handbook.*

## Combinations

To ensure fairness in the driving test, examiners are only permitted to ask the questions in the following combinations:

| Combination no. | 1 | 2 | 3 | 4 | 5 | 6 | 7 | 8 | 9 | 10 | 11 | 12 | 13 |
|---|---|---|---|---|---|---|---|---|---|---|---|---|---|
| 'Show me' question | S8 | S9 | S2 | S4 | S1 | S3 | S7 | S6 | S14 | S15 | S16 | S9 | S17 |
| 'Tell me' question | T10 | T5 | T12 | T5 | T12 | T18 | T13 | T13 | T10 | T11 | T19 | T11 | T19 |

The vehicle safety questions and answers shown in this appendix are valid from 1 July 2008 and sourced from the Driver and Vehicle Standards Agency. Check with your instructor for any recent changes, and make sure that you understand how the safety questions apply to the car used for your driving test.

# Appendix 2
## Checkpoint answers and progress record

## Answers to checkpoints

### Checkpoint 1

| | | | |
|---|---|---|---|
| 1. b | 6. d | 11. b | 16. b, d |
| 2. d | 7. d | 12. a, c | 17. b, d, e |
| 3. d | 8. b | 13. c | 18. b |
| 4. b | 9. b, d | 14. b, c, d | 19. b |
| 5. b, c | 10. a | 15. c, d, e | 20. c |

### Checkpoint 2

| | | | |
|---|---|---|---|
| 1. a, b | 6. b | 11. d | 16. b |
| 2. b, c | 7. a, d, e | 12. a | 17. a, d |
| 3. b, c | 8. b, c | 13. a, c, d | 18. a, b |
| 4. a, d | 9. a, c, e | 14. c | 19. b |
| 5. c | 10. c, d, e | 15. c | 20. b |

### Checkpoint 3

| | | | |
|---|---|---|---|
| 1. a, c | 6. b, c | 11. a, b, c | 16. a, b, c |
| 2. c | 7. b, c | 12. b | 17. c |
| 3. c | 8. a | 13. c | 18. b |
| 4. c | 9. a | 14. a, d | 19. c |
| 5. a, b, d | 10. a | 15. a, c | 20. c |

## Checkpoint 4

| | | | |
|---|---|---|---|
| 1. a | 6. b | 11. a, d | 16. b |
| 2. d | 7. b, d | 12. a, c | 17. c |
| 3. d | 8. a | 13. b, c | 18. a, d |
| 4. c | 9. c | 14. a, b | 19. d |
| 5. c | 10. c | 15. b, c, d | 20. b, c |

## Checkpoint 5

| | | | |
|---|---|---|---|
| 1. b | 6. d | 11. c | 16. c |
| 2. d | 7. c | 12. c | 17. a |
| 3. b | 8. a, b | 13. d | 18. c |
| 4. c | 9. c, d | 14. c, d | 19. a, d |
| 5. c | 10. b | 15. b, c | 20. c |

## Checkpoint 6

| | | | |
|---|---|---|---|
| 1. b | 6. b, d | 11. a, b, d | 16. b, c |
| 2. b | 7. c, d | 12. c | 17. b, d |
| 3. b, d | 8. d | 13. c | 18. b |
| 4. a, d | 9. b, c | 14. b, c | 19. d |
| 5. a | 10. a, d | 15. a | 20. a, c |

## Checkpoint 7

| | | | |
|---|---|---|---|
| 1. b, c | 6. b | 11. b | 16. b, d |
| 2. a, d | 7. b | 12. a, b | 17. b |
| 3. a | 8. a, d | 13. a, d | 18. b, c |
| 4. a | 9. b | 14. b | 19. b, c |
| 5. b | 10. a | 15. b | 20. b, c |

## Checkpoint 8

| | | | |
|---|---|---|---|
| 1. b, d, e | 6. a, b, d | 11. a | 16. b |
| 2. a, d | 7. a, d | 12. b | 17. d |
| 3. b, d | 8. b | 13. c | 18. a |
| 4. c | 9. a, c, d | 14. b | 19. c, d |
| 5. b, c | 10. b, c | 15. a, e | 20. a, c, d |

## Checkpoint 9

| | | | |
|---|---|---|---|
| 1. b | 6. a | 11. b, c | 16. d |
| 2. a, b | 7. b | 12. d | 17. a, d |
| 3. d | 8. b | 13. b | 18. b, d |
| 4. a, c | 9. a, d | 14. c, d | 19. b, c, f |
| 5. b | 10. a, d | 15. b, c, d | 20. c |

## Checkpoint 10

| | | | |
|---|---|---|---|
| 1. b | 11. b | 21. b, c, d | 31. b |
| 2. b | 12. a, d | 22. d | 32. c |
| 3. a | 13. b, d | 23. b, c, d | 33. b, c, d |
| 4. d | 14. a | 24. a | 34. c, d, f |
| 5. b, d | 15. b | 25. b | 35. c |
| 6. c | 16. c | 26. a, c | 36. a |
| 7. a | 17. c | 27. b, e | 37. a, b, c |
| 8. a, b | 18. b, d | 28. a, b | 38. b, c |
| 9. a, c, e | 19. b | 29. b | 39. a |
| 10. b | 20. a, d | 30. b | 40. b |

# Checkpoint scores

This section of *Learn to Drive* is designed to help you build up a picture of your progress. It should help you understand whether you are ready to apply for your driving test or highlight any areas that need further revision and practice.

It is in your own interest not to cheat. You should have answered the questions at the end of each stage honestly. This will show where there are any weaknesses in your knowledge.

Your instructor or supervisor should also have been frequently checking by asking you questions on the rules and regulations.

As you complete the checkpoint at the end of each stage, record your scores below. If you cannot answer all of the questions, revise those you are not sure about and try again.

| Stage | 1st try | 2nd try | 3rd try | |
|-------|---------|---------|---------|---|
| 1 | | | | |
| 2 | | | | |
| 3 | | | | |
| 4 | | | | |
| 5 | | | | |
| 6 | | | | |
| 7 | | | | |
| 8 | | | | |
| 9 | | | | |
| 10 | | | | |

# Progress record

The driving test is designed so candidates will be able to show they can drive competently and safely, making decisions that will ensure their own safety and that of other road users.

The 'Can do' statements in this section should help you understand and measure your learning achievements. Learning about the rules should help you to make sensible decisions. Your confidence and ability should grow with plenty of practice. There are three levels of ability that you can note in this progress record:

- Talk through. To begin with, your instructor will control your actions and tell you exactly what to do.

- Prompted. As you improve, your instructor should only need to give you prompts, sometimes just by asking a question.

- Unaided. Finally, your ability and confidence should have developed so much that all your instructor has to do is check on your performance and give any corrective advice necessary. This is the level you need to aim for – the responsibility for making decisions has been passed to you, and you should be ready for taking your driving test.

You might feel self-assessment is too much bother! However, to get the best value from your training, you will need to reflect on what went well in your lessons, the things that need improvement and your goals for the next lesson. You may be surprised to discover that your own marking would not differ too greatly from your instructor's.

As you work your way through the text of this book, fill in the dates in the 'Can do' statements table below to chart your progress at each lesson or practice session.

| Subject | Talk through | Prompted | Unaided |
|---|---|---|---|
| Starting precautions | | | |
| *Make proper use of:* | | | |
| accelerator | | | |
| clutch | | | |
| gears | | | |
| footbrake | | | |
| parking brake | | | |
| steering | | | |
| Move off safely | | | |
| Emergency stop | | | |
| Reverse left | | | |
| Reverse right | | | |
| Turn in the road | | | |
| Reverse park | | | |
| Bay parking | | | |
| Use of mirrors | | | |
| Use of signals | | | |
| Act on signs/signals | | | |
| Making progress | | | |
| *Side roads and T-junctions:* | | | |
| MSM | | | |
| speed on approach | | | |
| observations | | | |
| position/left | | | |
| position/right | | | |

| Subject | Talk through | Prompted | Unaided |
|---|---|---|---|
| *Crossroads:* | | | |
| MSM | | | |
| speed on approach | | | |
| observations | | | |
| position/right | | | |
| position/left | | | |
| position/ahead | | | |
| *Roundabouts:* | | | |
| MSM | | | |
| speed on approach | | | |
| observations | | | |
| position/right | | | |
| position/left | | | |
| position/ahead | | | |
| Meet others | | | |
| Safety clearances | | | |
| Crossing path of others | | | |
| Pedestrian crossings | | | |
| Overtaking | | | |
| Dual carriageways | | | |
| Railway crossings | | | |
| Parking | | | |
| *Anticipating:* | | | |
| pedestrians | | | |
| cyclists | | | |
| other drivers | | | |

Tick the appropriate column and make a note of the dates until you improve to the point where you can carry out most of the skills without any help.

# Index